Matthew Harrison

The Rise, Progress, and Present Structure of the English Language

Matthew Harrison

The Rise, Progress, and Present Structure of the English Language

ISBN/EAN: 9783337086503

Printed in Europe, USA, Canada, Australia, Japan

Cover: Foto ©Thomas Meinert / pixelio.de

More available books at **www.hansebooks.com**

THE

RISE, PROGRESS, AND PRESENT STRUCTURE

OF

THE ENGLISH LANGUAGE.

BY THE

REV. MATTHEW HARRISON, A. M.,

RECTOR OF CHURCH OAKLEY, HANTS; AND LATE FELLOW OF QUEEN'S COLLEGE, OXFORD.

Third American Edition.

PHILADELPHIA:
E. C. AND J. BIDDLE AND CO., No. 508 MINOR ST.
1861.

PUBLISHERS' ADVERTISEMENT

TO

SECOND AMERICAN EDITION.

In meeting the call for a second edition of this work, the American publishers desire to offer a few remarks in relation to it, intended for those into whose hands it may fall for the first time.

The increasing attention paid by intelligent American teachers to the grammatical and etymological structure of the English language, has recently demanded the publication of many works on these subjects. The knowledge that Mr. Harrison's work has met the decided approval of a very large number of this class, that it has been adopted as a text-book in some of the first class academies of our country, and that it has received warm commendation in the critical notices of the most respectable portion of the American press (see notices on printed lining paper of this volume), is satisfactory evidence to the publishers that it measurably supplies a desideratum.

Mr. Harrison is not one of the class who would decry or underrate the value of classical studies; but he claims for the study of the English language, a portion of that time and attention which he believes to have been generally too exclusively given to them. His views are clearly exhibited in the following extract from this work:—

"The purification of the English language is worthy of our holiest and never-ceasing devotion. It will bear to future ages the sentiments of a free, generous, and singularly energetic race of men. It already overspreads a large portion of the world, and is diffusing itself east, west, north, and south. It carries with it the cherished and sanctified institutions of its native soil, and, under the influence and adventurous spirit of the parent and her vigorous offspring in America, is materially changing, or modifying the destinies of mankind.

"In all the great essentials of language, we have arrived at a degree of copiousness such as few languages possess. But English literature furnishes us with no positive and recognized standard of grammatical accuracy. What was the result of the well-founded pride of Greece in the excellency of her own language? What the result of the unwearied pains which her orators, poets, historians, and philosophers bestowed upon their compositions? The delicate perceptions of the Grecian ear would not allow a word, a syllable, a letter, to be out of its place, to form a disagreeable collision of sounds, or a cadence which did not leave a pleasing effect upon the senses. The result was a language which, perhaps, will never be equalled in the future generations of mankind; a language which has become as necessary to the intellectual wants of European civilization as bread is for bodily support.

"The French and Italians have paid great and praiseworthy attention to the formation and accuracy of their respective languages, and Germany is following their example. We have societies of various descriptions, founded on the intellectual, social, or physical wants of the community; but we have no society of a purely literary character, to which the language can appeal in the case of doubt or difficulty. The consequence is that the vagaries of affectation, and sometimes even of ignorance, will be seized on as authorities worthy of confidence and imitation, words will be moulded in their spelling to accord with the transitory and ever-varying pronunciation of the day, etymology will be lost sight of, and error present a front of brass against the hand of correction. But if the very 'salt shall have lost its savor,' if men of high literary character shall think the grammatical structure of the English language a secondary consideration only, we must not be surprised if the sickness of the head should communicate itself to each individual member. It is no unusual thing for men of great classical attainments to say: 'I can understand the grammatical construction of a Greek or a Latin sentence, I can comprehend its syntactical arrangement, and the mutual dependence of its several parts, but in English I see nothing but the force of custom, and the unsettled licentiousness of idiom.' But, it may be asked, have these gentlemen ever paid a fiftieth part of the attention to the construction of the English language which they have paid to that of classical literature? The Greek and Latin languages to them have been the study of a life; the English frequently little more than an incidental acquisition, a matter of ear and imitation rather than of grammatical precept.

"But surely, there is much in our native English which deserves a separate attention on the part of those to whom the education of youth is entrusted. And no men would be more likely to apply themselves with success to the grammatical analysis of their native tongue, than those who already have made language their study, and pondered over the complex combinations of Greek and Roman sentences."

PREFACE.

The following work was begun some years ago. In the course of his occasional reading, the author was forcibly struck with the numerous grammatical errors scattered over every department of English literature with which he happened to be acquainted. For the purpose of private instruction, he noted down, from time to time, such errors as he considered liable to a marked and decisive condemnation. In doing this, he found that examples rapidly accumulated; and he felt that a systematic arrangement of those examples, accompanied by critical observations, would prove advantageous, to himself at least, in an intellectual point of view. Before he entertained any serious thoughts of publication, the remarks of others were sometimes embodied with his own, without any stringent references to the sources from which they were derived. To seek to remedy this afterwards would have been a hopeless task. When instances of this kind occur, more particularly in a work in which authors spread over so wide a space of time were to be consulted, he must crave the reader's indulgence. In the case of any historical fact, he ventures to affirm that no single assertion has been made which is not founded on recognized authority. He must beg also to observe that, where quotations are necessarily so numerous and so varied, he has occasionally availed himself of the labors of others, and taken such quotations at second-hand. In such cases, he can only claim the merit of compilation. To read book after book, for the express purpose of finding the misapplication of some particular term, would be tedious indeed, and very often unsuccessful. The purpose of utility is fully answered by the production of such an example as may bear directly upon the point at issue. It would have been an easy matter for the author to set up men of straw, and to knock them down; but he thought it better that examples of error should be brought forward plainly and indubitably existing, even though he might sometimes be indebted to others for their discovery. Candor, he hopes, will allow that such a liberty is pardonable, when it is generally acknowledged, and redeemed by a great variety of examples which, as far as the author knows, have never before been noticed.

As his attention had thus been directed to a grammatical analysis of such passages in English authors as he considered of faulty construction, it occurred to him that an *Introductory Discussion on the Rise and Progress of the English Language*, and another on its *Genius and Character*, would at least give a consistency to the work as a whole, however imperfect the execution. On the *Rise and Progress of the English Language*, he acknowledges himself infinitely indebted to the Anglo-Saxon Dictionary, and the Anglo-Saxon Grammar, of the Rev. J. Bosworth; also to Thwaite's translation of Lappenburg's "History of England under the Anglo-Saxons"—books, upon these subjects, of the highest value. With respect to the early migrations of our forefathers on the Continent of Europe, as affecting our language, he is under obligations to Laing's translation of the "Heymskringla, or Chronicle of the Kings of Norway," and often to comparatively obscure and sometimes anonymous, tracts and dissertations, pointing to higher authorities.

In accordance with these views, he has given a *Dissertation on the Rise and Progress of the English Language, and the changes which it has undergone*, confining himself, as much as possible, to strongly marked and leading features. This is followed by a *Dissertation on the Genius and Character of the Language, and on the Sources of its Corruption*. He has then brought under consideration all the separate parts of speech consecutively; examined the application and misapplication of each; and has also given a variety of examples in which the repetition or the omission of connecting particles has been judiciously and effectively exercised; and he cherishes a hope that his very failures may call forth the attention of abler heads to the still fluctuating and unsettled idioms of our language. In this last department, he begs to acknowledge the assistance which he has occasionally derived from the subtle genius of Harris, and the sound judgment of Lowth.

It is notorious, that, at our public schools, every boy has been left to pick up his English where and how he could; and many of the old exercise books, put into his hands to be translated into Latin, would often serve the equally useful purpose of *exercises to be turned into English*, though the authors themselves have either been insensible to this double advantage, or too modest to hold it forth to the public. The rigid, and almost exclusive attention which has hitherto, with few exceptions, been paid to classical literature, at our public schools, diverts the attention of the student from the construction of his own language; and it is surprising that he should ultimately succeed as well as he does. No man can, however, be conversant with the systematic construction of the Latin and Greek languages, without gaining a general knowledge of the principles of grammar, and a habit of grammatical analysis, which he carries with him into languages of looser texture. But let no one flatter himself that the mere knowledge of Latin and Greek will serve him, as an unerring guide, in the structure of the English language. Let the example of Bentley, great in his generation, and really great as a classical critic, serve as a warning against the admission of such a fallacy. Let him place Bentley and Cobbett in juxtaposition, and he must, in every page, be convinced, how far superior the latter is to the former in clearness and precision of terms, in grammatical accuracy, and in the construction of his sentences. Let him take care, lest, while he is wandering in imagination on the banks of the Tiber, the Ilyssus, or the Meander—while he is gathering the sweets of Hybla—or drinking at the fountains of Helicon, he may be recklessly and profanely trampling under foot the vigorous, the rich, and the varied productions of his own soil.

In the following work, the author has been sparing of reference to classical illustrations, because he had principally in view the English reader. Such illustrations have been introduced only when they have borne immediately, either by forcible parallelism, or by contrast, upon the question under consideration.

Nothing would give him greater pleasure than to find that this work, notwithstanding all its imperfections, should still prove useful in our public schools. His feelings, sympathies, and early associations are there; and he cannot but think that a more decided and systematic attention to the structure of the English language would form an advantageous appendage to the course of education pursued in those great and national establishments.

In presuming to criticise the works of others, the author is well aware that he may have laid himself open, perhaps on too many occasions, to the taunts, "Physician, heal thyself;" "Take the beam out of thine own eye." He is prepared to submit to them with decent resignation, whenever the chastisement shall be inflicted, not from a malignant instinct for punishment, but with the view of correcting the offender. In the language of Erasmus: "Nos ad utrumque juxta parati sumus, ut vel rationem reddamus, si quid recte monuimus, vel ingenue confiteamur errorem, sicubi lapsi deprehendimur."—*Præfatio ad Novum Testamentum.*

With this feeling he casts his mite into the treasury of English literature.

Church Oakley, Basingstoke, Hants,
Nov. 17, 1848.

CONTENTS.

PART I.
HISTORICAL.

		Page
Chap. I.	Introduction	15
II.	Original Seats of our Forefathers	17
III.	Comparison of the Tartaric, Saxon, Gothic, and English Languages	20
IV.	Migration of Odin and his Followers Westward	22
V.	Reciprocal Migrations	26
VI.	Character of the Northmen or Norsemen	27
VII.	The Amalgamation of the German and Scandinavian Tribes	29
VIII.	Accession of the Normans under William the Conqueror	32
IX.	Social Distinctions of the Tribes that settled in Britain	33
X.	Reasons why the Anglo-Saxon Language was neglected	35
XI.	Similarity between the German and Scandinavian Languages	38
XII.	Migrations	43
XIII.	The Changes that the Anglo-Saxon has undergone in England	44
XIV.	Simplification of Inflexions	47
XV.	Summary of Changes	51
XVI.	Names of Things in common Use generally Anglo-Saxon	55
XVII.	Names of Places	60

PART II.

PHILOLOGICAL.

SECTION I.

OF THE GENIUS AND CHARACTER OF THE ENGLISH LANGUAGE.

		Page
Chap. I.	The Principles on which Languages are formed	68
II.	The Language of Greece	75
III.	The Anglo-Saxon Language	78
IV.	Monosyllabic Character of the English Language	79
V.	Flexibility of the English Language	92
VI.	A Principle of Economy observed in the Formation of our very Monosyllables themselves	92
VII.	Process of Contraction and Simplification	94
VIII.	Want of Inflexion a Cause of greater Variety of Termination	96
IX.	Modification of Foreign Terms by Modern Languages	97
X.	Effects of the Cultivation of Classical Literature	101
XI.	Advantages arising from the Judicious Introduction of Classical Terms	104

SECTION II.

SOURCES OF CORRUPTION.

Chap. I.	Introduction of Foreign Terms, Phrases, and Idioms	108
II.	Unauthorized Terms	111
III.	Inflated Terms	112
IV.	Incongruity of Terms	114
V.	Talkee-talkee	116
VI.	Corruption arising from Words altogether extraneous	117

Chap.		Page
VII.	Effects of Colonization	119
VIII.	Summary	121

PART III.

GRAMMATICAL.

SECTION I.

THE PRESENT STRUCTURE OF THE ENGLISH LANGUAGE.

Chap. I.	Introduction	124
II.	Origin of the Parts of Speech	128
III.	Grammar regards construction only	135

SECTION II.

GRAMMATICAL CONSTRUCTION OF NOUNS.

Chap. I.	Numbers of Nouns	136
II.	Cases of Nouns	141
III.	Nominative Case	145
IV.	The Genitive, or Possessive Case of Nouns	150
V.	Compound Terms joined by Hyphen	155
VI.	Objective Case	159
VII.	Genders of Nouns	162
VIII.	Principle of Genders in the English Noun	163

SECTION III.

GRAMMATICAL CONSTRUCTION OF PRONOUNS.

Chap. I.	Their Irregularities	167
II.	Personal Pronoun	169
III.	Inconsistency of Number and Gender	179

CONTENTS.

Chap.		Page
IV.	Proper Use of the Personal Pronoun	181
V.	On the Use of Ye, You, and Thou	183
VI.	Pronouns Enclitic and Emphatic	187
VII.	The Relative Pronouns—Who and Which	190
VIII.	Relative Pronoun omitted idiomatically	197
IX.	Ambiguity arising from the Plurality of Antecedents	198
X.	Pronominal Adjectives	200
XI.	Repetition of the Pronoun—its Effect	206

SECTION IV.

ARTICLE.

Chap. I.	Anglo-Saxon Article	214
II.	Distinction of Articles	215
III.	English Article compared with the Greek Article	218
IV.	Irregular Use of the Definite Article	219
V.	English Article compared with the German Article	220
VI.	The Definite Article improperly omitted	224
VII.	The Definite Article, not only Superfluous, but Mischievous	228
VIII.	The Definite Article properly repeated	229
IX.	The Indefinite Article properly repeated	235
X.	The Indefinite Article improperly omitted	236
XI.	Confusion of Articles	237

SECTION V.

ADJECTIVE.

Chap. I.	The Adjective—its Properties	239
II.	Confusion of Pronominal Adjectives	241
III.	Adjective in the Place of the Adverb	245
IV.	Adjective in the Place of the Noun	249
V.	Preventive—Particular—Peculiar	250
VI.	Comparison of Adjectives	251
VII.	Adjectives not admitting Comparison	253
VIII.	Confusion of Comparatives	256

SECTION VI.

THE VERB.

		Page
Chap. I.	Its Moods and Tenses	259
II.	The Auxiliary Verbs	262
III.	General Remarks on the Auxiliaries	278
IV.	The Neuter Verb	280
V.	Irregular Verbs	284
VI.	The Subjunctive Mood	293
VII.	Examples of the proper Use of the Subjunctive Mood	301
VIII.	Examples of the proper Use of the Indicative Mood	306
IX.	Improper and confused Use of the Indicative and Subjunctive Moods	309
X.	Promiscuous Errors in the Use of the Verb	315

SECTION VII.

THE PARTICIPLE.

Chap. I.	Its Character	329
II.	Verb in the Place of the Participle	330
III.	Proper Use of the Participle	333
IV.	Confusion of Nouns and Participles	334
V.	Prefix before the Participle	336
VI.	Participles ending in *en, ing, ed, t*	339

SECTION VIII.

ADVERB.

Chap. I.	Its Nature	347
II.	Examples of Adverbs	348

SECTION IX.

PREPOSITION.

		Page
Chap. I.	Its Nature	359
II.	Adoption of Latin, Greek, and French Prepositions	360
III.	Place of the Preposition	362
IV.	Double Prepositions	365
V.	Compound and Simple Prepositions	366
VI.	Terms compounded with Prepositions	370
VII.	Errors in the Use of Prepositions	371
VIII.	Repetition of the Preposition	373

SECTION X.

THE CONJUNCTION.

Chap. I.	Its Nature	375
II.	Correlative Conjunctions	376
III.	Conjunctions Copulative and Disjunctive	377
IV.	Omission of Conjunction	383
V.	Repetition of the Conjunction	387

SECTION XI.

THE INTERJECTION	390
Concluding Remarks	392

ON THE ENGLISH LANGUAGE.

PART I.
HISTORICAL.

CHAPTER I.

INTRODUCTION.

It seems natural to suppose that the early history of our ancestors would be one of the most interesting studies in which we could engage. Yet, even in the case of great and powerful tribes, the subject is often involved in mystery, and it is upon incidental circumstances and discoveries that we must depend, rather than on any authentic records, or creditable traditions. Such, at least, is the case with respect to the original seats of many of the scattered tribes and nations that now people the different quarters of the globe. The want of written records in the early period of the world, the strong and absorbing influence of present circumstances and occupations, the novelties springing out of migratory and roving habits, would all tend to produce that uncertainty which, even at this distance of time, we ourselves are more anxious to clear up than those who lived much nearer to the sources of correct information. Within the memory of living man, the human mind has been turned to the investigation of subjects which seemed doomed to everlasting sleep in the lap of time. On every side, we see an energy and a perseverance which are big with unseen and unknown results. We feel ourselves individually hurried along with the stream to regions dark, mysterious, and undeveloped; and, if we do not take part in the stirring scenes and business of life, we must still suffer ourselves to be cast, in a state of helpless resignation, into the vast and fermenting caldron of human passions. In this race, to an unknown goal, our countrymen are taking a decided part; and, when we contrast the present widely-extended power and influence of Great Britain with her state in the palmy days of Rome—when we were described as

—— "penitus toto divisos orbe Britannos,"

(the Britons cut off from intercourse with the whole world)—we would fain lift the veil of futurity, and anticipate those changes which, as yet, remain hidden in the counsels of Divine Providence. In the days of her greatness, Rome had clutched within her grasp a large portion of the civilized world; but, when her power gave way, under the ferocious assaults of the Gothic nations, she was obliged to call home her legions from Britain, for her own defence. The Britons, then unable to cope with the Picts, were induced to call in the assistance of the Saxons. From that moment, their independence received a fatal blow; and, with the exception of a comparatively small part, Britain fell into the hands of a different race, under which she has arrived at her present giddy height of political and moral greatness. The Saxon and Scandinavian races, originally one and the same, have occupied the whole of Great Britain, with the exception of the Highlands of Scotland and Wales, the Highlanders being of Irish and Celtic extraction. The history of a people is, in fact, the history of their language. The scenes, the circumstances, the occupations, through which they pass, will ever form the materials from which their language must be drawn.

CHAPTER II.

ORIGINAL SEATS OF OUR FOREFATHERS.

It must, therefore, be interesting to us, not merely to know that we are Saxons, Danes, Norwegians, Swedes, Icelanders; that we are members of the Gothic or Teutonic family;—we are desirous of pushing our researches beyond this point, and of penetrating, as nearly as we can, to the original seats of the fair-skinned, light-haired race that is now playing so conspicuous a part on the theatre of the world. In former times, the empire of Rome crumbled before them into dust; and, in the present day, mighty nations are springing from them in regions whose existence, but a few ages ago, was beyond the reach of conjecture. Now, a single glance at any individual of this great Northern family who bears the characteristics of the race will convince us that he is not a child of the sun—of climes "that breathe of the sweet South." His stature, his fair complexion, the rigidity and massiveness of his frame, all indicate the absence of those causes which gradually give a darker tinge to the skin, and a delicacy and suppleness to the limbs. He must, for ages prior to his migration to the British isles, have been the child of cloudy skies, and of a rigorous climate. Can we then fix upon any region from which it is probable that a race of men possessing these characteristics might migrate westward, till stopped by the Atlantic Ocean? Can we, anywhere, discover a region which would be likely to generate those tastes, and occupations, and propensities which distinguish the race to which we belong? But, above all, can we find any traces of our language amongst those hordes which, issuing from the East, carried their conquering arms westward, and possessed themselves of a large portion of Europe? If we look to the nautical skill and the reckless daring of the piratical sea kings of the north, we should at once point to the Black Sea as the place in which this spirit had been generated and nursed amongst their forefathers; and is indeed the only place, except the Caspian, in which it could have been nursed. Then, again, the Saxon and Scandinavian population have always been agricultural, and not nomadic, wandering tribes; and it is on the borders of the Black Sea, more particularly about the Crimea, that we find one of the finest corn countries in the world. Again, the English population have always been remarkable for their attachment to horses. The first Saxon chiefs that landed in England, the brothers Hengist and Horsa, bore on their banners a white horse, on a red field. The Cossacks of the Tanais or Don, which falls into the Black Sea, on the northern side, are noted as possessing a breed of horses distinguished for their speed and hardihood. It is said that the Cossacks, in cases of no very pressing emergency, do not scruple to eat horse-flesh. The eating of horse-flesh formed a part of the religious festivals of our forefathers, and was never abolished till the introduction of Christianity. This is so decidedly a Tartar custom, that it would be difficult to trace it to any other source. These considerations, independent of any historic records, are certainly very strong grounds for supposing the neighborhood of the Black Sea to have been the more remote locality of our forefathers.

If, however, we can discover a similarity of terms in the Saxon, the Gothic, and the language of Crim-Tartary, bordering on the Black Sea; and if those terms are household words, or words of every day occurrence, the supposition amounts to a certainty. Now Busbequius, who was ambassador at the Porte from Ferdinand, Emperor of Germany, and who paid great attention to the subject, has the following passage :—

"Non possum hoc loco praeterire, quae de gente accepi, quae etiamnum incolit Tauricam Chersonesum, quam, saepe audiveram sermone, moribus, ore denique ipso, et corporis habitu, originem Germanicam referre."

"I cannot omit, in this place, what I have heard of a nation, that as yet inhabits the Tauric Chersonese; and which, I had often heard, indicated a German origin, in language, in manners, in countenance, and habit of body."

He then proceeds to give a list of these Tartaric words, which he took from the mouth of this Tartar envoy, at Constantinople. Most of them, with slight variations, are common to the Tartar, Gothic, Saxon, and the English language of the present day. The resemblance is minute and indisputable, and leaves no doubt of the more remote locality both of ourselves and of our language.

CHAPTER III.

COMPARISON OF THE TARTARIC, SAXON, GOTHIC, AND ENGLISH LANGUAGES.

Tartary	Saxon	Gothic	English
Brot.	Bread.		Bread.
Plat.	Blod.	Bloth.	Blood.
Stul.	Stole.	Stols.	Stool.
Hus	Hus.	Hus.	House.
Wingart.	Wingard.	Weinagards.	Vineyard.
Regen.	Regn.	Rign.	Rain.
Broder.	Broder.	Brothr.	Brother.
Schwester.	Swester.	Swister.	Sister.
Alt	Eald	Ald.	Old.
Wind.	Wind	Winds.	Wind.
Silver	Seolfor.	Silvbr.	Silver.
Goute.	Gold.		Gold.
Korn	Corn	Kaurn.	Corn.
Salt	Sealt	Salt.	Salt.
Fisch.	Fisc.	Fisk (h by the Danes.)	Fish.

Tartaric.	Saxon.	Gothic.	English.
Hoef.	Heafod.		Head.
Sune.	Sunna.	Sunno.	Sun.
Mine.	Mona.	Mene.	Moon.
Tag.	Dage.	Tags.	Day.
Œghene.	Eaghen.	Augon.	Eyes.
Handa.	Hond.	Handus.	Hand.
Brunne.	Byrne.	Brunna.	Bourne.
Schliper.	Sclaper.	Zlepar.	Sleep.
Singhen.	Singar.		Sing.
Lachen.	Lohan.	Hlaghan.	Laugh.
Criten.			Cry.

To *greet*, in the Northern counties, signifies to *cry*.

The numerals are still more remarkable:—

Tartaric.	English.	
Itt.	One.	Not a whit, a tittle.
Twa.	Two.	Scotticè, twa.
Tria.	Three.	
Fyder.	Four.	
Finf.	Five.	
Seis.	Six.	
Sevene.	Seven.	
Athe.	Eight.	
Nyne.	Nine.	
Tune.	Ten.	

So striking a coincidence of terms seems amply sufficient to establish a common origin; but a remark, with which Busbequius prefaces his observation, in making this comparison of the Tartaric, Gothic, and Saxon languages, establishes a still more remarkable affinity.

" Omnibus vero dictionibus præponebat articulum *tho*, aut *the* nostratia, aut parum differentia."

" Before all his words he placed the article *tho* or *the*, like those of our country, or differing from them but little."

The envoy probably meant *nominibus* and not *dictionibus*. We cannot suppose that the article *tho* or *the* was prefixed to every *word*. It is more likely that he did so before every *noun*, or before so many of his nouns as to strike the attention of the envoy; just as the Germans say, *der* Mann, *die* Frau : or we, *the* man, *the* woman. If we join this *tho* or *the* to the Tartaric nouns just mentioned, we have the broe, the bread; the plut, the blood; the stul, the stool; the hus, the house, &c.

In looking at these extraordinary coincidences, we are reduced to the necessity of concluding, either that a portion of the Saxons migrated eastward, towards the Tauric Chersonese, or that they originally came from those regions, and that some of their forefathers still remained in some of their former habitations about the shores of the Black Sea.

CHAPTER IV.

MIGRATION OF ODIN AND HIS FOLLOWERS WESTWARD.

Nothing certain is known of the Gothic language till a short time before the Christian era. Odin, or Wodin, with his followers, migrated from the eastern side of the lake Maeotis, being driven out, as is supposed, by the fear of the Roman arms. Pompey had subdued Mithridates, King of Pontus, in the immediate vicinity. To avoid them, Odin retired towards the north-west, and ultimately reached Saxland and Scandinavia.

"Unicam gentium Asiaticarum immigrationem in orbem Arctoum factam nostræ antiquitates commemorant, sed eam tamen non primam, verum circa annum tandem, XXIV. ante Christum, Romanis exercitibus auspiciis Pompeii Magni, in Asiæ parte Phrygiâ Minoris grassantibus: illâ enim epochâ, ad hanc rem, nostri chronologi utuntur."—*Arngrim Jonas:* "*Crymogæa.*"

The Gothic tribes possessed themselves of a large part of Europe, and in the end subverted the Roman Empire. Odin and his countrymen were not the first that migrated in a westerly direction. He and his followers were kindly received by the then existing inhabitants. He introduced amongst them many useful arts, and also that of letters, which form what is termed the Runic alphabet. He was reputed to be a great magician; and we have the coincidence that he came from the neighborhood of Colchis, the seat of sorcery and magic incantations, according to Grecian story. This migration took place twenty-four years before the Christian era, when Gylfe was king of Sweden.

"In cujus tempore incidit Odinus Asiaticæ immigrationis, factæ anno vicessimo quarto ante natum Christum."—*Arngrim Jonas:* "*Crymogæa.*"

This account agrees exactly with that given in the "Heymskringlia, or Chronicles of the Kings of Norway," translated from the Icelandic of Snorro Sturleson, by Samuel Laing:—

"There goes a great mountain barrier from north-east to southwest, which divides the Great Sweden from the other kingdoms.

South of this mountain ridge, it is not far to Turkland,* where Odin had great possessions. But Odin, having fore-knowledge and magic-sight, knew that his posterity would come to settle, and dwell in the northern half of the world. In those days, the Roman chiefs went wide round the world, subduing to themselves all people, and on this account many chiefs fled from their domains. Odin set his brothers, Ve and Viter, over Asgaard, the capital of the country east of the Tanais; and he himself, with all the gods, and a great many other people, wandered out first westward to Gardaridge, (Russia,) and then south to Saxland. He had many sons; and, after having subdued an extensive kingdom in Saxland, he sent his sons to defend the country. He himself went northward to the sea, and took up his abode in an island which is called Odinso in Fyen. Then he sent Gefyon across the sound to the north, to discover new countries, and she came to king Gylfe, who gave her a plough-gate of land."

It appears, from this, that Scandinavia was inhabited, at the time that Odin arrived in those regions, by a prior immigration, the elder Asi; and that, at the head of the warlike Asi, he settled amongst them, and drove northwards the Fins and Laps, the earliest inhabitants of those regions, and a comparatively diminutive race. This latter immigration of the Asi thus amalgamated with the former. Previous to the irruption of the latter Asi from the East, Thor, and not Odin, was the principal god of the Scandinavian Goths. Odin and his followers became the dominant party, and, in some degree, supplanted the former religion, Odin now taking precedence over Thor, and, as it is said, over a more ancient Odin, deified by the first Goths, that took possession of Scandinavia.

* Not Turkland, in the time of Odin, but which bore the name, after the conquest of the Turks.

This Odin, with his gods and followers, settled in the regions about the Malar Sea, or Lake Lögur, at Sigtun: on this lake, Odin built a temple, and instituted sacrifices, introducing fresh religious rites. He assigned their respective places to the chief priests. This was the last and most complete state of the Scandinavian mythology; and in this state it was professed by our forefathers amongst the Norsemen as late as the *eleventh* century, and amongst the Anglo-Saxons till their conversion to Christianity in this country. The following observations on this subject appear in Mr. Urquhart's "Revelations of Russia:"

"But, however this may be, and whether we see reason to look upon the Caucasus as the cradle of mankind or not, to us men of the north, these mountains ought to inspire that feeling of veneration which is naturally inspired by contemplating the tombs of our progenitors, the hallowed soil where the race which gave rise to our own mingled its dust with the earth from which it sprang, for successive generations, when the spirit which animated it had passed away; for it is from these mountains that the *Teutonic* and *Scandinavian* families, to which we owe our origin, are as clearly made out to have spread over Europe, as any fact concerning the early history has ever been established. It is a fact abundantly confirmed by the similitude of feature to the descendants of the German and Scandinavian off-shoot of their parent tree, which the Therkessian and Ossetinian nations, at present inhabiting the Caucasus, continue to exhibit—retaining, in its purity and beauty, in remarkable contrast to the races which surround them, the original type from which we have far degenerated."—Vol. ii. p. 281.

CHAPTER V.

RECIPROCAL MIGRATIONS.

According to Jornandes, the hostile tribes which inhabited Scanzia, or Scandinavia, under their king Filimer, the fifth in descent from Berich, under whom the Goths first took possession of that country, made their way as conquerors—

"Ad extremam Scythiæ partem, quæ Pontico mari vicina est"—

to the extreme part of Scythia, which borders on the Pontic Sea. So that, in fact, we have reciprocal migrations between the Pontic and the Baltic Seas; that is, we first have a migration from the East to the Baltic, under Berich, the first leader of the Asi westward; then from Scandinavia back again, under their leader Filimer, to the Black or Pontic Sea; then, in the year 21 before the Christian era, from the borders of the Black Sea, east of the Tanais, back to Scandinavia, under the conduct of Odin, where he and his followers again amalgamated with their kindred, representing themselves, as was really the case, as of the family of the elder Asi, who first took possession of Scandinavia, under Berich. We find a connection kept up between Scandinavia and the regions of the Black Sea even as late as the 11th century; and it is this connection, and these reciprocal migrations, which have in some degree perplexed this part of Gothic history. In the 11th century, Harald Hardrade, Harald the Stern, reigned from 1046 to 1066. He was son of

Sigurd Syr, brother of Olaf the Saint, King of Norway. He entered into the military service of Zoe the Great, at that time empress of Greece. In her service, Harald, with his Norsemen, fought no less than eighteen pitched battles.

> "In eighteen battles fought and won,
> The valor of the Norsemen shone."

He fought against the Saracens, in Africa. He fought in Sicily, and various parts of the Grecian seas. He marched to Jerusalem, destroying bands of robbers and disturbers of the peace. He also passed through Ellepalta, or the Hellespont, into the Black Sea. After all these services, he returned home to Scandinavia.

CHAPTER VI.

CHARACTER OF THE NORTHMEN, OR NORSEMEN.

These Norsemen were very extraordinary men, possessing great physical strength; reckless, daring, and ferocious. Before the discovery of gunpowder, when much depended upon personal prowess, they were irresistible. They were in a state of perpetual warfare, either against one another, or along the coasts of Europe, and were therefore always practised and experienced in arms. Being thoroughly acquainted with the harbors, and creeks, and rivers, on the coast of Norway, the Baltic, and the English Channel, their attacks were often made under the cover of night. They, at such times, left their ships, advanced to a given point, surrounded a house or village, plundered, burned, butchered, and committed the most dreadful atrocities. Such was the terror excited by them, along the northern coast of France, in that part which they afterwards subdued, and which has since gone under the name of Normandy, (a name derived from those Northmen,) that it formed a part of the liturgy, or public daily prayers to God, that they might be delivered from the fury of the Northmen:—

"A furore Normannorum, libera nos, Domine."

A horrible mode of death was practised by these Northmen, called cutting the spread eagle "at vista örn á bak einom," (to describe an eagle on the back of any one,) from the supposed resemblance of the sufferer to a spread eagle. Snorro thus describes it:—

"Ad speciem aquilæ, dorsum ita ei laniabat, ut, adacto ad ponam gladio, costisque omnibus ad lumbos, usque a tergo divisis, pulmones extraheret." *Lappenberg's note, Anglo-Saxons, Thorpe's Translation, vol ii. p. 31.*

They divided the ribs from the spine, down to the loins, and then dragged out the lungs.

These men of violence delighted in frightful names; such as were synonymous with Bloody-axe, Skull-cleaver, &c.

Mere handfuls of them, comparatively speaking, possessed themselves of populous kingdoms, and kept them. The works of their Scalds breathe nothing but blood and slaughter. Sigvat the Scald writes of King Olaf:—

"On with the king—his banner's waving;
On with the king—the spears he's braving;
On, steel-clad men, and storm the deck,
Slippery with blood, and strew'd with wreck."

Again:—

"Into the ship our brave lads spring;
On shield and helm their red blades ring;
The air resounds with stroke on stroke;
The shields are cleft, the helms are broke:
The wounded boarder o'er the side,
Falls shrieking in the blood-stain'd tide;
The deck is clear'd, with wild uproar;
The dead crew lie about the shore."

CHAPTER VII.

THE AMALGAMATION OF THE GERMAN AND SCANDINAVIAN TRIBES.

LET us now see how the blood of the Gothic nations, and the dialects of the Gothic language became amalgamated on the soil of Britain.

The first Saxons landed in England about the year 450. Their religion was identical with that of the Northmen, who afterwards landed in England about the year 787. In 550, *i. e.* a century from the time that Hengist and Horsa landed on the Isle of Thanet, the Heptarchy was in existence. In 640, Christianity was generally established. In 787, the pagan Northmen made a complete conquest of the kingdom of Northumberland, that is, of England north of the river Humber, which they continued to hold under the independent Danish kings until 953. In Domesday-Book, made under the direction of William the Conqueror, the lands of Northumberland, which then comprehended the northern counties, are omitted, as if not forming a part of the conquest. They were, in fact, already in possession of Scandinavians, the kinsmen of William, Duke of Normandy, who was descended within a short interval from Hrolf Ganger, the Norwegian pirate—this Hrolf Ganger falling upon the coast of Normandy, as it was afterwards called, at the same time that other pirates were ravaging and occupying different parts of the coast of England. So late as the eleventh century, the Northmen were still pagans. In 1017, Canute the Dane became sole monarch of England. The kingdom of Northumberland comprehended the present Northumberland Proper, Durham, Yorkshire, Cumberland, Westmoreland, and part of Lancashire. East Anglia, comprehending the Isle of Ely, Cambridgeshire, Norfolk, and Suffolk; Essex, Middlesex, and part of Hertfordshire; and the extremities of the Anglo-Saxon kingdom of Mercia, were so entirely occupied by Danes, or people of Danish descent, that they were under Danish, and not under Anglo Saxon laws. From 787 to the Norman Conquest, 1066, or nearly 300 years, the laws of the Northmen prevailed over this large portion of the island. The Northmen, immediately previous to the Norman Conquest, had conquered the whole of England, and held it from 1003 to 1041, for four successive reigns; viz, that of Swein, Canute the Great, Harold Harefoot, and Hardicanute. The Saxon line was restored in 1042, and continued to 1066, when Harold fell before William, Duke of Normandy, at the Battle of Hastings. Here the Saxon line ceased; and the Anglo-Saxon language underwent some change, by the mixture of Norman terms, and the rejection of many of its inflections. Hrolf Ganger, the conqueror of Normandy, was the son of Rognvald, Earl of More. The first in descent from him was William; yet in his time the language of the Northmen was not spoken at Rouen, for he sent his son Richard to learn the language of his forefathers at Bayeux; so soon had the language of these Northmen fallen into disuse at the court—Normandy being a conquest, and not a colony. The fourth in descent was also Richard; the fifth, Richard; the sixth, Robert; the seventh William the Conqueror. The third Richard was the father of Emma, wife of Ethelred, King of England, aunt to William the Conqueror. The battle of Hastings, by which William gained the kingdom of England, was, in fact, a family quarrel, decided by an accidental shot, resulting in the death of the then King of England.

CHAPTER VIII.

ACCESSION OF THE NORMANS UNDER WILLIAM THE CONQUEROR.

Here, then, are united, under William, various branches of one and the same family: 1st, the Jutes, who came into Kent in 449; 2d, the South Saxons, who came into Sussex in 491—the West Saxons, into Hampshire in 519—the East Saxons, into Essex in 527—the Angles, into Anglia, Norfolk, in 527; into Bernicia, Northumberland, in 547; into Deira, Yorkshire, in 559; and into Mercia, Derbyshire, in 586. Added to these, we have the repeated incursions of the Norse pirates, and their conquest, first, of all the country north of the Humber and the Mersey; and then the conquest of the whole kingdom, under Canute the Great; and then, again, the conquest of England under William, Duke of Normandy. From these various sources we might naturally expect a mixed and unsettled language, and a strange jumble of dialects—the dialects which we now have in different parts of England having, in all probability, been partly introduced by the various tribes which thus from time to time settled in England and entirely dispossessed the ancient Britons from that which we now call England, i. e. the land of the Angles or Angles' land.

CHAPTER IX.

SOCIAL DISTINCTIONS OF THE TRIBES THAT SETTLED IN BRITAIN.

The names of their social boundaries warrant the supposition of the existence of different dialects amongst the tribes that settled in Britain. According to Lappenberg, the whole of England north of Hartford, Northampton, and Warwick, was first occupied by the *Angles*. The counties, under the *Angles*, were divided into *Wappentakes*. Amongst the *Saxons*, they were divided into *Hundreds*. The term *Ward*, met with in Cumberland, Westmoreland, Northumberland, and Durham, is probably of later origin. The Jutes occupied Kent, the Isle of Wight, and a part of Wessex. They had the law of *Gavelkind*. Kent is not divided into *Hundreds* or *Wappentakes*, but into *Lathes*. Sussex is divided into *Rapes*. From this, it would appear that distinctions in their social regulations existed amongst these tribes *before* they landed in Britain. These distinctions still continue.

The whole of Britain was comprehended under the term *Anglia*, for the first time, by Ecgberht, with the sanction of a Witenagemot, held at Winchester in the year 800.

"Egbertus, rex totius Britanniæ in Parliamento, apud Wentoniam, mutavit nomen regni de consensu populi sui, et jussit illud, de cætero, vocari *Angliam*."—*Lappenberg's Quotation from Hist. Fundationis Hospit. L. Leonardi*, vol. vi. p. 608, *Thorpe's Translation*.

"The compound word 'Anglo-Saxons' occurs first in Paul Warnefrid, lib. 6, c. 15; 'Cedoaldus, rex *Anglorum Saxonum;*' consequently, before the time of Ecgberht."—*Note from Lappenberg.*

To these dialects must be added words taken from the Normanno-Franco-Celtic language of Normandy, and, in later ages, terms, in great abundance, introduced from the Latin and Greek. It is out of this chaos, this fermentation of speech, this chemical amalgamation of elements, that the English language is formed. In its early and unsettled state, for some centuries after the establishment of the Saxons in this island, no language was ever more barren of every species of composition, and of all recognized principles of orthography and grammar: the written language, whenever distinguished by such an honor, being such as a laborer of the present day would write, who could do little more than write his name and place of abode—he being, at the same time, perfectly and blissfully ignorant that, in grammar and spelling, there is such a thing as a right and a wrong. The language, in the mean time, was full of terse, bold, and nervous expressions, occasionally rugged; but the limbs were the limbs of a young giant, requiring only time and discipline, in order to cover them with manly beauty. As an example of the unsettled state of spelling, the word signifying to "give" is found spelt in eleven different ways; as, gif, yef, if, yf, yeve, yeoven, given, giffs, geive (*vin ye will*) (gi'me). The reason why Anglo-Saxon literature—or, rather, language, for no literature existed—remained uncultivated and unheeded during many centuries, was the perpetual state of war in which the country was engaged, and because Christianity had been introduced by foreign missionaries totally ignorant of the language of the people at large. While, however, the Anglo-Saxon tongue was neglected, the Churchmen, in many instances, were well versed in the Latin language. The verses of Wulstan, bishop of Winchester, on the punishment of a parricide, show a perfect command of that language:—

> "Nam occidit proprium crudeli morte parentem,
> Unde reo statim præcepit episcopus urbis
> Ferreus ut ventrem constringeret acriter omnem
> Circulus, et similem paterentur brachia nænam.
> Continuosque novem semel cruciando per annos
> Atria sacrorum lustraret sæpe locorum,
> Viseret et sacri pulcherrima limina Petri,
> Quò veniam tantæ mereretur sumere culpæ."
> *Acta Benedicti: note from Lappenbery,* vol. ii. p. 21.

CHAPTER X.

REASON WHY THE ANGLO-SAXON LANGUAGE WAS NEGLECTED.

But, as the services of the Church were conducted entirely in Latin, and all communication with the See of Rome, the then head of the Church, was held through the medium of the same tongue, the Saxon Churl was left to grovel in ignorance, and abject, unreasoning superstition. The fierce spirit of independence and of conquest, which characterized the Saxons as pagans, when they first landed on the coast of

Britain, had been crushed under a load of ceremonies, and an unbounded spiritual domination. Large portions of the country had passed into the hands of the emissaries of Rome, and the revenues of church property were, from time to time, sent out of the kingdom. When, therefore, England was invaded by the pagan Norsemen, the Saxons had little to lose, as a people, except their lives: that hardihood and daring, on account of which some of the German tribes were said to be a match for the very gods themselves,* succumbed to the ferocity of the followers of Odin, ever practised in bloodshed, and eager for conquest. Into the higher ranks of the Saxons, Christianity had diffused a milder and more peaceful disposition. Sigeberht, King of the East-Angles, gave the first instance of an Anglo-Saxon royal monk.

"So deep rooted was the conviction that led the East-Anglian to a renunciation of earthly sway, that not even the danger of his native land, at that time suffering under the cruel ravages of Penda, King of Mercia, could induce him to forsake the quiet of his cloister. When forcibly brought forth by his subjects, in the hope that the sight of a leader, once honored for his valor, might cheer and stimulate his warriors, he stood still amidst the raging battle, with a staff in his hand, until he was slain, together with his brother Egric." *Thorpe's Translation of Lappenberg's History of England under the Anglo-Saxon Kings.*

"So soon had the time passed away when the son of Woden knew no greater disgrace than to die in a bed. But to the nation, the then increasing longing after the cowl was more pernicious than the use of harness." *Idem.*

From these causes, the cultivation of the Anglo-

* "Sunt quae Suevis concedere, quibus ne Dii quidem immortales pares esse possunt."—*Cæsar, De Bello Gallico,* lib. iv. c. 7.

Saxon tongue was entirely neglected, and we have the extraordinary fact that, whilst not a single fragment of Anglo-Saxon literature existed, or even had been called into existence, a Scandinavian literature had existed for ages in Iceland—the remotest habitation of man; and that literature full of a fiery and poetic daring. Under its influence, the Norse warrior was stimulated to court every extremity of danger, and to despise every extremity of suffering. He lived in the alternations of drunkenness and slaughter, gloating with a diabolical satisfaction over the bodies of his enemies, given as food to the wolf and the raven, or floating, in bloated putrefaction, the sport of wind and wave.

When these Norsemen took possession, therefore, of various portions of the kingdom, we might naturally expect that their language, originally of the same family with the Anglo-Saxon, though now diversified by time and circumstances, would mix itself with the language of the more ancient inhabitants of the soil.

That a considerable similarity existed between the Anglo-Saxon and the Scandinavian, both originally, and by subsequent amalgamation, is proved by the fact that about the time of the conversion of the followers of Odin, in later ages, a Saxon priest was sent from England to assist in the conversion of the Scandinavians, as being sufficiently acquainted with the Scandinavian language.

Mr. Bosworth has given various examples, which perfectly establish the similarity that existed amongst all the Germanic languages. The Dutch V, it may be premised, is sounded like the English F.

CHAPTER XI.

SIMILARITY BETWEEN THE GERMAN AND SCANDINAVIAN LANGUAGES.

English.	*Anglo-Sax.*	*Dutch.*	*Fris.*	*Ger.*	*Mœs.*	*Dan.*	*Swed.*	*Icel.*
A Fish	[illegible]	[illegible]	Fisk.	[illegible]	Fisks.	Fisk.	Fisk.	Fiskr.
A Fish's	[illegible]	[illegible]	Fiskes.	[illegible]	Fiskis	[illegible]	Fiska.	Fiska.
To a Fish	[illegible]	[illegible]	Fiske	Fische.	Fiska	Fisk.	Fisk.	Fiske.
A Fish	Fisc	[illegible]	Fisk.	Fisch	Fisk	Fisk.	Fisk.	Fisk.
Fishes	[illegible]	[illegible]	Fiskar.	Fische.	Fiskos.	Fisk.	Fiskean.	Fiskar.
Fishes'	[illegible]	[illegible]	Fiske.	Fische.	Fiskl.	Fiskes	Fiskars.	Fiskar.
To Fishes	[illegible]	[illegible]	Fiskum.	Fischen.	Fiskar.	Fiske.	Fiskar.	Fiskum.
Fishes	[illegible]	[illegible]	Fiskar.	Fische.	Fiskans	Fiske.	Fiskar.	Fiska.

English.	*Anglo-Sax.*	*Dutch.*	*Fris.*	*Ger.*	*Mœs.*	*Dan.*	*Swed.*	*Icel.*
I	Ic	Ic	Ik.	Ich.	Ik.	Jeg.	Jag.	Ek.
Mine	Min	Mijn	Min.	Mein.	Meins.	Min	Min.	Min.
To Me.	Me	Mij	Mi	Mir.	Mis.	Mij.	Mej.	Mér.
Me	Me.	Mij	Mich.	Mich	Mik	Mig	Mig	Mik.
We	We.	Wij	Wi.	Wir	Weis.	Wi.	Wi.	Wer.
Our	Ure.	Onser.	Use.	Unser.	Unsara	Vor.	War.	War.
To Us	Us.	Ons.	Us	Uns.	Uns.	Os.	Oss.	Oss.
Us	Us	Ons	Us.	Uns.	Uns.	Os.	Oss.	Oss.

Irregular Verbs.

But perhaps the strongest proof of an identity of origin, in all the German languages, is to be found in the case of irregular verbs and comparisons. Take, for instance, the verb *come*, English; present, come; perfect, came; past participle, come. Anglo-Saxon, cume, com, cumen. Fris. kem, kom, kemen. Low Dutch, kom, kwam, ge komen. Mœsic, quima, quam, quiman. German, komme, kam, (ge) kommen. Icel. kem, kom, kommen. Dan. kommen, kam, kummen. Swed. kommen, kom, kommen.

Irregular Comparisons.

English, good, better, best. Anglo-Saxon, god, betra, betst. Fris. gód, bettre (betere), beste. Dutch, goed, beter, best. Mœs. goths, batiza, batist. Ger. gut, besser, beste. Icel. gód, bettri, bestr. Dan. god, bedre, beste. Swed. god, bättre, bäst.

Many nouns may be traced through all these languages, with very insignificant variations. For example: Anglo-Saxon, meole. Plat. Dutch, melk. Ger. milch. Icel. meolk. Danish, malk. Swed. mjölk. English, milk.

Anglo-Saxon, rec. Plat. Dutch, rook. Fris. rec. Ger. rauch. Icel. reykr. Dan. rog. Swed. rok. English, reek.

A Dalecarnian boy, brought over by the Swedish ambassador, is said to have easily understood the language spoken by the peasantry of the north of England. The Dalecarnian is the mountain dialect of Norway. It is also said that some Scotch farmers, who have taken up their abode in Norway, have little difficulty in understanding the Norwegians, or being understood by them. In making the comparison, we must not look to the spelling, but to the general sound of the word. As a proof of the strong similarity between the English and the Danish languages, we cannot perhaps have a better specimen than the following quotation, taken from the beginning of a national song, which is to the Danes what "God save the King" is to the English:—

English.

"King Christian stood by the lofty mast,
    In mist and smoke;
His sword was hammering so fast,
Through Gothic helm, and brain it pass'd;
Then sank each hostile hulk and mast
    In mist and smoke.
Fly, shriek'd they, fly he who can;
Who braves of Denmark's Christian
    The stroke?"

Danish.

"Kong Christian stod ved höien mast,
    I Rog og Damp;
Hans Værge hamrede saa fast,
At Gothens Hielm, og Hierne brast;
Da sank hver fiendligt Speil og Mast
    I Rog og Damp.
Flye, skreyde flye, hvad flye can;
Hvo staar for Danmark's Christian
    I Kamp?"

Some of these words resemble the Anglo-Saxon more than they do the English of the present day; as fiendligt, the Anglo Saxon being feondlic, signifying hostile; hver, in Anglo-Saxon, æghwæher, each.

In the same song, the following words occur in one line:—

    "Han heisede det röd flag."
    "He hoisted the red flag."

Modern:—

    "Hans mad var græ hopper, og vild honning."
    "His meat was the grasshopper, and wild honey."

    "Han sad til dem, følger efter mig."
    "He said to them, follow after me."

In the national song we see not only a close similarity

of terms, but a capability of mutual translation, almost word for word, with the same metrical arrangement.

Some stanzas by the Countess of Blessington on Life and Death, which appeared in the "Book of Beauty," in 1834, have been translated by Mr. Bosworth into the present Friesic language, and resemble the Anglo-Saxon so closely, that the mere English scholar may at once comprehend the greater part of it:—

> "Dead, hwat bist dou,
> Ta hwaem allen buisgje,
>   Fen de scepterde kening ta da slave?
> De lætste bæste freon,
> Om uns soargen to eingjen,
>   Dyn gebiet is in t' græf."

> "Death, what art thou,
> To whom all bow,
>   From sceptered king to slave?
> The last best friend,
> Our cares to end,
>   Thy empire is in the grave."

"When Wilfrith, Bishop of York, was accidentally thrown upon the coast of Friesland, he preached to them the Gospel of Christ, in the intelligible dialect of the Anglo-Saxons, and baptized nearly all the princes, with many thousands of the people."—*Lappenberg.*

The Friesians, from the earliest ages, have occupied the same country, bordering on the Ems, and stretching into Jutland. They were neighbors of the Angles, from whom we derive our name of Anglesmen or Englishmen; and, being a maritime people, most probably joined the Angles in their irruptions into Britain. We have then all these various streams, issuing from the great Gothic reservoir, again collected on the soil of Britain, receiving an accession from the Norman, and, as the progress of arts, and sciences, and literature require, admitting various additions from the Latin and Greek, and occasionally from the modern languages of Europe. In the northern counties of England, the language of the common people is to this day Dano-Saxon, and differs very materially from the language of the South both in terms and pronunciation. There is in the North a striking peculiarity in the use of the definite article. The Southern imagines that it is dropped altogether before words beginning with a consonant. This, however, is not the case. It is always mentally, and to a certain extent audibly, pronounced in such cases. In the South it would be said, for example, fetch THE cows; in the North, fetch t' cows. Even in words beginning with a vowel the same principle is adopted, as, drive t' ass out of t' orchard.

The origin of this custom we find in the phrase, which occurs in the stanzas on Death, already quoted, in t' graf, in t' grave, in *the grave*. In the Hindelopian Calendar for seamen, we find the dialect of Westmoreland so clearly marked, that whole lines would be understood there without difficulty, whether spoken or written. For example:—

"As we tommelje ower t' watter."
"As we tumble over the water."
Westmoreland. "As we tummel ower t' watter."

As a general summary, then, we have these results.

CHAPTER XII.

MIGRATIONS.

First Migration.

THE Gomerian or Celtic race, migrating from the East, and occupying a considerable portion of Europe. These were the first occupants, and from these are derived the following languages:—

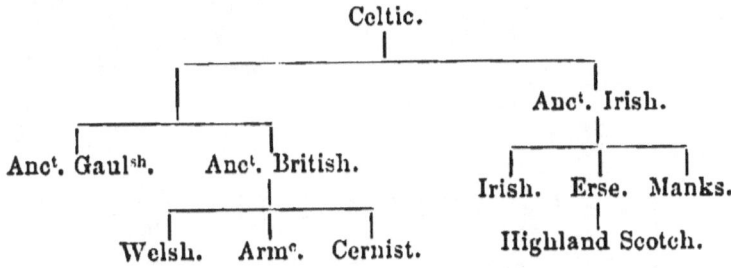

Second Migration.

The next migration from the East took place about 700 years before the Christian era, and this consisted of the Gothic or Teutonic tribes. The bulk of Europeans are descended from these. From the Gothic are derived the following languages:—

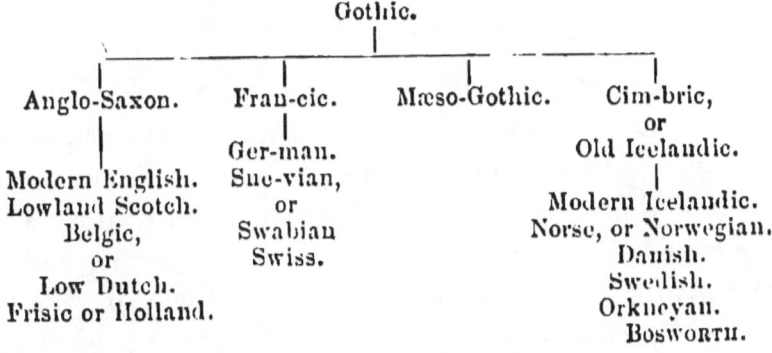

Last Migration.

The *last* stream of population from the East was the Sclavonic, which overflowed Russia, Poland, Eastern Prussia, Moravia and Bohemia. With the Celtic and Sclavonic the English language has very little, if any affinity. The blood of all the Gothic tribes flows in its veins. The bone, and sinew, and muscle are Gothic: its filling up and polish, and adaptation to the progressive exigencies of the times, are from the Roman and Grecian models.

CHAPTER XIII.

THE CHANGES THAT THE ANGLO-SAXON HAS UNDERGONE IN ENGLAND.

The *First Change* that took place was from the partial introduction of Scandinavian terms from Norway, Sweden, and Denmark.

Names of Places.

It is almost a general rule, that the names of towns and villages ending in *by* are of Scandinavian origin, as Derby, Whitby. Such names abound in the northern parts of England, whilst few, if any towns or villages in the south of England, have names ending in *by*, Rugby excepted. *By*, in Danish, signifies a town or village. Thus *By*, combined with a term descriptive of some local feature or peculiarity, would form the proper name of a town or village; as, *Whitby*, White-*By*, White-Town; Deor-*By*, the habitation or place of Deer, Deer-*By*, Derby.

Names of Persons.

The proportion of names ending in *son* preponderate greatly among the Dano-Saxon population of the North. Such names were originally of Scandinavian origin, though the principle was afterwards extended to Anglo-Saxon names, and obviously must have been so in the case of names derived from Scripture; as, Johnson, John son. The names Arneson, Arason, Haraldson, Harald-Sigur*dson*, Harald son of Sigurd, were common in Scandinavia, before we hear of such terminations in England. Swein still exists in the present name, Swainson. Swend was born of *Alfila*, a daughter of Earl Alfrim, and was also called Swend Alfila*son*. Olafson, son of Olaf the Saint. Eric, Ericson. Ulf, Ulfson.

Ing was the Anglo-Saxon termination denoting son; as Ethelwulf Ecbright*ing*, Ethelwulf the son of Ecbert or Ecbright; Bryn*ing*, Bryn's son.

Amongst the Northmen, who took possession of that region which is now called Normandy, such names as ended in *son* generally took the prefix *Fitz* or *Fits*, a contraction of *Filius*, in the place of son; thus Gerald-son would become *Fitz* or *Fitz-Gerald*.

The *Second Change* commenced with the accession of William the Conqueror, and progressed to about the time of Henry the Third.

"The foundation indeed of Norman influence, in England, was laid in the reign of Edward the Confessor, who, having passed his youth, and having received his education, at the court of his uncle Duke Richard, returned to his native country with a train of Norman favorites. This Norman faction was opposed by the Saxons, under Earl Godwin; but the battle of Hastings put an end to the struggle, and the French ascendancy became complete."—*Hippesley; Chapters on English Literature*, p. 9.

Property and official dignities were occupied by the Normans. The language of the court and of public business was Norman; and a knowledge of that language became a necessary qualification for the discharge of public duties. It consequently became a part of school and university education to translate Latin into French.

"In the reign of Edward the Third, the fate of French, as a national language, was sealed. Soon after the plague in 1348, the practice of translating into French was discontinued by schoolmasters." . . . "By a statute of 1362, all pleas in courts of justice are directed to be carried on in English."—*Hippesley*, p. 11.

The *Third Change* came on about the reign of Elizabeth.

The *Fourth*, from that time has been, and is now in progress; consisting chiefly of the application of numerous classical terms to the literature, and the arts and sciences of the day.

Chaucer, Spenser, Shakspeare are the great landmarks of English poetry, each exercising no inconsiderable influence over the age in which he lived.

The most important change was begun by the Danes, because it was a structural change: they disregarded inflexions. According to Hicks, Henley, and Rask, the Anglo-Saxon had six declensions; according to Thwaites seven, Manning four, Lye three, which last number is also adopted by Bosworth. Judging from so wide a diversity of opinion, there must have been multitudes of exceptions to any general rule on the subject of declensions. The Anglo-Saxon had four cases in each number, nominative, genitive, dative, and accusative, determined by the ending of the word. As

Singular.
N. Smith, a smith.
G. Smith-es, of a smith.
D. Smith-e, to a smith.
A. Smith, a smith.

Plural.
N. Smith-as, smiths.
G. Smith-a, of smiths.
D. Smith-um, to smiths.
A. Smith-as.

CHAPTER XIV.

SIMPLIFICATION OF INFLEXIONS.

In the time of Chaucer, about the year 1350, the six declensions of Anglo-Saxon nouns were reduced to one, and the cases from four to two—the genitive case being formed from the nominative, by the addition of *es*, in the singular number; and, in the plural, all the cases being invariable. In the plural number of nouns we have some exceptions to the general rule; as ox, *oxen;* and, in some parts of the country, amongst the common people, we still hear house, *housen.* From the present structure of our own language, we know that the relation of words to each other may be expressed by the use of prepositions, without the assistance of these variable and complex terminations. The Normans also, finding the cases and the remaining inflexions of nouns inconvenient, dispensed with them altogether, except in the expression of the genitive case; and this is often formed by the use of the preposition *of* before the noun, instead of the abbreviated Saxon genitive; as, Christes, Christ's, of Christ. In dispensing with these variable terminations, the language was returning to the principles of the Hebrew language, which expressed the relation of words by *prefixes*, the same prefix being applicable to any noun, and each noun remaining invariable, except in the difference between the singular and the plural numbers.

The Hebrew says:—

Singular.	*Plural.*
seq, a sack.	sequim, sacks.
le-seq, of a sack.	le-sequim, of sacks.
me-seq, from a sack.	me-sequim, from the sacks.
be-seq, in a sack.	be-sequim, in sacks.

Here the noun itself is invariable, except as far as it is requisite to distinguish the plural from the singular number by the addition of *im*, as we do by the addition of *s*; seq, sequim, sack, sacks. The Northmen, therefore, in avoiding trouble, by simplifying, were in fact returning to an old and philosophical principle, which has been adopted to a certain extent in modern Greek, and in the Italian language.

Again, the Anglo-Saxon had its arbitrary genders, like the Greek, Latin, French, and German of the present day; than which nothing can be more unphilosophical, or gratuitously troublesome. Why, for instance, should *fle* be of the masculine gender in Latin, *water* in the feminine, *air* in the masculine, *earth* in the feminine, and *heaven* in the neuter? As a principle, the English language has discarded these absurdities; and, except in the case of figurative personification, all creatures of the male sex are of the masculine gender, those of the female sex of the feminine, and things without life are of neither gender, or *neuter*. The English language determines the gender by the signification of the term, without any respect to the termination. The ancient languages, except the Hebrew, determined the gender by the termination, without respect to the signification, but with innumerable exceptions and inconsistencies; and it would be a bold assertion to say that, in Latin and Greek, or in many modern languages, there is any such thing as a general rule on the subject of genders.

Again, in the Anglo-Saxon, adjectives had their singular and plural numbers, and their masculine, feminine, and neuter genders distinguished by the termination, and agreeing with their respective nouns; but, as the adjective, both in the Anglo-Saxon and modern English, is in juxta-position with its nouns, of which it expresses the quality, there would be no necessity for any variation at all. We can say, a tall man, a tall woman, a tall spire; or tall men, tall women, tall spires. It is not necessary to alter the word *tall*, either as to number, case, or gender. This useless variation was also discarded.

Again, in Anglo-Saxon, adjective pronouns were declined like nouns adjective, and varied in number, case, and gender. *Mine*, for example, in English has no variation whatever. We say the house is mine, the field is mine, the horse is mine, or the houses are mine, the fields are mine, the horses are mine. The word *mine*, however applied, has no variable termination. It is true we say, *my* house, using *my* before a noun; but the word *my* is in a different position, and, though *mine* in the position of *my* would now be somewhat antiquated, still there is no impropriety in using *mine*, as *mine* host, *mine* arm.

But in the Anglo-Saxon we had

	Singular.			*Plural.*	
	Masc.	Fem.		Masc. Fem.	Neut.
Nom.	Min.	Mine.	Nom.	Mine.	
Gen.	Minnes.	Minre.	Gen.	Min-a.	
Dat.	Minum.	Minre.	Dat.	Min-um.	
Acc.	Minne.	Mine.	Acc.	Min-e.	

Ba, both.   Tig, Twenty.

Nom. Ba.	Nom. Tig.
Gen. Begra.	Gen. Tigra.
Dat. Bam.	Dat. Tig-um.
Acc. Ba.	Acc. Tig.

The Anglo-Saxon verbs had a greater variety of terminations than the present English verbs. About the time of Chaucer they had assumed much of their present simplicity. The final *n* of verbs was dropped about the time of Henry VIII.: as, we loven, ye loven, they loven, *i. e.* we love, ye love, they love. Ben Jonson regrets the loss of the final *n*: —

"All to tell you my opinion, I am persuaded that the lack hereof will ere it be long be found a great blemish to our tongue."

CHAPTER XV.

SUMMARY OF CHANGES.

The first material change, then, that took place in the Anglo-Saxon, was by the introduction of the Dano-Saxon, operating, more or less, according to the regions occupied by the Northmen. This Danish influence was felt chiefly from the year 900 to 1070. They introduced new terms, and dealt with inflexions, at their own will and pleasure. After the conquest, the particolored Norman-French, a mixture of the Gallic and the language of the Northern adventurers, mingled itself, more or less, with the already altered language of the country, again gradually casting aside what remained of inflexions and variable terminations. This process went on from two to three centuries: the orthography of the language, long after this date, remaining very different from its present state. From the period of the translation of the Scriptures into English, no very material alteration has taken place. Verbs ending in *eth*, as loveth, hateth, have been changed into loves, hates, at the same time that the termination *ed* has, in many cases, been contracted, so as to coalesce with the root of the verb, as *lov'd*. In some cases, such a coalition would be cacophonous; in others, as in words ending in *t*, impossible; we cannot pronounce hate, hated, hat'd. Both these changes, as far as the euphony of the language is concerned, are to be lamented. The *th*, almost peculiar to the English, in modern European languages, and lost to its affinities, is the gentlest and most pleasing of all sounds. Take the following passage: "Whoso love*th* fa*th*er or mo*th*er more *th*an me is not wor*th*y of me." The *th* occurs five times in this short sentence, and the whole is peculiarly soft and tender. Change the *th* of loveth into loves, and we at once pass from the note of the dove to the hiss of the serpent. Take, again, the following beautiful description of the Pelican and her young, from Rossewell's "Armourie of Honour," quoted by Mr. Lower:—

"The Pelicane fervently *loveth* her young byrdes, yet when thei ben haughtie, and beginne to wax hotte, they smite her in the face, and wounde her, and she *smiteth* then againe, and *sleaeth* them. And after three days, she *mourneth* for them, and then striking herself in the side, till the blonde runne out, she *sparpleth* it upon theire bodyes, and by virtue thereof thei quicken againe."

The word byrdes should be here pronounced as a word of two syllables—a pronunciation still found among our Southern peasantry.

"There was there a dragon grete, and grimme,
Full of fyre, and also very nime,
With a wide throte and *tushis* grete."— *Warton's Poetry.*

The Lord's prayer, now dating back more than eleven hundred years, gives us a good specimen of early Saxon. It is valuable, as affording us a subject for comparison with the different modes of expressing the same sentiments, at different periods:—

"Uren Fader, thic arth in heofnas.
Sie gehalgud thin noma, to cymeth
thin ric. Sie thin willa, sue is in
heofnas, and in eortho. Urenhlaf

ofer wirtlic* sel us to daeg, and
forgef us scylda urna, suc we for-
gefan scyldgum urum, and do inlead†
usith in custnung. An gefrig vrich
from ifle."

Of the date of 890:—

"Fæder ure thu whe eart in heofenum.
Si thin nama gehalgod.
To be-cume thin rice
Gefurthe thin willa on corthan, swa swa
on heofenum.
Urne dægramlicam hlaf syle us to dæg,
And forgif us ure gyltas, swa swa we forgifath
urum gyltendum.
And ne gelædde thu us on costenunge,
Ac alys us of yfell. Sothlice."

Taking intermediate ground between the Saxon of 890 and the present day, we have the following form of words:—

" Our Fadir that art in Hevenys.
Halewid be thi name,
Thy kingdom come to,
Be thi wil in erthe, as in hevene.
Give to us this day our breed ovir other substauce,
And forgive to us our dettis, as we forgive our dettouris,
And lede us not into temptacioun.
But delyvere us from yvel. Amen."

In 1611, the only difference between the Lord's Prayer of that date and of the present day, is in the sentence "and forgive us our *dettes*, as we forgive our detters," some of the other words also being differently spelled.

* "Ofer wirtlic." translated super-substantial.
† "Inlead," not lead.

We come then to the conclusion, that the Gothic is the root from which branched out a variety of dialects, each undergoing certain changes in the course of time, according to circumstances: that England having become the battle-field of the Gothic tribes, in after ages, these dialects became amalgamated; and that out of that amalgamation was formed the English language, modified and simplified in its construction, according to the genius of the people, and enriched from the copious stores of Latin and Greek, in terms of art, science, and philosophy, according to the rising wants of the age. It is apparent, also, that the English language has lost its declensions, its variable termination of nouns, in a great degree; its arbitrary genders; its inflection of adjectives, both in gender, case, and number. Its verbs also have been simplified, in their tenses, by the general adoption of the auxiliary verb, in the place of variable terminations. These are important changes, and render the language much easier of acquisition. No uneducated man could have written a line of verse in Latin or Greek; accurate composition could only be the result of rule and discipline. From the comparative absence of variable terminations and inflexions, and the substitution of accent for quantity in the English language, verse is frequently written, and that of no ordinary merit, by those who possess but a very slight knowledge of the grammatical structure of the language.

A knowledge of the English language, as it exists at the present time, would therefore embrace a knowledge of the Anglo-Saxon to a certain extent, of Greek and Latin, and such French terms as have established themselves in our literature; the Anglo-Saxon terms forming the bulk of the language, in about the proportion of $\frac{13}{20}$ths, and still constituting, in a very great degree, the language of the common people. The progress of discovery is every day demanding new terms, in addition to our vocabulary.

CHAPTER XVI.

NAMES OF THINGS IN COMMON USE GENERALLY ANGLO-SAXON.

THE names of things in common use are almost universally Anglo-Saxon. The names of the days of the week are still pagan, and, with a slight difference in orthography, are the same as they existed amongst our forefathers before they were converted to Christianity. Thus we have *Sun*-day, the day sacred to the sun; *Moon*-day, or Monday; *Tuisco*-day, or Tuesday; *Wodens*-day, or Wednesday; *Thors*-day, or Thursday; *Friga*-day, or Friday; *Seater*-day, or Saturday.

The idols, to which these days were sacred, were all represented under appropriate emblems. The figures are all given by Verstegan, and described in the following beautiful language:—

" *Idoll of the Sun.*

"It was made, as here appeareth, like half a naked man, set upon a piller, his face, as it were, brightened with gleames of fire, and holding with both his arms stretched out a burning wheele upon his breast, the wheele being to signify the course which he runneth round about the world, and the fiery gleames and brightnes, the light and heat wherewith he warmeth and comforteth the things that live and grow."

"The Idoll of the Moone.

"The form of this idoll seemeth very strange and ridiculous; for, being made for a woman, shee hath a short coat, like a man; but more strange it is to see her hood, with such two long eares. The holding of a moone before her breast may seem to have been to expresse what she is; but the reason of her chapron, with long eares, as also her short coat, and pyked shooes, I do not find."

"The Idol Tuisco.

"The next unto the idolls of the two most apparent planets, was the idoll of Tuisco, the most antient and peculiar god of all the Germans, here described in his garment of a skinne, according to the most antient manner of the Germans' clothing. Of this Tuisco, the first and chiefest man of name among the Germans, and after whom they do call themselves Tuytchen, that is, Duytches or Duytch people, I have already spoken in the first chapter; as also shewed how the day, which yet amongst us retaineth the name of Tuesday, was especially dedicated unto the adoration and service of this idoll."

This Tuisco is said to have been the son of Assenez, the son of Gomer, the son of Japhet, and to have been the first who conducted the Germans into *Tuitchland*. The Netherlanders, changing T into D, have made it *Duytchland*, and we now call the Duytch, Dutch. From Tuisco we have Tuisco-day, or Tuesday.

"The Idoll Woden.

"Woden was the military god of the Saxons. He was, while sometime he lived amongst them, a most valiant and victorious prince, and captaine, and his idoll was, after his death, honoured, prayed, and sacrificed unto, that, by his ayde and furtherance, they might obtaine victory over their enemies; which, when they had obtained, they sacrificed unto him such prisoners as in battell they had taken. The name Woden signifies furious, and in like sence we yet retaine it, saying, when one is in a great rage, that he is *wood*, or taketh on as if he were *wood*:" from *wedun*, to rage, *wod*, mad.

Chaucer uses the word in this sense:—

"He loved to drinke strong wine, as rede as blood,
Then wolde he speke and crie as he were *wood*."

An abjuration of Woden preceded baptism in Germany, on conversion to Christianity.

"Ek forsakno diabole, ende Woden."
"I forsake the Devil, and Woden."

"*The Idoll Thor.*

"This great reputed god, being of more estimation than many of the rest of like sort, though as little worth as any of the meanest of that rabble, was majestically placed in a very large and spacious hall, and there set, as if he had reposed himself upon a covered bed.

"On his head he wore a crowne of gold, and round in compasse above, and about the same, were set or fixed twelve bright, burnished, golden stars, and in his right hand he held a kingly scepter.

"He was of the seduced pagans beleeved to be of most marvellous power and might, yea, and that there were no people, throughout the whole world, that were not subjected unto him, and did not owe him divine honour and service.

"That there was no puissance comparable to his: his dominion, of all others, most farthest extending itselfe, both in heaven and earth.

"That in the air he governed the winds, and the clouds ; and being displeased did cause lightning, thunder, and tempests, with excessive raine, haile, and all ill weather. But being well pleased with the adoration, sacrifice, and service of his suppliants, he then bestowed upon them most fair and seasonable weather, and caused corn abundantly to grow, as also all sorts of fruits, &c., and kept away from them the plague, and all other evil and infectious diseases. Of the weekly day, which was dedicated to his peculiar service, we yet retain the name of *Thursday*, the which the Danes and Swedians doe yet call *Thorsday*. In the Netherlands, it is called *Thunders-dagh*, which being written according to our English orthography is *Thunders-day*, whereby it may appear that they antiently therein intended the day of the god of thunder; and in some of our old Saxon bookes, I find it to have been written Thunres-deag. So, as it seemeth, that the name of *Ther*, or *Thor*, was abbreviated of *Thunre*, which we now write *thunder*."

In the North of England, the old term still remains—*thunre*, and not thunder.

"The Idoll Friga."

"The idoll Friga represented both sexes. In her right hand she held a drawne sword, and in her left a bow, signifying thereby that women, as well as men, should, in time of neede, be ready to fight. Some honoured her for a god and some for a goddesse, but she was ordinarily taken rather for a goddesse than a god, and was reputed the giver of peace and plenty, as also the causer and maker of love and amity, and of the day of her special adoration we yet retain the name of Friday; and as, in the order of the dayes of the week, Thursday commeth betweene Wednesday and Friday, so (as Olaus Magnus noteth), in the septentrional regions, where they made the idoll *Thor* sitting or lying, in a great hall, upon a covered bed, they also placed on the one side of him, the idoll *Woden*, and on the other side the idoll *Friga*; and her day our Saxon ancestors called Friga-deag, from whence our name now of Friday in deed commeth."

"The Idoll Seater.

"The last, to make up the number seven, was the idoll Seater, fondly of some supposed to be Saturn.

"First, on a piller was placed a pearch, on the sharpe prickled backe whereof stood this idoll. He was leane of visage, having long haire and a long beard, and was bare-headed and bare-footed. In his left hand he held up a wheele, and in his right he carried a paile of water, wherein were flowers and fruites. His long coat was girded unto him, with a towel of white linnen. His standing on the sharpe finnes of this fish, was to signify, that the Saxons for their serving him should passe stedfastly and without harm in dangerous and difficult places. By the wheele was belikened the knit unity and conjoined concord of the Saxons, and their concurring together in running one course. By the girdle, which with the wind streamed from him, was signified the Saxon's freedome. By the paile with flowers and fruites was declared, that with kindly rain he would nourish the earth, to bring forth much fruites and flowers. And the day unto which we yet give the name of Sater-day, did first receive, by being unto him celebrated, the same appellation."

Out of seven days in the week, three correspond, in the origin of their names, with the Roman calendar; Dies solis, Sun-day; Dies lunæ, Moon-day; Dies Saturni, Saturn-day; Seater-day, Saturday.

We have, however, discarded all the Anglo-Saxon designations of the months, and adopted the Roman. The origin of some of the latter may be found in the Fasti of Ovid. Different explanations are given of the names of the Anglo-Saxon months, which probably arise from the different periods to which they have reference. In a comparatively unsettled social system, different names might also prevail in different districts, as in the social partitions of hundreds, wapentakes, lathes, &c., already noticed.

The Saxons had many other idols, which it is not necessary to particularize, as no trace of them is left in the language. Of the fearful reality, which entered into the belief of our forefathers in these false gods, we have a proof in the fact of their offering human sacrifices to them for particular purposes. Harold the First, King of Norway, sacrificed two of his own sons, in order to obtain such a tempest at sea as might disperse the fleet of Harold, King of Denmark.

There is a peculiarity, also, in our mode of reckoning time, which has come down to us from our Saxon forefathers. We reckon time, in some cases, by *nights*, and not by days. We say, for instance, this day *se'nnight*, that is, this day seven nights. We also say, this day, or to-morrow *fort'night*, that is, this day or to-morrow fourteen nights.

CHAPTER XVII.

NAMES OF PLACES.

The names of places are generally to be looked for in Anglo-Saxon. In our researches here, we must pay little regard to the spelling. The sound deducible from the letters must be our guide. It has already been stated, that the word *give* is spelled in thirteen different ways. Even later than the time of Elizabeth there was no settled orthography. The different members of the same family would spell the family name in different ways. Dr. Chandler, as quoted by Lower, states that Waynflete had seventeen modes of orthography; and Dugdale, in his collections respecting the family of Mainwaring of Peover, in Cheshire, has the extraordinary number of 131 variations of that single name.—

(Lower.) The same uncertainty prevailed in the names of places, and frequently they are only to be dimly perceived. There are a few general terms, however, which will always be found useful in discovering the origin of the names of places.

The names of places ending in *chester*, or *caster*, denote that a Roman camp has been situated there, being derived from the Latin castra; as, Silchester, in Hants; Colnchester, in Essex; Lancaster, corrupted from Lunecaster, a camp on the river Lune, as Colnchester is a camp on the river Colne; Winchester, the Roman term of which was Vindonia. The V has been changed into W, as in the case of *vinum* into *wine*. From this we get Win, which, with the addition of chester, indicating a camp, makes Winchester.

Burg, Burh, Byrig, Bury, a town, a fort, a city; as, Canterbury, Salisbury, Scarborough, a town on a rock or Scar.

Bourne, a brook; as, Selbourne, Titchbourne, Sherbourne, &c. "Ofer tha bur-nan Cedron," over the brook Cedron, John xviii. 1. Places, into the names of which this word enters, under different modifications, are situated on brooks. The secondary signification of this word is a boundary, because streams form the natural boundaries of a region.

Butts. When the bow formed the chief weapon in war, many towns and villages had a field set apart for practice, usually called the *butts* or *butt*-close; the butt being the object at which the arrow was discharged. Hence, we say that a man is made the *butt* of the company, that is, an object or mark for the discharge of pointed jokes.

By, bye, Danish, a town, or village, or habitation, as already observed.

Bottom, a deep valley; a depression of the ground. Mr. Lower, on the authority of "an intelligent correspondent," supposes the personal name *Ramsbottom* to be a corruption of the word *Romsbottom.* *Roms,* in Lancashire, signifies a kind of wild onion, which is produced in two bottoms or dales near Bury, in Lancashire, in great abundance; hence *Romsbottom,* corrupted to *Ramsbottom.* *Ramps* is the term applied to this filthy pasture-weed, in the northern counties. *Ram,* however, enters into the composition of other names of places; as, *Rams*dale in Hants, *Rams*gate in Kent, where the same etymology would not perhaps apply.

Car, a marshy place, where alders grow.

Carn, or *Cairn,* a Druidical heap of stones.

Coomb, Combe, a wooded valley. Coombe Hurst, a wooded valley in Surrey.

"Sylvan Combes."—*Wordsworth.*

Croft, a small inclosure. A poor man described proverbially—

"He had no *loft,* no *croft,*"

i. e. homestead or field.

Cross had references to places at which a cross was erected, on the junction of different ways, to point out the proper road. Crosses were in use in Mexico for this purpose, before the introduction of Christianity, and are in use in China. We also apply the term to roads that cross each other. The erection of a cross, in any particular locality, would be sufficient to give a name to a place; as, Waltham Cross, Charing Cross, a cross having been erected at the village of Charing. *Crosby-Ravensworth*, that is, Cross-by Ravensworth; worth, according to Mr. Bosworth, signifying land, a farm, street, public way, hall, palace. According to Mr. Lower, some etymologists have given it the convenient signification of *place;* if so, Crosby-Ravensworth would signify the Cross by the Raven's Place.

Dale, a valley; as, Kendal, a corruption of Kent dale: the river Kent running down the valley, and dividing the town Kendal; Ravenstonedale, the dale of the Raven's Stone; Sleddel, Slate-dale; Kirby Lonsdale, Kirk by Lune's dale.

Dene, Deane, and *Den* have all the same origin, and signify a valley or low place:—

"Ale denu byth gefylled."
"Every valley shall be filled."—*Luke* iii. 5.

Singly, it is generally spelled deane or dean, as Dean, in Hants, also Bramdean; in composition, sometimes den, as, Arden, Ardean, in Warwickshire.

Donne, Don, Dun, Dune, and *Down,* as we now write it, are all the same. The term signifies a *hill*, stretching out in a gentle slope. Sand-banks in Holland are called *dunes*. Dunkirk had its name from its situation on the *dunes* or sand-banks. We still have the term *downs* in the South Downs.

Fell, in the northern countries, a term applied to mountains; *Stainmore, Stan, Stone-moor Fells.*

Ford, the passage of a river, as Ox*ford,* Hart*ford;* not to be confounded with *fort,* as Roch*fort.*

Frith, from *fretum*. In England, a plain amidst woods: in Scotland, a strait between two lands.

Grange. According to Lower, a large farm, kept in hand by a religious fraternity, with buildings, and occasionally a chapel attached. Nicotius interprets it a *barn*. It is usually applied to a lone farm-house.

Gill, a stony watercourse or ravine.

Ham, a very common termination to the names of places, signifies home; in the Southern counties pronounced *home*, but in the North retaining much of its original pronunciation, as if written *heam*. The original form still remains in *hamlet*, and in the various compounds of *ham*; as Den*ham*, Ded*ham*, Hig*ham*, Lang*ham*, and also in Sout*ham*pton or South*ham*-ton, South-home-town, compared with Winchester, the seat of some of the Anglo-Saxon kings, or compared with England at large; so also *Ham*tunscire abbreviated to *Ham*pshire. In Swedish, it is written *hem*; Danish, *hiem*; German, *heim*, from *heimen*, to cover; originally signifying a place of shelter.

Hatch, a flood-gate, such as used in the irrigation of meadows, a gate, or door, on a game-warren.

Hide, as much land as one plough can plough, in a year, with one team.

Hough, a green plot in a valley.

Hou, according to Lye and Bosworth, a mountain; from the Anglo Saxon *how*.

Holm, plain grassy ground, by the side of a river.

Holt, a hanging wood, a grove.

"Abraham planted a *holt*."— *Gen.* xxi. 33.

Holt-hana, a wood-cock.

Hurst, or *Hyrst,* a wood; as, Tyee*hurst,* Crow*hurst,* Bang*hurst,* Yew*hurst.*

Ing, a meadow, field, tract of land; as, Read*ing,* Red*ing,* Birmingham, Broom-*ing*-ham or home, Godalming, Basing: Danish, Anglo-Saxon, and German.

Knoll, the top of a hill.

Lee, leigh, lea, lye, all have the same signification, and denote pasture-ground. We say pasture-ley, clover-lea, sainfoin-lea. It meets us under various combinations; as, *Bramley, Bramble*-ley, *Oakley, Oak*-ley, *Bromley, Broom*-ley, *Nutley, Nut*-ley. This word so frequently forms a surname in Cheshire, that Mr. Lower, on the authority of a correspondent, gives the following proverb—

"As many Leighs as fleas, Massies as asses, and Davenports as dogs' tails."

Ness, a promontory projecting like a nose.

Pen, the top of a hill. British.

Slack, a depression between two hills; the form assumed by a slack rope.

Scar, a word common in the North, to denote a craggy eminence or precipice. *Scar*borough, a town upon a scar.

Shaw, a small wood or coppice; applied often to signify a broad hedge-row.

Shot, a keep.

Slow, slough, a miry place.

Spital. Spital Inn, on the wildest part of Stainmore Fells: an abbreviation of hospital, a place for the reception of strangers. *Hospitium*, Lat. Such a place was necessary for the shelter of travellers in that stormy region.

Sted, Dutch, *Stad*, a station. Homestead.

Strand, the bank of a river, as the Strand in London.

Staple, as Barnstable, Barnstaple, a place, a mart for merchandise, where goods were placed under the King's staple. See "Halle of John Hall," by the Rev. Mr. Duke.

Stoke signifies in itself a place, and is generally combined with some other description, or distinctive word; as, Woodstock, Wode-stoc, a woody place. Laverstoke, Alverstoke, Basingstoke.

In the word Basingstoke, we have *stoke* as a generic term, and *Basing* as a distinctive term. By Basingstoke is meant a place near Basing; as, in other cases, it is said, Stoke-by-Clare, Stoke-by-Nayland. So, in this case, it might have been said, Stoke-by-Basing, or Basingstoke. Basing might perhaps derive its name from Baize-Ing, or Baize meadow, supposing that particular kind of cloth to have been exposed there. But the word *Basing* occurs, as a whole term, in Joshua vii. 21, in the sense of *cloak* or garment, as " Je geseah, wurm-readne basing," I saw a shell-fish-reddened cloak —a purple cloak, dyed from the shell-fish—a Babylonish garment—*wurm* signifying a shell-fish, the fish from which the celebrated purple of old was obtained. Wurm-readne thread, scarlet thread.

Thrup, a village; a name prevailing in various parts of the country, sometimes simply, sometimes with a distinctive addition; as Bishops-*thorp*, Mil-*thorp*, by metathesis Milthrop. Crackenthorp, by the same change Crackenthrop. Anglo-Saxon *thorp*, Dutch *dorp*, Ger. *dorf*, Swedish and Danish *torp*, Fris. *therp*. We need not be surprised that this word should have established itself over various parts of England, as it prevailed in all the countries of our progenitors.

Thwaite, used in the North, supposed to be derived from the Dutch *hwoit*, a pasture.

Tor, a rock having a castellated form. In this sense, it occurs in Derbyshire, where we meet with so many heights having the form of *towers*, or castles. This word occurs in fifteen different languages in the same sense, though with variations in spelling. *Turris* in Latin, in English *tower*.

Ton, tun, a garden, or small inclosure, a town, a number of habitations within prescribed limits. *Wyrt-tun*, a garden of worst, or herbs. Luke xiii. 19.

Wick, wich. Dan. *vig*, and Swedish *vig*, a bay, Dutch *wyk*. A creek formed by the curve of a river, a station or place of retreat. Its meaning will therefore vary with attendant circumstances; as Aln-*wick*, a dwelling on the Aln; Green-*wic*, or *wich*, the green village; Gypes-*wic*, Ips-*wich*, the curve of the river Gipping; Nor-*wich*, north village; Sand-*wich*, sand village; Here-wic, *Her*-wic, *Har*-wich, the army station, from *here*, an army; Ing-here, In-here, native troops; Ut-here, Out-here, foreign troops; Gangend-here, walking troops, infantry; Ridende here, riding troops, cavalry.

PART II.
PHILOLOGICAL.

SECTION I.
ON THE GENIUS AND CHARACTER OF THE ENGLISH LANGUAGE.

CHAPTER I.
THE PRINCIPLES ON WHICH LANGUAGES ARE FORMED.

On looking at a landscape, diversified as it may be by trees and shrubs, we are not at the first impulse disposed to go back in our researches, and to find fault with it simply because it may not consist of purely indigenous productions. The poplar of Ontario or of Lombardy, the oak of Africa, the cypress of the East, the cedar of Lebanon, by the peculiarities of their growth and foliage when mixed with the natives of the forest, may all tend to produce one general and harmonious effect. To the eye of the savage, or half-civilized man, these additional ornaments were not wanted; but the uses, the conveniences, and the taste of a more refined age have adopted them, and they continue to flourish in a soil congenial with their habits and properties. It is just so with language. All languages must originally have been scanty; in the first place, simply expressive of visible objects. Grammatical inflexions, philosophical principles, and subtle distinctions must have been unknown. Language would not outstrip the wants of a community. Words would not be invented to express things which did not visibly exist, or combinations of ideas which the human mind had not yet formed. We must first, therefore, contemplate language in its skeleton condition, imperfectly jointed, uncovered with the softer integuments, not yet moulded into symmetry and just proportions, not yet graced by the poet's fancy, warmed by the patriot's ardor, enriched from the vast stores of nature and of science, or regulated by logical and grammatical criticism. If the word tree, or any equivalent term, expressed that vegetable production which we now understand by the term tree, a repetition of the word (*tree, tree, tree*) would express a forest, till some arbitrary word should be invented expressive of a number of trees as a whole. The Australian savage, sent back along the trail to recover a young man who had been left to perish in the bush, in giving an account of his journey, does not say that he proceeded so many hours along the sea-shore, and so many hours through the wood; but he travelled by *the sea*, by *the sea*, by *the sea*, or through *the wood*, through *the wood*, on *the plain*, on *the plain*, leaving you to form an opinion of the extent of each region over which he travelled by the number of repetitions; the whole forming a simple and interesting topographical description by this child of the wilderness. As mankind advanced in civilization, convenience would dictate abbreviation, and the adoption of arbitrary forms of speech; and language would thus gradually become more artificial. As new objects and new combinations of ideas presented themselves, new terms would be invented; and the language would thus become more copious and more connected. The language of a pastoral people would be confined to the objects with which they were surrounded; but, if this people, by conquest or any other cause, should become identified with a maritime people, the common language would be a mixture of both, hereafter to be modified and amalgamated by time and circumstances. The language of every people would thus be strongly tinctured by the nature of the objects with which they were surrounded. If they were conversant with clouds and storms, and those objects which present the features of a rude and harsh sublimity, the language would be formed in accordance with those objects. If, on the other hand, nature was presented under a more lovely aspect, with sunny skies and green and flowery valleys,

> " And summer seas
> Kiss'd by southern winds,"

the language of the people would soon harmonize with these gentler spirits of nature. In obedience to this principle, we find the Sclavonic, German, and Scandinavian languages abounding in consonants, so clustered and condensed as to be difficult of enunciation, except to a native; the Greek, Latin, and Italian, the Spanish and Portuguese, more flexible; the English and French holding a middle rank. Languages are thus subject to modification by climate and circumstances. The Attic dialect was softer than the Doric, or mountain Greek. The Ionic, the offspring of the voluptuous regions of Asia Minor, was softer and more sinuous than the Attic. Many of the South Sea Islands enjoy a heavenly climate, and are clothed with the most beautiful natural vegetation. The language is moulded accordingly; and whole chapters of the New Testament, translated into some of these languages, do not possess one word ending with a consonant, except the proper names of the originals. The English language, as spoken in the North of England, is much harsher, and that by a gradual progression, than that spoken in the Southern districts; and the mountainous regions of the North present us with a still ruder and harsher dialect than the plains. The republic of Tlascala was situated in the high volcanic regions between Mexico and Vera Cruz. The Tlascalans were a race of hardy and independent mountaineers. They belonged to the same great family as the Aztecs; they came on the great table-land of Mexico about the same time. But "the Tlascalan tongue," says the national historian, "simple as beseemed that of a mountain-region, was *rough* compared with the polished Tezcucan, or the popular Aztec dialect, and therefore not so well fitted for composition."*

In Norfolk and Suffolk, the English language is spoken with a very peculiar, and an almost inimitable,

* Prescott's Conquest of Mexico.

attenuated whine. In Devonshire, it is spoken with a splutter, as if the tongue were too large for the mouth, and the organs of articulation generally and inconveniently turgid. These organs in man are in fact of the most delicate construction, and are affected by the most trifling circumstances. To the same effect is the opinion of Henselius, for which he quotes Olaus Borichius, in his Synopsis Universæ Philologiæ, page 30, and quoted by Parsons in his "Remains of Japhet:"—

"Instrumenta ordinaria (loquendi) cum plura sint, pulmones, thorax, arteria, trachea, &c., fieri non potest, ut (quin) hæc ipsa climatis variatione, afficiantur, alibi ex frigore, alibi ex calore, humore, siccitate, aliisque locorum proprietatibus et in perigrinitatem quandam degenerent. Diversitatis causa non residet in solis parentibus, sed et in cibo, potu, aëre, aquis, et locis, quód crassiora hæc omnia obtusiores plerumque reddant sensus, habetiora organa, impeditiorem linguam, subtiliora, his contraria. Hinc experimur populos climatibus septemtrionis subjectos, ad duriusculas, tardas, atque asperas inclinare dialectos; ex opposito, autem, alios, qui in meridiem vergunt, ad molliora atque celeriora loquendi genera magis propensos esse."

That is,

"The organs of speech being many, as the lungs, thorax, trachea, &c., it is impossible that they should not be affected by the difference of climate, and degenerate into some corruption; in some places from heat, in others from cold, moisture, dryness, and other peculiarities of situation. The cause of this diversity is not in parents alone, but in meat, drink, water, and situation; for when all these are of a more dense nature, they for the most part make the senses duller, the organs heavier, and the tongue more slow; when more refined, they produce contrary effects. Hence, we find that those people who are subjected to the influences of northern climates, incline to hard, slow, and rough dialects; and, on the other hand, that others who verge towards the south, have a strong tendency to a softer and a more rapid way of speaking."

The impress given in early life to the organs of utterance by these causes can never be totally obliterated. Pain, pleasure, grief, joy, languor, energy, every bodily and mental affection and modification, has its peculiar and appropriate expression. The air we breathe, and the temperature in which we live, and the objects with which we are surrounded, acting from day to day upon body and mind, necessarily produce an effect upon the organs of utterance, and mould them for harsher or softer expression. To imagine the daring sea-kings of Scandinavia, cradled on the ocean and rocked by the storm, speaking in melting accents adapted to the Lydian lute, would be a monstrous and an unnatural supposition: it would be as much out of place as if Prometheus, riveted to the bleak Scythian rock, and defying the vengeance of Jove, should express himself in the liquid melody of an Anacreontic love-song. Whatever, therefore, might be the scanty vocabulary of the early progenitors of mankind, it is obvious that it would be amplified in some cases, and changed in others, and that generally it would be modified in substance, form, and enunciation by the influences of external circumstances.

"To form a just notion of the formation of language," says Mr. Ingram, "we must consider man in the infancy of society, and in the infancy of life. We must divest him of his eight parts of speech, and hear him deliver his thoughts with little more assistance than that of a noun and a verb only. We must tear from him, however reluctantly, that gaudy plumage, those borrowed wings, επεα πτεροεντα, composed of soft and beautiful feathers, hermetically adjusted, by which he has been enabled to soar with triumphant glory to the highest regions of human fancy. We must behold him a poor, defenceless creature, surrounded by wants which he struggles to express, and agitated by sensations which he labors to communicate. We shall then see how various causes of a local and temporary nature have influenced his ideas, and the language in which he has embodied them."

Thus, then, the language of a mere pastoral people would differ widely from that of a maritime people; that of the mountaineer from that of the inhabitant of the plain; that of the wanderer of the burning desert from that of the rude and hardy barbarian of the cold, dark, and damp German forest. Language being the spontaneous result of human organization, would everywhere be influenced by geographical position. The wants of a people merely pastoral would be few, and easily expressed: but a people whose territories might branch out into mountain, and plain, and forest; who might have their flocks, and herds, and corn-fields, and vineyards; their rivers, and lakes, and seas, and mines, and minerals; and who might be daily establishing some interchange of production with other communities more or less remote, would be constantly increasing their stock of words by the introduction of new commodities, and the adoption of their concurrent names. The language would thus not only become more copious, but more polished, divested of its asperities, worn down and rounded by use, by collision, and attrition—like pebbles on the sea-shore, tossed by every returning tide.

CHAPTER II.

THE LANGUAGE OF GREECE.

Hence, from the position of Greece, for example, we should expect to find a language at once copious and polished. Situated in the most favored latitude, and enjoying a beautiful climate—intersected by bays and creeks, and possessing an extraordinary extent of seacoast, compared with her area—broken into great diversities of surface—the sublimities of Olympus and Pindus contrasting with the fens of Bœotia—Greece enjoyed every variety of natural scenery. Divided again into various independent communities, each following the bent of its own policy, and influenced by its own peculiar locality, she presents us with the hardy mountaineer, the ponderous Theban, the volatile and subtle Athenian, the luxurious Corinthian, and the stern and frugal Spartan—in fact, with every variety of human character. Her seas were studded with the most beautiful islands, yielding the choicest gifts of nature; whilst she held an easy intercourse with the whole southern coast of Europe, the northern coast of Africa, and the soft and luxurious regions of Asia Minor. She possessed a copious mythology, derivative and invented—gods, and goddesses, and demigods, and nymphs, and fawns, and satyrs, all favorable to the spirit of poetry; while, from all the scattered Grecian communities, and their colonial dependencies, the most enterprising spirits were collected periodically into one focus, at the Olympian and Pythian games. There they joined in bodily and mental conflict, not for filthy bags of gold, but for the simple olive crown, which, entwined around the brows of the victor, made him at once the proudest and the happiest man on earth. The Greek language is therefore precisely what, from the preceding principles, we should have expected—copious, as having been fed from various sources; subtle and complicated, and intriguing, according to the genius of the people; and harmonious, as having received the last degree of cultivation.

From the facility with which it admits of composition of noun with noun, and preposition with other parts of speech, of combinations under the most diversified aspects, it is capable of expressing the most delicate shades of meaning, the nicest points of physical and metaphysical distinctions, impalpable to the touch of ruder speech. In the plenitude of its greatness, and the age of its purity, it was the language of philosophy and science, of history, poetry, and oratory —of the sublimest productions of human genius. It enters greatly into the composition of most European languages. It is most exclusively the language of our sciences; and so it will continue to be, till man shall again retrograde to the food of the beech-mast, and the shelter of the wigwam. It is fortunate for mankind that a language should thus exist, which is the common property of all, and peculiar to none; that it should enter, more or less, into the constitution of the language of all civilized nations; and that the nomenclature of the most important sciences in which mankind have been engaged, should possess an identity quite independent of a barbarous and a contracted provincialism. Take, for instance, the science of Geology, which, half a century ago, had no words to express its meaning, and yet it has already arrived at such a pitch of copiousness and variety in its Grecian nomenclature, as to require a distinct glossary. We have here a science springing up 2,000 years after the Greek language was spoken in its purity; and yet that language, from its extraordinary capabilities of combination, has been adopted, as if it were a matter of course, and by general consent, to express the varied conditions of the organic and inorganic matter of ages past and gone, and lost in the darkness of antiquity. We need not, therefore, be surprised that a language found so convenient in expressing the terms of philosophy, of science, and of arts, should be adopted, not only in those particular departments, but that it should also enter materially into the composition of all languages, wherever Grecian literature has been cultivated. Yet Greek in its construction is not a practical, every-day language. It is the language of the scholar rather than the language of the common people: it never could be the language of an ordinary people. The incalculable variety of its terminations, its singular, dual, and plural numbers, its declensions and cases, its capricious irregularities, its arbitrary genders, its verbs active, passive, and middle, barytons, contracted, ending in $\mu\iota$, and anomalous, many of them with their participial terminations running through about twelve hundred Protean changes and complexities, render it a matter of astonishment that it should ever have been the spoken language of a mixed community. With four variations only in the English regular verb, and with a pronoun far more simple than that of the Greek language, we seldom take up a book, even of the last century, without perpetually meeting with a confusion of the preterite tense of the verb with the passive participle, and of the nominative with the objective case of the pronoun—and this, too, amongst the standard authors of English literature. The frequent occurrence of such errors constitutes them errors of ignorance, and not of inadvertence.

CHAPTER III.

THE ANGLO-SAXON LANGUAGE.

In the formation of the Greek language, we see the principles here laid down fully borne out. It is the language of an acute and ingenious people, framed, enriched, polished, and embellished under peculiar circumstances. The language of our continental forefathers was framed under circumstances the very reverse. It was the language of fierce and untamed barbarians, hemmed in by tribes as barbarous as themselves, cut off from foreign intercourse, or roving as sea-wolves only to plunder and destroy. It was the language of a people conversant only with gloomy forests and stormy seas, and naturally prone to taciturnity; we may therefore expect a language harsh and monosyllabic. *A priori*, we should be led to suppose that such would be the character of the Anglo-Saxon language. Such it was—a vigorous stock, destined to receive the grafts of more sunny and softer climes, to throw out its branches far and wide, and to blossom and bear abundant fruit.

CHAPTER IV.

MONOSYLLABIC CHARACTER OF THE ENGLISH LANGUAGE.

In the simple specimens of our written language, and in common colloquial intercourse, it is computed that the average of Anglo-Saxon words, compared with those of foreign origin, is as 15 to 5; and Dr. Hicks has observed that, of 58 words of which the Lord's Prayer consists, 55 are derived from the Anglo-Saxon. In the opening of the Gospel of St. John, the proportion is perhaps greater, and in the first sentence of Paradise Lost, out of 41 consecutive words, there are but 7 not of Saxon origin.

As a principle in the construction of language, we can see no reason why the simple name of a thing should not be expressed by a monosyllable, as *tree*, except when the term is expressive of the thing itself, as *chatterer;* or why the action of a verb should not be expressed in the same way, as *fly*, *run*, except when the sound is an index to the sense, as to *babble*, to *prattle*. Now this monosyllabic principle is peculiarly characteristic of the Anglo-Saxon language. In this respect it differs widely from the Greek and Latin. A few comparisons with the Latin of terms in common use will fully establish this point. Take, for instance, the parts of the human body;—

English.	Latin.	English.	Latin.
Head,	Caput.	Hand,	Manus.
Skull,	Cranium.	Thumb,	Pollex.
Hair,	Crinis.	Hip,	Coxendix.
Ear,	Auris.	Knee,	Genu.
Tongue,	Lingua.	Skin,	Cutis.
Cheek,	Gena.	Throat,	Guttur.
Scalp,	Pericranium.	Back,	Tergum.
Brain,	Cerebrum.	Arm,	Lacertus.
Eye,	Oculus.	Finger,	Digitus.
Nose,	Nasus.	Nail,	Unguis.
Lip,	Labrum.	Thigh,	Femur.
Chin,	Mentum.	Toe,	Digitus pedis.
Neck,	Cervix.	Blood,	Sanguis.
Breast,	Pectus.	Nerve,	Nervus.
Lungs,	Pulmo.	29.	70.

Eye-brow, eye-lid, nostrils, are compound words from monosyllabic roots; the last derived from nose, and thyrlian, to bore: thyrl-hus signifies a turner's shop, needle-thyrel, a needle's eye, as in Mark x. 28.

Take the senses:—

English.	Latin.	English.	Latin.
Sight,	Visus.	Smell,	Olfactus.
Hearing,	Auditus.	Taste,	Gustus.
Touch,	Tactus.	6.	12.

Infirmities.

English.	Latin.	English.	Latin.
Lame,	Claudus.	Deaf,	Surdus.
Blind,	Cæcus.	Dumb,	Mutus.
		4.	8.

Domestic Animals.

English.	Latin.	English.	Latin.
Dog,	Canis.	Cat,	Felis.
Rat,	Sorex.	Horse,	Equus.
Cow,	Vacca.	Pig,	Porcus.
Hen,	Gallina.	Duck,	Anas.
Goose,	Anser.	Bull,	Taurus.
		10.	21.

Elements, and their Properties.

English.	Latin.	English.	Latin.
Fire,	Ingis.	Earth,	Terra.
Air,	Aër.	Clouds,	Nubes.
Water,	Aqua.	Hail,	Grando.
Rain,	Pluvia.	Frost,	Gelu.
Storm,	Procella.	Wind,	Ventus.
Thaw,	Glaciei solutio.	Cold,	Frigus.
Heat,	Fervor.	14.	35.

Hence, it appears that, in the names of certain things constantly before us, or in common use, the Latin language requires 146 syllables to express that which is expressed in English by 63.

The same monosyllabic principle is carried out in the construction of our verbs. Take the exercise of our faculties—to see, hear, taste, touch, smell: the exercises of the body—to walk, run, leap, jump, hop, skip, trip: in the water, we swim, float, dive, sink, drown; in the air, we soar, fly. With the hand, in gentle action, we touch, stroke, smooth—in doubtful, we strike, smite, pinch—in violent, we thump, bang, gripe, fell, cuff. The fire is said to burn, glow, parch, dry, scorch, blast, scathe. Water is said to flow, glide, run, roll, lash, dash, splash, gush, rush, seathe, foam. To mourn, sigh, groan, weep, moan, laugh, smile, smirk, express affections of the mind. In the sky, we have sun, moon, and stars. The earth yields grass, corn, hay, straw, wheat, rye, oats. Our ordinary food is bread, fowl, flesh, fish: our fuel coal, wood, peat, turf. These, and such like words as these, form the staple of the English language, and more particularly of English poetry. The language even of a semi-barbarous people has more force and fire than the language of a mincing and fastidious refinement. The pompous march of blank verse admits the accompaniment of rolling and diffusive expression; but energy, and condensation, and tenderness must be sought for in the pithy, monosyllabic Saxon of our forefathers. It would be easy to multiply examples on these separate points; but it is the monosyllabic principle which is at present the chief object of illustration; and under this principle we find some of the most condensed and some of the tenderest passages in the English language. Take the journey of the fallen Angels from Milton:—

EXAMPLES.

"Through many a dark and dreary vale
They passed, and many a region dolorous,
O'er many a frozen, many a fiery Alp,
Rocks, caves, lakes, fens, bogs, dens, and shades of death—
A universe of death."

Where is the language that, in the same number of words, can present such a picture of

"Th' unreal, vast, unbounded deep
Of horrible confusion!"

> "That is a step
> On which I must fall down, or else o'erleap,
> For in my way it lies. Stars, hide your fires;
> Let not light see my black and deep desires.
> The eye winks at the hand. Yet let that be
> Which the eye fears, when it is done, to see."
>   SHAKSPEARE'S *Macbeth*.

Here we have fifty-two words, and but two dissyllables; one of the two a compound Anglo-Saxon word, o'erleap; the other a derivative from the Latin, desire.

> "Here lay Duncan.
> His silver skin *laced* with his golden blood,
> And his *gash'd stabs* looked like a breach in nature
> For ruin's wasteful entrance. There the murderers
> *Steeped* in the colors of their trade, their daggers
> Unmannerly *breeched with gore.*"   *Macbeth*.

The *silver skin laced* with blood, the *gashed stabs*, the murderers *steeped* in the colors of their trade, and the daggers *breeched;* that is, covered to the very hilt with gore, place the mangled body of Duncan and his blood-stained murderers before us in all their fearful realities.

> "And by his bloody side
> The noble Earl of Suffolk also lies.
> Suffolk first died, and York, all *haggled* over,
> Comes to him, where in *gore* he lay *insteeped*,
> And takes him by the beard, kisses the *gashes*
> That bloodily did *yawn* upon his face."   *Henry V*.

The field of battle also "sups full of horrors:"—

> "For many of our princes, woe the while!
> Lie *drown'd* and *soak'd* in mercenary *blood*."
>   "Their wounded steeds
> *Fret fetlock deep in gore*, and with *wild rage*
> *Yerk* out their armed heels at their dead masters,
> Killing them twice."   *Henry V*.

Again:—

> "Peace! Peace!
> Dost thou not see my baby at my breast,
> That *sucks the nurse to sleep?*"
>
> SHAKSPEARE's Cleopatra.

The gentle, monosyllabic language, and the tenderness of the imagery in which Cleopatra here describes the baby at her breast, the fatal asp in her bosom, contrasted with the deadliness of purpose, make the very blood run cold.

Take the old man's song from Wordsworth, a beautiful specimen of smoothness of versification, and simplicity of language. He is supposed to be reclining by the side of a fountain on a summer's day.

> "Down to the vale the water steers;
>   How merrily it goes!
> 'Twill murmur on a thousand years,
>   And flow as now it flows.
>
> And here, on this delightful day,
>   I cannot choose but think
> How oft a vigorous man I lay
>   Beside this fountain brink.
>
> My eyes are dim with childish tears,
>   My heart is idly stirr'd
> For the same sound is in my ears
>   Which in those days I heard.
>
> Thus fares it ill in our decay,
>   And yet the wiser mind
> Mourns less for what it takes away,
>   Than what it leaves behind.

> The blackbird in the summer trees,
>   The lark upon the hill,
> Let loose their carols when they please,
>   Are quiet when they will.
>
> With nature never do they wage
>   A foolish strife; they see
> A happy youth, and their old age
>   Is beautiful and free.
>
> But we are press'd by heavy laws,
>   And often glad no more:
> We wear a face of joy, because
>   We have been glad of yore.
>
> If there be one who need bemoan
>   His kindred laid in earth,
> The household hearts that were his own,
>   It is the man of mirth."

Graceful, tender, thoughtful, melancholy. Contrast this with the animated apostrophe of the same author to Toussaint.

> "Toussaint! the most unhappy man of men!
> Whether the whistling rustic bend his plough,
> Within thy hearing, or thy head be now
> Pillow'd in some deep dungeon's carless den.
> O miserable chieftain! where and when
> Wilt thou find patience? Yet die not: do thou
> Wear rather in thy bonds a cheerful brow,
> Though fall'n *thyself*, never to rise again.
> Live and take comfort. Thou hast left behind
> Powers that will work for thee, air, earth, and skies:
> There's not a breathing of a common wind
> That will forget thee. Thou hast great allies:
> Thy friends are exultations, agonies,
> And love, and man's unconquerable mind."

Here we have the expression of lofty and indignant sympathies contrasted with the tender simplicity of the preceding verses, each example bearing testimony to the *versatility* and the *capability* of the language.

The monosyllabic principle of the language pervades those exquisitely beautiful stanzas composing the "Adieu, adieu, my native Land," by Lord Byron.

> "Adieu! adieu! my native shore
>   Fades o'er the waters blue,
> The *night-winds sigh, the breakers roar*,
>   And *shrieks the wild sea-mew.*
>
> Yon sun, that sets upon the sea,
>   We follow in his flight;
> Farewell awhile to him and thee,
>   My native land, good night.
>
> With thee, my bark, I'll swiftly go
>   Athwart the foaming brine;
> Nor care what land thou bear'st me to,
>   So not again to mine.
>
> Welcome, welcome, ye dark blue waves!
>   And when ye fail my sight,
> Welcome, ye deserts and ye caves!
>   My native land, good night!"

Take out *native* and *desert*, which are Latin, and *Adieu*, French, and we have English in its purity. Welcome is a compound English term. The third and fourth lines are pure English, and paint the scene to the very life; the *soft sighing* of the *night-winds*, the *roaring* of the *breakers*, and the *shrieks* of the *wild sea-mew*, cannot be surpassed. They fall on the ear like enchanting melody; and we sympathize in the deep and tender melancholy of the poet.

In the "Destruction of Sennacherib," we have the animated anapæstic measure totally different from that of the "Adieu," but still exhibiting the same principle of diction:—

> "For the angel of death spread his wings on the blast,
> And breathed in the face of the foe as he pass'd;
> And the eyes of the sleepers wax'd deadly and chill,
> And their hearts beat but once, and forever lay still.
>
> "And there lay the steed with his nostrils all wide,
> And through them there roll'd not the breath of his pride,
> And the foam of his gasping lay white on the turf,
> And cold as the spray on the rock-beating surf."

Out of 89 consecutive words, 79 are monosyllables, and the roots of all the others monosyllabic; and yet how beautifully and harmoniously are all these monosyllables linked into the majestic and animated movement of the anapæstic measure! With the exception of *angel* and *face*, and those reduced in the number of syllables, the materials are Saxon.

Surely Lord Byron, who has adhered to the Anglo-Saxon terms so much in his various works, and with so much force and beauty, ought to be the last man to compliment other tongues at the expense of his own:—

> "I love the language, that soft bastard Latin,
>   Which melts like kisses in a female mouth,
> And sounds as if it should be writ on satin,
>   With syllables that *breathe* of the *sweet* south,
> And *gentle liquids* gliding all so pat in,
>   That not a single accent seems uncouth,
> Like our *harsh, northern, whistling, grunting guttural*,
> Which we're obliged to *hiss*, and *spit*, and *sputter* all."

This very stanza alone is sufficient to rescue the English language from the charge his lordship has endeavored to fix upon it. If it is expressive of harshness in one part, it is equally expressive of gentleness in another. The first five lines are full of liquids, the gentlest of all sounds. The "gentle liquids gliding," and the repetition of "th" in "breathe of the sweet south," are soft and beautifully descriptive. The smoothness and softness of the words exactly represent the poet's meaning. When we come to the word *uncouth*, and the two following lines, Lord Byron would have looked in vain to the "sweet south" for terms so applicable to the purpose which he had in view as the terms *harsh, northern, whistling, grunting, guttural, hiss, spit* and *sputter*. The hand that possesses strength and power may have as delicate a touch, when needed, as the hand of nervous debility. Where the poet wished to represent the smooth, liquid, gentle, he finds in his own language terms perfectly adapted to his purpose; where he wished to express harshness and *uncouthness*, he is equally fortunate. The materials of the English language are abundant for all purposes, and only require a judicious application. It can drop the honeyed words of peace and gentleness, and it can visit with its *withering, scathing, burning, blasting* curse. Wherever it breaks forth through the foreign fripperies with which it is overlaid, it possesses all the strength of elemental nature.

Listen to the language of contemptuous scorn:—

"Thou liest, thou thread, thou thimble,
Thou yard, three quarters, half-yard, quarter, nail,

Thou flea, thou nit, thou winter-cricket, thou:—
Braved in mine own house with a skein of thread!
Away, thou rag, thou quantity, thou remnant."
Taming of the Shrew.

Hear the tender, the earnest, the irresistible appeal of Eve, when she is imploring the forgiveness of Adam. In its simplicity and feminine tenderness, it descends to the very fountain of human sympathies; and if Adam had remained obdurate under such an appeal, he must have been more or less than man:—

"Forsake me not thus, Adam! Witness, Heaven,
What love sincere, and reverence in my heart,
I bear thee, and unweeting have offended,
Unhappily deceived! Thy suppliant,
I beg, and clasp thy knees; bereave me not
Whereon I live, thy gentle looks, thy aid,
Thy counsel, in this uttermost distress,
My only strength and stay! Forlorn of thee,
Whither shall I betake me; where subsist?
While yet we live, scarce one short hour perhaps,
Between us two let there be peace!"

Contrast this language of repentant, earnest, humble, and affectionate supplication, with the fiery indignation of the Welsh Bard, as he stands upon a rock (his gray hair streaming in the troubled air), and looks down upon the invaders of his country:—

"Ruin seize thee, ruthless king!
   Confusion on thy banners wait!
Though, fann'd by Conquest's crimson wing,
   They mock the air with idle state.
Helm, nor hauberk's twisted mail,
Nor e'en thy virtues, tyrant, shall avail
To guard thy secret soul from nightly fears,
From *Cambria's curse*, from *Cambria's tears.*"

Read the tender and touching appeal of Joseph to Pharaoh's chief butler:—

"But think on me when it shall be well with thee, and shew kindness, I pray thee, unto me, and make mention of me unto Pharaoh, and bring me out of this house: for indeed I was stolen away out of the land of the Hebrews: and here also have I done nothing that they should put me into the dungeon."—*Gen.* xl. 14, 15.

Contrast this humble and suppliant appeal with the animated burst of the Chorus, in the opening of Shakspeare's "Henry V.:"—

> "O, for a muse of fire, that would ascend
> The brightest heaven of invention!
> A kingdom for a stage, princes to act,
> And monarchs to behold the swelling scene!
> Then should the warlike Harry, like himself,
> Assume the port of Mars, and *at his heels*
> *Leash'd in like hounds, should famine, sword, and fire*
> *Crouch for employment.*"

How wide the contrast between these passages in feeling and diction, yet how true to nature are all of them!

Listen to the aged Priam, begging the body of his son of the ruthless Achilles:—

> "Ah think, thou favor'd of the powers divine!
> Think of my father's age, and pity mine;
> In *me* that father's reverend image trace,
> Those silver hairs, that venerable face.
> His trembling limbs, his helpless person see;
> In all my equal, but in misery."   *Il.* 24.

Contrast with this the Raid of Glen-Fruin, from "The Lady of the Lake:"—

> "Proudly our pibroch has thrill'd in Glen-Fruin,
> And Banochar's groans to our slogan replied,
> Glen-Luss and Ross-Dhu, they are smoking in ruin,
> And the best of Loch Lomond lie dead on her side.
> Widow and Saxon maid
> Long shall lament our raid,
> Think of Clan-Alpine with fear and with woe;
> Lennox and Leven Glen
> Shake when they hear again
> Roderigh Vich-Alpine Dhu, ho! iero!"

Here we have the language of sorrow and supplication contrasted with that of barbarous triumph.

Take the following passage from Pope's "Essay on Man," and try to translate it into any other language, so as to bring it into the same compass, preserving the same variety of ideas, the force of expression, and the spirit of the original:—

> "Ask for what end the heavenly bodies shine,
> Earth for whose use; Pride answers, 'tis for mine.
> For me kind Nature wakes her genial power,
> Suckles each herb, and spreads out every flower;
> Annual for me the grape, the rose, renew
> The juice nectareous, and the balmy dew;
> For me the mine a thousand treasures brings;
> For me health gushes from a thousand springs;
> Seas roll to waft me, suns to light me rise;
> My footstool earth, my canopy the skies."

The whole passage is bursting with meaning, yet under perfect control; the rhymes all strictly legitimate, the rhythm and the alternation of pauses all that the most fastidious ear could desire.

CHAPTER V.

FLEXIBILITY OF THE ENGLISH LANGUAGE.

For the purpose of versification, no language possesses greater capability of adaptation to the infinite forms of rhythm than the English. The man of genius stamps upon it any impression that he pleases; tenderness, passion, elegance, sublimity, withering scorn. Each master mind gives to it his own coloring, and develops its peculiar aptitudes. Milton, Shakspeare, Thomson, Cowper, Potter, and many others, each has his characteristic style in blank verse; Dryden, Pope, Byron, Southey, Wordsworth, Moore, Scott, and many others in rhyme. At one time, we see the verse running like an impetuous torrent; at another, falling gently like the dews upon the green slopes of Hermon.

CHAPTER VI.

A PRINCIPLE OF ECONOMY OBSERVED IN THE FORMATION OF OUR VERY MONOSYLLABLES THEMSELVES.

But not only is the principle of the Anglo-Saxon monosyllabic, but even in the construction of our monosyllables a principle of economy is observed, and we produce words of a totally different meaning by the simple change of *a, e, i, o, u;* as bat, bet, bit, bot, but; bag, beg, big, bog, bug; ball, bell, bill, boll, bull; far, fir, for, fur. The same effect is produced by the change of consonants; as, bat, cat, fat, gat, hat, mat, pat, rat, sat, vat; fight, light, might, night, right, tight; dash, hash, lash, gash, rash, wash, with many others that might be added. Voltaire is reported to have said that the English gained two hours a day by clipping words, to which he might have added two hours more by punctuality, and something by the I. O. U. of the commercial world. The principle of clipping prevails to a very great extent in proper names, more particularly in common conversation. Foreign names must be satisfied to be reduced to English proportions and to English estimate of utility. How much valuable time would be lost in reading, speaking, or thinking of such a string of titles as Jenkin ap-Griffith ap-Rogers ap-William ap-Rees ap-Evans. No: Ap-Rogers must be Prodgers; Ap-Richard, Pritchard; Ap-Rice, Price; Ap-Howell, Powell; Ap-Robert, Probert. This is a quiet mode of rebuking a useless parade of genealogy. An Englishman calls cheese cheese, and is satisfied; a Welshman must give its genealogy:—

> "Cheese, Adam's own cousin-german by its birth;
> Ap-curds ap-milk ap-cow ap-grass ap-earth."
>
> LOWER.

> "O, should this mincing fashion overspread
> From names of living heroes to the dead,
> How would Ambition sigh and hang her head,
> As each loved syllable should melt away!
> Her Alexander turn'd into great A,

A single C her Cæsar to express,
Her Scipio shrunk into a Roman S,
And nick'd and dock'd to these new modes of speech,
Great Hannibal himself, a Mister H."
Prologue to the Farce of Mr. H.

CHAPTER VII.

PROCESS OF CONTRACTION AND SIMPLIFICATION.

But, independent of the monosyllabic principle of the English language, and even the economy of its monosyllables, it has in other respects been undergoing a perpetual process of simplification. Dissyllables have in many cases been reduced to monosyllables, as in the perfect tense and the past participle of verbs, and all unnecessary variations in case have been abolished. The articles, adjectives, and participles have no variation in case, gender, or number; an immense advantage compared with many modern languages, and humane when compared with the twisting and turning, the fantastic gyrations and the indefinite declensions of the German noun. The genders, again, are not arbitrary and capricious, as in the Greek, Latin, and most modern languages, but founded on principle; things masculine being of the masculine gender, things feminine of the feminine, and things without life of the neuter. This is the general principle; and, as the noun adjective, the participle, and the article have no variation in the expression of gender, it is only the pronoun that can ever require to be marked by a distinction of gender at all. In poetic diction, where strength or softness is required, or when objects possess some natural and distinctive peculiarities, as *Sun*, *Moon*, the masculine or feminine gender is applied to things without life. It is this simplicity of principle which renders the English language, though difficult of pronunciation to a foreigner, easy of acquisition in many essential particulars, and which causes it to be spoken with tolerable accuracy by persons who never had any grammatical education at all; the chief stumbling-blocks being in the variations of the verb *to be*, in the confusion of the preterite tense of the verb with the passive participle, and in the irregularities of the pronoun. Whilst the Gothic languages, therefore, and more particularly the Anglo-Saxon, have borrowed liberally from the Greek and Latin, in the use of terms not needed in former times by a comparatively barbarous people, these ancient and complex languages have borrowed in simplicity of construction from the Gothic and their derivatives. Modern Greek and Italian have discarded much of their former complexities; the Italian having assumed the prefix applicable to all nouns, instead of a variation of case; and the modern Greek having reduced its number of cases, and formed its verbs more after the Italian model.

"Th' abundant Latin then old Latium lastly left,
Both of her proper form, and elegancie reft,
Before her smoother tongue their speech that did prefer,
And in her tables fixt their ill-shape't character."
                                        DRAYTON, *Polyolbion*, song 5.

CHAPTER VIII.

WANT OF INFLEXION A CAUSE OF GREATER VARIETY OF TERMINATION.

It might be supposed that, from the comparative absence of inflexion and variation in the cases, genders, and numbers of our nouns, and the simplicity that prevails in the construction of our verbs, our language would be monotonous, and deficient in variety of termination. The *very reverse*, however, is the fact. In Greek or Latin, the adjective very frequently terminates like the noun, with which it agrees; so do the article and the participle, in many cases; at the same time that personal verbs, in the first person singular, all end in *o* or *or*. Take the following example, quoted by Cicero in his "De Naturâ Deorum:"—

    Clamo, postulo, obsecro, oro, ploro, atque imploro fidem.

If translated into English, all these words would have different terminations. So also from the Greek.

    ὡς τας ἀδικφας τας δι τας ιμας χιρας.   SOPHOCLES.

Here are six consecutive words ending in αs, with the slight exception of the enclitic δι. Such a coincidence in English would be impossible. In Italian, a language formed for song, it is not uncommon to meet with a whole series of words ending in *o*.

CHAPTER IX.

MODIFICATION OF FOREIGN TERMS BY MODERN LANGUAGES.

Even in modern languages, which are not so encumbered with inflexions as the ancient, strange liberties have been taken with proper names, when they happen not to harmonize with the genius of the language into which they have been adopted. From Cromwell, the Spaniards have Caramuel; from Oswald, Ossubaldo; from Ethelwalde, Etelubalde. From Oxford, Froissart has Aquesufford. The term Welsh, applied by the Saxons to the Ancient Britons, arises from a corruption of a similar kind. They rightly believe the Welsh, or Ancient Britons, to be of Gallic, or, according to the genius of their own language, of Gallish extraction. This term, like many others, in which the initial G was changed into W, became Wallish, and was further contracted into Walsh and Welsh. The ancient French writers, reversing this, called our Edward Prince of Wales, Edouard Prince de Gaulles.

It is the very simplicity observed in the construction of the English language, which enables it to adopt, with perfect ease, terms which do not easily amalgamate with languages of more complexity. If a term be adopted into the English language, the addition of *s* or *es* in the plural number, and of *s* with the apostrophe in the possessive case, comprises all the modifications which, with trifling exceptions, it is destined to undergo. If a foreign word was admitted into the Greek language, it had to undergo a considerable alteration, in order to adapt it to the genius of that language. It had to pass through the grammatical crucible, from which it issued purified of what might be considered its barbarism, but with modifications and amalgamations to which it had hitherto been a stranger. A ludicrous instance of the change of words to suit the genius of another language is related in the case of Sir J. Hawkwood, a renowned English knight, who died at Florence. Some Englishmen passing through Florence observed an epitaph to Johannes *Acutus*, Eques. The Latin word *acutus* signifying *sharp*, they naturally enough translated the words John Sharp, Knight, or, as we say, Sir John Sharp. Who this Sir John Sharp could be, they were at a loss to tell; but, on investigation, found that, as the Latin had neither *k* nor *w*, and the initial aspirate H in Hawkwood did not seem of much importance, the Florentines had taken the word most nearly resembling Hawkwood in sound, *Acutus*, which an Englishman would naturally translate Sir John *Sharp*.

From the Hebrew, we have Jacob; in Greek, Ιακωβος; in Spanish, Jago; in Italian, Giacomo; in French, Jacques; and in English, James. Where compound transmutations have taken place, in some cases scarcely any trace of the original root can be discerned.

From the Greek preposition ἐξ, from out, we have the Latin *ex*, with the same meaning; from this is derived *extra*, without; from *extra* the French have got *étranger*, from which we have the term *stranger*, possessing all the air of an Anglo-Saxon term; though a fourth remove from the Greek. It is thus that corruption added to corruption leaves little trace of original parentage, and that words which national vanity may suppose to be the offspring of its own soil, may often be traced, through successive variations, to some remote original. Thousands of languages might thus branch out from one original stock, bearing an affinity, more or less, to that stock in general; but in some cases losing, perhaps, all traces of their original parentage.

Words in common use, and more particularly those which are expressive of domestic objects, would be more likely than any others to be transmitted through successive generations of men, whether stationary or migratory. In the Sanscrit, for instance, the most ancient, and, according to high authorities, the most philosophical language in existence, we have, for example *Pitr;* Greek, πατηρ; Latin, pater; Persian, padr; German, vater; Anglo-Saxon, fæder; Dutch, vader; Danish, fader; English, father. Again, in Sanscrit, we have *Mātre;* Persian, madr; Russian, mater; Celtic, mathair; Greek, μητηρ; Latin, mater; German, mutter; Dutch, moader; Anglo-Saxon, moder; Danish and Swedish, moder; English, mother. The word brother is still more remarkable. Sanscrit, *Bhratre;* Irish, bratha; Greek, φρατηρ; French, frêtre, frère; Persian, bradr; Tartaric, bruder; German, bruder; Russian, bratr; Celtic, brawd; Erse, brathair; Mœsic, brothar; Dutch, brœder; Danish and Swedish, broder; Icelandic, brodur; Armoric, breur; Anglo-Saxon, brodor; English, brother; the same word, with slight variations, in *seventeen* languages.*

* Bosworth's Preface to Anglo-Saxon Dictionary.

These are household words, interwoven with our earliest and purest affections, the first to be learned, the last to be forgotten; at the same time, they beautifully illustrate the continuous tide of human population, as it rolls over the earth's surface with the progress of time. Words, which sprang up at Agra, and Delhi, and Benares, four thousand years ago, are but now scaling the Rocky Mountains of Western America.

At the same time, if, from any peculiar circumstances, as from commercial intercourse or territorial occupation, a term drawn from another language should be really wanted, and should always harmonize, or be made to harmonize, with the language into which it may be adopted, we cannot look upon it as a case of corruption. It is a rupee melted down, and stamped with the impress of the current coin. It is an article of foreign commerce, admitted into the general stock of national conveniences. With respect to the language into which it may have been adopted, it is often nothing more than a matter of precedence, a question of time. Its novelty gradually wears off, and its features become more and more familiar. Over many accessions of this kind, time has already spread a dark and impenetrable mantle. In this way, as commerce and foreign conquests have been continually adding to the riches of the English nation, so the intercourse arising from commerce and conquest has been continually adding to the English vocabulary.

CHAPTER X.

EFFECTS OF THE CULTIVATION OF CLASSICAL LITERATURE.

Wherever classical literature has been cultivated, there we may expect to find numerous terms, which have been adopted from necessity, convenience, or taste. We must not look upon such adoptions as the result of *necessity only.* Terms taken from the Latin and Greek languages have been incorporated with those of our own, and that, too, in many cases, where the meaning might have been expressed in the Anglo-Saxon. We have, for instance, periphery from the Greek, and circumference from the Latin; but have lost *embegang,* from emb, about, and begang, to go, a going-about. We have adopted hydrophobia, but have lost *wæter-fyrthnys,* water-fright; dropsy, but have lost *wæter-adl,* water-ill. We have lexicon and dictionary, one from the Greek, the other from the Latin, which might have been expressed by *word-book.* From the Greek we have geometry, but have lost *eorth-gemet,* earth-measure. We have arithmetician from the Greek αριθμος, number, but have lost *gerim-cræftig,* skilful in numbers. We have lunatic, but have lost *monath-seoc,* month-sick. For *witena-gemot,* we have adopted the French term parliament; "an assembly of the wise," for "a talkee-talkee:" and, in the place of the beautifully descriptive word *eorthling or yrthling,* earthling, we have got agriculturist, and the unmeaning term farmer. Numerous examples of this kind might of course be added.

It is not always necessity, therefore, that has been the cause of our introducing terms derived from the classical languages. The capability of varied combination is not wanting in the English language; but the very fact of our having availed ourselves of classical combinations in lieu of our own, and often in conjunction with them, has rendered it not only more copious and more flexible, but more easy of acquisition to other nations, with whom we may have territorial or commercial intercourse, at least, wherever classical literature has been cultivated. We gain a technical nomenclature easily recognized and understood by all nations conversant with those models of antiquity, Greek and Latin. Every Englishman knows what is meant by the word *net;* no explanation would make it better understood; but a *reticulated* texture, English words adopted from the Latin, makes the definition perfectly intelligible at once to a classical scholar of any country. If it is praiseworthy in a nation to adopt useful discoveries in arts and sciences, though of foreign origin, it is not only praiseworthy, but necessary, for that nation to enrich its native tongue with such terms as the progress of arts and sciences may require.

When our forefathers issued from the forests of Germany or Scandinavia, and quitted the shores of the Baltic or the stormy coasts of Norway, they possessed a language sufficient to express their wants, but not sufficient for the exigencies of a refined and scientific people. Their language was rude, harsh, and pithy, with an air of savage independence, that regarded not those nicer grammatical and syntactical discriminations which a more civilized state of society requires. The alterations and additions that have been introduced, have given copiousness and flexibility, without injuring the original texture of our language. We have not imitated the grammatical complications of the Greek or Latin; whilst those languages, in their modern condition, have gradually approximated more closely to the structure of the English language.

In the adoption of classical terms, the English language has done nothing more than that which has been done by the other languages of Europe. It is not a question of fact, but of degree. The Greek word λινον, for example, has been adopted into nine European languages. Greek, λινον; Latin, linum; French, lin; Italian, lino; Spanish, liño; Portuguese, linho; German, lein; Norwegian, lun; Swedish, lin; whilst every European language, except the Danish, uses *lin*, when speaking of the seed. From this word *line*, we have several secondary meanings. When we speak of direct extension, we call it a *line*, because line is the common material from which ropes or cords used in direct measurement would be usually formed. From this term also we have *lining*,—line, or linen, being the material from which the under-garment was generally made, or with which the outer-garment was internally covered. From the term *line* we have also *lineage*, a direct succession; and *lineaments*, the distinct characters or boundary lines of the features.

CHAPTER XI.

ADVANTAGES ARISING FROM THE JUDICIOUS INTRODUCTION OF CLASSICAL TERMS.

The judicious admixture of Anglo-Saxon and classical terms constitutes the style of our best authors. It gives a legitimate variety of composition, formed upon peculiar tastes and education. In this respect, Swift and Johnson may be considered as placed at opposite extremes; the style of the former being peculiarly *English*; that of the latter being formed upon the classical models, and imitating not only the phraseology, but the polish and rotundity of their periods. Swift would say, "The thing has not life enough in it to keep it sweet;" Johnson, "The creature possesses not vitality sufficient to preserve it from putrefaction." How widely different is the phraseology of these sentences! yet they both express the same meaning, and we call them both English. To court classical terms too much, or to avoid them too much, would generally lead to a mode of expression bordering on affectation. In words compounded with prepositions, we have borrowed largely, and necessarily so, from the Latin; and, from these borrowed terms, primary and secondary meanings are obtained with a happy discrimination. Take, for instance, the verb *sisto*, I stand, itself derived from the verb ίστάω. We then have, in the first place,

Sisto, I stand.

Compounded with Ad, Adsisto,	I stand to or near,	Assist.
Con, Consisto,	I stand with, agree with,	Consist.

Compounded with De, Desisto, I stand off, Desist.
— Ex, Existo, I stand forth, Exist.
— In, Insisto, { I stand over, upon, take my stand on, Insist.
— Per, Persisto, I stand through, Persist.
— Re, Resisto, I stand back, Resist.
— Sub, Subsisto, I stand under, Subsist.

From *traho*, to draw, is derived *tractus*, drawing, from which we have:—

Compounded with Ad, Attract, to draw to.
— Con, Contract, to draw together.
— De, Detract, to draw from.
— Dis, Distract, to draw asunder.
— Ex, Extract, to draw out of.
— Pro, Protract, to draw forward.
— Re, Retract, to draw back.
— Sub, Subtract, to draw from under.

From *tendo*, I stretch, when compounded with prepositions, are derived *attend, contend, distend, extend, intend, pretend, portend*. The verbs *teneo, venio,* and *fero,* with many others, admit of being compounded with prepositions, and then run through diversities of meaning, both in Latin and English, with a clear and beautiful discrimination. If these words alone were blotted out of the English language, how could their places be supplied?

Again, take such a word as asylum, for example. How shall the mere English scholar deal with it? He may not, it is true, misapply it, and so far it serves his purpose; but he cannot understand, without explanation, why it signifies a place of refuge, which is in fact only a secondary meaning. Its primary meaning is a place from which you *cannot drag* an object—hence a place of refuge, a sanctuary not to be violated. Absurd, *ab surdo*, coming from a deaf man, who mistaking the question that is put to him, returns an answer quite foreign to the purpose. Calamity, from *calamus*, a reed, a stalk of corn. Calamity, destruction of the stalks (of corn); hence, a great misfortune, a calamity. Imbecility, *im* (in) *baculus*, *imbecillus*, one leaning on a staff; hence, imbecility, weakness, dependence for support.

It is only when we enter into the *anatomy* of such words as these that we become sensible of their perfect adaptation to express our ideas; and we feel that their services in the English language cannot be dispensed with. As children of softer climes and gentler aspect, they have been received into the family inheritance, and add grace and elegance to the land of their adoption. If we must borrow at all, it is surely better that we should borrow from these pure fountains of antiquity than from the polluted streams of more modern times; and if we are to be accused of piracy on this account, what European language can furnish partisans bold enough to throw the first stone? From intercourse and from conquest, all the languages of Europe participate with each other. The modern French is a compound of the ancient Gallic; of Greek, partly derived from the Greek colony that founded Marseilles, and partly through the medium of the Latin, introduced by the long residence of the Roman legions in Gaul; of the Francic, introduced by the Franks, who entered Gaul under Faramund, and gave their name to France; of the Norman, or northern dialect, with which the peculiar pronunciation of the letter *r* is supposed to have been introduced, just as a similar peculiarity was introduced into Northumberland by the Danes. Language, in fact, is the mere child of circumstances; "words," as it has been beautifully expressed, "being the daughters of earth," whilst "things are the sons of heaven," the one changeable and perishable, the others stable and permanent. We see language in various stages of its progress, in its rude formation, its acquirements, its plenitude, its corruption, and its decay.— But the English language has shown no wanton or capricious adoption of foreign terms or foreign idioms. In the simplicity of its construction, it has cut out a path for itself; and neither by the introduction of classical terms, nor by words or phrases derived from any other source, has it ever suffered its onward process of simplification to be impeded, or its leading principles to be overpowered.

"Trampled upon by the ignoble feet of strangers, its spring still retains force enough to restore itself; it lives and plays through all the veins of the language; it impregnates the innumerable strangers entering its dominions with its temper, and stains them with its color; not unlike the Greek, which, in taking up Oriental words, stripped them of their foreign costumes, and bid them appear as native Greeks."—*Halbertsma*, quoted by Bosworth.

SECTION II.

SOURCES OF CORRUPTION.

CHAPTER I.

INTRODUCTION OF FOREIGN TERMS, PHRASES, AND IDIOMS.

Foreign Terms.

In the time of Chaucer, the French language flowed in copiously upon the Anglo-Saxon. His popularity as a poet gave authority to the introduction of new terms. "He was, indeed," says an ancient author, "a great mingler of English with French, unto which by like, for he was descended of French, or rather Wallon race, he carried a great affection."

"And he hadde be long time in *chevachie*,
In Flanders, and Artois, and Picardie." *Cant. Tales.*

Again:—

"And to ben holden *digne* of reverence." *Ibid.*
"Of which *achetours* mighten take ensample." *Ibid.*

This propensity acquired for Chaucer the nickname of "The French Brewer."

Besides introducing French terms, Chaucer accented many of his syllables after the French form, and made disyllables out of monosyllables; a principle quite contrary to the genius of the English language, and, as it has proved, incapable of sustaining itself:—

> "A clerke there was of Oxenforde also,
> That unto Logicke haddé long ygo,
> And lené was his horse, as is a rake,
> And he was not right fat, I undertake." *Cant. Tales.*

Some excuse may be found for the introduction of French terms by Chaucer, in the comparative poverty of the English language at the time in which he lived. What might even be excusable in his day would be an affected and mischievous principle in the present state of our language. If the French invent some new instrument, as *guillotine* or *bayonet*, we use the same term to express those objects, rather than have recourse to a circumlocution, or invent a new term. Upon the same principle, we call a Turkish sword a *scimitar;* the burning of a widow in India, a *suttee;* a noisy instrument invented by the Chinese, a *gong.* If we introduce a foreign material, we in most cases adopt its concurrent name, as *gutta percha.* Such terms are already made to our hands, and offer themselves for their adoption. In this there is nothing worthy of blame: it is the practice of all countries. But this is very different from that silly, pedantic affectation of interlarding our language with foreign terms, where there is no occasion for it; very different from that heterogeneous mixture which no process, however laborious, can ever triturate into a state of amalgamation. We wish not the manly form of our language to be tricked out in a coat of many colors. It has arrived at vigorous and majestic proportions, and spurns from it that officiousness which would hide its dignity under a load of foreign frippery.

Foreign Phrases.

"I was *chez moi*, inhaling the *odeur musquée* of my scented *boudoir*, when the Prince de Z. entered. He found me in my *demi-toilette, blasée-surtout*, and pensively engaged in solitary conjugation of the verb *s'ennuyer*; and, though he had never been one of my *habitués*, or by any means *des nôtres*, I was not disinclined, at this moment of *délassement*, to glide with him into the *crocchio ristretto* of familiar chat."—*Lady Morgan, New Monthly*, No. 116.

Again :—

"And where did I give this notable rendezvous? 'Je vous le donne en une- je vous le donne en quatre,' as Madame Savigne says. Why, in the church of the Quirinal at Rome, and at the cardinal's. *Perdì*, my cardinal was none of your ordinary cardinals, who come with a whoop and a call, and take a cover at your table, and fill your little anteroom with *la famiglia*. The cardinal *par excellence*, the Cardinal Gonsalvi, was of another *étoffe*."

Here are the sweepings of a tailor's shop, the shreds and patches of a harlequin's jacket. It is fit to be put into competition with the address of Jemeno, the priest, to Mr. Coleridge, at Dominica :—

"Como esta, Monsieur? J'e père que usted se porte vary well. Le Latin est good ting, mais good knowledge, sin el Latin, rien to be done."

Foreign Idioms.

Foreign idioms ought as strenuously to be avoided as foreign terms and phrases. They derange and interfere with the natural order of the language. This sort of corruption is well exemplified in Hannah More's "Satirical Letter from a Lady to her Friend, in the Reign of George the Fifth :"—

"DEAR MADAM, *Alamode Castle.*

"I no sooner found myself here than I visited my new apartments, which are composed of five pieces; the small room which gives upon the garden, is practised through the great one, and there is no other issue. As I was exceeded with fatigue, I no sooner made my toilette than I let myself fall upon a bed of repose, where sleep came to surprise me. My lord and I are in the intention to make good cheer, and a great expense, and this country is in possession to furnish wherewithal, to amuse oneself. All that England has of illustrious—all that youth has of amiable, or beauty of ravishing, sees itself in this quarter. Render yourself here, then, my friend, and you shall find assembled all that is of best, whether for letters, whether for mirth," &c. &c.

Here the words are English, but the idiom altogether French. It is intelligible; but, as English, ridiculous.

CHAPTER II.

UNAUTHORIZED TERMS.

WE sometimes find that particular authors presume too much upon their own authority, and make use of strange and unauthorized terms. Mr. Coleridge, in his "Constitution of Church and State," uses the following words, *influencive, exhaustive, extroitive, retroitive, productivity*. Minds not so subtile or metaphysical as that of Mr. Coleridge would scarcely recognize the necessity of such terms as these.

Bentley uses *commentitious, aliene, negoce, exscribe*, as English words. When, however, words perish on the page on which they were written, it is a proof that they were not wanted. He finds fault with his opponent for using *cotemporaneous* instead of *contemporaneous*, on the principle that the Latins used *co* instead of *con*, when followed by a vowel, as, coire, coercere; but they wrote congratulare, constituere, componere, &c., retaining the *n* when the next word began with a consonant. Cotemporary, as a matter of euphony, is, however, struggling against contemporary, and principle and analogy may yet succumb before the authority of custom.

- - - -

CHAPTER III.

INFLATED TERMS.

There is an inflated or stilted style of composition, embodying terms altogether disproportionate to the subject, and which is often so unfortunate as to combine in one sentence, or one paragraph, the pompous, the offensive, and the ridiculous:—

"The night, now far advanced, was brilliantly bright with the radiancy of lunar and astral effulgence—a most lovely night—a death like stillness prevailed over nature, sound asleep, and the fair moon, taking her nocturnal promenade along the cloudless azure, and stellar canopy of heaven, walked in all the resplendency of her highest and brightest glory—the very night, according to fiction's tales and romance, of imagination's fantastic records, as that would have suited a melancholic pensiveness, a sentimental solitude, a chivalrous spirit, bent on some Quixotic deed of bold adventure." *Visit to the Metropolis of France. By G. Cayton, Esq.*

The same gentleman speaks of houses that "run eight

stories in ascent;" basins of " translucent water, in which gold and silver fish disport leapingly, with vaulting somersets."

Francis Moore would say that a style like this had been generated under a " malific configuration of deleterious planets." Not, however, that this style and this kind of phraseology are altogether to be avoided. When there is an *intentional* disproportion between the subject and the diction, as in " The Battle of the Frogs and Mice," or in the case of a *Puff*, the hyperbolical may be made productive of considerable humor. Thus, when M'Alpine, after dilating in high-flown phraseology on the superiority of his bear's-grease, boldly throws himself into the field of competition for empire, and proclaims, to the consternation of inferior aspirants, "The Rubicon is passed—aut M'Alpine aut nullus," we are amused with the disproportion between the object and the diction—the contrast between the man of empire and the man of hair. The hyperbole, with its concomitant phraseology, is a dangerous figure, when used seriously. It is constantly quivering on the verge of the ridiculous. The aspirant who says to himself,

"Sublimi feriam sidera vertice,"

but too often meets with the fate of the unhappy Icarus. Thus Blackmore:—

"Up to the stars the sprawling mastiffs fly,
And add new monsters to the frighted sky."

We are apt to follow these flying dogs in imagination,

and, were it not for the trifling anachronism, to trace the position of Sirius and Procyon to an English bull-bait.

CHAPTER IV.

INCONGRUITY OF TERMS.

To these may be added the startling incongruities which we meet with in the "Memoirs of Dr. Burney," by the authoress of Evelina.

"Mrs. Cibber herself he considered as a pattern of perfection in the tragic art, from her *magnetizing* power of *harrowing* and *winning* at once, every feeling of the mind."

"Six heartless, nearly desolate years of lonely conjugal chasm had succeeded to double their number of unparalleled conjugal enjoyment; and the *void* was still *fallow*, and hopeless, when the yet *very-handsome-though-no-longer-in-her-bloom* Mrs. Stephen Allen of Lynn, now become a widow, decided, for the promoting (of) the education of her eldest daughter, to make London her winter residence."

Again :—

"By a fearful and calamitous event, which made the falling leaves of Autumn *even nearly sepulchral* to Dr. Burney."

Again :—

"Scarcely had this harrowing filial separation taken place, ere an assault was made upon his conjugal feelings, by the *sudden-at-the-moment-though-from-long-previous-illness-often-previously-expected* death of Mr. Burney's second wife."

Here, *eleven* words connected by hyphens form one rambling adjunct to *death*—an example of what the English language may be made to bear, but no credit to the executioner.

Mr. Willis, an American writer, in his "Dashes at Life with a Free Pencil," is full of overstrained and incongruous imagery and expressions. As,

"My heart was as prodigal as a *Croton Hydrant*."—p. 48.

"She was *consumedly* (consummately?) good-looking."—p. 50.

"They might have known, indeed, that the *chain of bliss* ever so far extended, breaks off, at last, with an imperfect link—that, though *mustard and ham may turn two slices of innocent bread into a sandwich, there will still be an unbuttered outside.*"

"Phœbe at last believed that in the regions of space there existed, wandering, but not lost, the aching worser half, of which she was the better; some lofty intellect, capable of *sounding* the *unfathomable* abysses of hers; some male essence, all soul and romance, with whom she could soar finally, *arm-in-arm* to their native star, with no changes *of any consequence* between their earthly and their astral communion."—vol. iii. p. 64.

"But virtue, if nothing more, and no sooner, is its own reward, and in time to *save its bacon.*"—p. 90.

"To the keeper of Congress Hall the restoration of the Millennium would have been a rushlight to this second *advent* of *fun and fashiondom.*"—p. 99.

"If she could have protruded from the flounce of her dress a foot more like a mincing little muscle, and less like a *jolly fat clam.*"—p. 117.

In addition to these, we have such terms as "*pocketually* speaking," "*unletupable* nature," *plumptitude, wideawakeity, betweenity, go-awayness.*

Mr. Brockden Brown, also an American, uses disproportionate epithets and pedantic expressions. Simple matters require simple terms, and such as are in common use. Mr. Brown, in such examples as the following, violates this obvious and natural principle. Thus:—

"I was *fraught* with the persuasion that my life was endangered."

"The outer door was ajar; I shut it with trembling eagerness, and drew every bolt that was *appended* to it."

"His brain seemed to swell beyond its *continent*."

"I waited till their slow and harsher *inspirations* showed them to be both asleep; just then, on changing my position, my head struck against something which *depended* from the ceiling."

The terms *fraught, appended, continent, inspirations, depended*, ill accord with the simplicity of the subject.

CHAPTER V.

TALKEE-TALKEE.

ANOTHER mode of corrupting a language, and one from which the English, as well as other languages, is liable to suffer, consists in adapting it to the standard and caprice of ignorance and vulgarity. Would it not have been much better, for instance, if the Moravian missionaries had adopted the simple authorized version of the New Testament amongst the Negroes, in the English West India Colonies, in preference to the hideous corruptions and abominations which they have sanctioned in print? Take the following specimens, extracted from the "Quarterly Review," No. 76. The subject is the Marriage Feast in Cana of Galilee.

"Drie deh na bakka, dem holi wan bruiloft na Cana, na Galilée, en mamma va Jesus been ee dapeh. 2. Ma dem ben kali Jesus, manga him disciple toe va kom na da bruiloft. 2. En tah wieni kaba, mamma va Jesus takki na him, dem no habi wieni morro. 4. Jesus takki na him nu mamma noeworko mi habi nanga joe. Tem va mi no ben kom jette," &c.

Translation. "Three days after back, them hold one marriage in Cana of Galilee, and mamma of Jesus been there. But them ben call Jesus with him disciples to come to that marriage, and when wine end, mamma of Jesus talk to him. Them no have wine more. Jesus talk to him, me mamma, how work me have with you. Time of me no come yet."

Tarrawan, in this jargon, stands for t'other one; nebrewantum, for never one time; man-voal, man-fowl, a boy; snekki-family, snaky-family, a generation of vipers. The whole is ridiculous, base, and shocking to the feelings. To confer upon such stuff the factitious dignity of print is a miserable degradation of a sacred subject, and a mistaken policy indeed.

CHAPTER VI.

CORRUPTION ARISING FROM WORDS ALTOGETHER EXTRANEOUS.

CERTAIN terms have been introduced into the English language which claim no kindred or acquaintance with it. They have no affinity either with the stock from which the language has sprung, or with its more recent ramifications. They are often vile mutilations of some remote and ill understood original. D'Israeli, in his "Curiosities of Literature," gives the following explanation of the phrase *run a muck:*—

"A strong spirit of play characterizes the Malayan. After having resigned everything to the good fortune of the winner, he is reduced to a horrid state of despondency. He then loosens a lock of hair, which indicates war and destruction to all whom the raging gamester may meet. He intoxicates himself with opium, and, working himself up to a fit of frenzy, he bites, or perhaps kills, any one who may come in his way. But as soon as this lock is seen flowing, it is lawful to fire at him, and destroy him as soon as possible."

The Malay term is *amuco,* which we have corrupted to *a muck,* and from this we have framed *to run a muck.* The phrase is used to designate a furious and indiscriminate onset :—

"Thus frontless, and satire-proof, he scours the streets,
An runs an Indian *muck* at all he meets." DRYDEN.

"Satire's my weapon; but I'm too discreet
To run a *muck,* and tilt at all I meet." POPE.

Night-mare. "Mara was a Finland elf, in the Scandinavian mythology. Varland, who ruled over the Upsal domain, was bewitched by this elf. He became drowsy, and laid himself down to sleep: but, when he had slept but a little while, he cried out, saying Mara was treading on him; but, when they took hold of his head, she trod upon his legs, and when they laid hold of his legs, she pressed upon his head, and it was his death.

"And Varland in a fatal hour
Was dragg'd by Grimchild's daughter's power,
The witch's wife, to the dwelling-place
Where men meet Odin face to face;

Trampled to death by Skyta's shore,
His corse his faithful followers bore,
And there they burn'd with heavy hearts,
The good chief killed—killed by witchcraft's arts."
Laing's *Chronicles of the Kings of Norway.*

Assassin. The word *Assassin,* according to Lane in his "Modern Egypt," is derived from the Arabic word *hhash-shash,* signifying a smoker, or eater of hemp, which has an intoxicating effect. The name was first given to Arab warriors in Syria, in the time of the Crusades, who made use of intoxicating and soporific drugs in order to render their enemies insensible. In such a state, they would be unprepared for resistance, and fall easy victims to the murderer.

Jacobite. The same author gives the following explanation of the origin of the term *Jacobite.* A sect of Christian Copts were called Ya-a-chibeh, or Ya-a-cheobees, Jacobites, from Jacobus Barodæus, a Syrian, who was a chief propagator of the Eutychian heresy. Those who adhered to the Greek faith were called *Melchees;* that is to say, *Royalist,* because they agreed in faith with the Emperor Constantine.

CHAPTER VII.

EFFECTS OF COLONIZATION.

Colonization has a tendency not only to add to the words of a language, but also to corrupt it. New scenes, new objects, new habits of life, call forth new expressions, at the same time that words, in many cases, deviate from their original signification. Many words have crept into the English language, in America, which are quite new to it; others have changed their meaning; others are merely fanciful. From America we have adopted to *progress*, to *effectuate*. *Clever*, in America, has gained a meaning which it does not express in England; as, a *clever house*, a *clever son*, a *clever cargo*. *Slick*, *kedge*, *loss*, *absquatulate*, are from America; nor do we quite understand what is meant by a *tall smell*. Political parties are there designated by terms which have never been applied to anything, living or dead, on this side of the Atlantic; so that, looking at the English language, as improved by Americanisms, there is some reason for a New York Negro barber's saying to Mr. Fearon, "You speak English pretty well, for a Britisher." The inhabitants of different localities receive their appropriate nicknames, understood and relished on the spot, but unmeaning to the uninitiated. What do we understand by *Suckers*, *Pukes*, *Wolverines*, *Hoosiers*, *Cornecrackers*, *Buckeyes*, and *Ring-tailed Roarers?* A man may have emigrated from the old country under the name of Jack Smith. It may, however, be in vain to inquire for him under this name, as, without a patent, he has perhaps assumed the name of *Populorum Hightower*, of Goose-creek.

These vagaries are, however, harmless in themselves; and, if they tickle the fancy of the communities into which they are from time to time introduced, they may be looked upon as minor contributions to the sum of human happiness. The world, without a dash of nonsense, would scarcely be worth living in, and our Trans-Atlantic kindred have their full share of dry humor.

― ― ―

CHAPTER VIII.

SUMMARY.

It is not, then, so much individual terms which tend to corrupt a language, for these have no effect on the structure of the language; it is rather the licentious and pedantic introduction of foreign *phrases* and *idioms*, never to be justified, except in peculiar cases of necessity. In a language so copious as the English is now, such necessity will seldom arise.

> "Surely, far more dear
> Is good plain English to an English ear
> Than lisp'd out phrases stol'n from every clime,
> And strangely alter'd to conceal the crime.
> Yet without French, how dull the page would look!
> Must no italics mark when speaks a duke?
> Must peers and beauties flirt in common print,
> And no small letters mark a statesman's hint?"
>
> *The Novel*, a Satire.

As Butler says, shall men

> "Be natives wheresoe'er they roam,
> And only foreigners at home?"

Hear the beautifully expressed lament of Arthur Golding on the too free introduction even of classical terms in his day. The verses are prefixed to Baret's "Alviarie," 1560:—

> "All good inditers find
> Our English tongue driven almost out of mind,
> Dismembered, hacked, maimèd, rent, and tornè,
> Defac'd, patch'd, marr'd, and made a skornè."

He then adds:—

> "No doubt but men would shortly find there is
> As perfect order, as firm certaintie,
> As grounded rules, to try out things amiss,
> As much sweet grace, as sweet varietie
> Of words and phrases, as good quantitie
> For verse and prose, in English every way,
> As any common language hath this daie.
>
> "And were we given as well to like our owne,
> And for to cleanse it from the *noisome* weede
> Of *affectation*, which hath overgrowne
> Ungraciously the good and native seed,
> As for to *borrow where we have no need*,
> It would prick near the learned tongues in strength,
> Perchance, and match me some of them at length."

If observations like these were called for in 1560; if so strong a protest as this was entered against the too free introduction of terms borrowed from the classics at that period, how much more strongly have we reason to protest against the introduction of continental frivolities in the present day? The language in which Shakspeare, Milton, Dryden, Pope, and Byron, and many other eminent poets, have sung; in which Hume, and Robertson, and Gibbon have narrated; in which Addison, Swift, and Johnson have written; in which Burke, and Pitt, and Fox, and Sheridan have spoken, needs not to ask alms of its neighbors. It has done with them, except where the improvements in arts and sciences, and the introduction of new commodities, render the use of adventitious terms necessary. It has already culled the sweets, and made them its own.

"The Italian," says Camden, "is pleasant, but without sinews, like a still fleeting water. The French delicate, but ever nice, as a woman scarce daring to open her lips, for fear of marring her countenance. The Spanish majestical, but fulsome, running too much on the *o*, and terrible like the divell in a play. The Dutch manlike, but withal very harsh, as one ready, at every word, to pick a quarrel. Now we, in borrowing from them, give the strength of consonants to the Italian, the full sound of words to the French, the variety of terminations to the Spanish, and the mollyfying of more vowels to the Dutch; and so, like bees, gather the honey from their good properties, and leave the dregs to themselves; and thus, when *substantialnesse combineth with delightfulnesse, and fullnesse with finenesse, seemlinesse with portlinesse, and currentnesse with stayednesse, how can the language that consisteth of all these sound other than most full of sweetnesse!*"

PART III.

GRAMMATICAL.

SECTION I.

THE PRESENT STRUCTURE OF THE ENGLISH LANGUAGE.

CHAPTER I.

INTRODUCTION.

AMIDST the multitudinous accomplishments of the present age, a knowledge of English grammar is by no means a common qualification. Many speak and write their mother tongue with general accuracy, it is true, who at the same time possess but a very superficial knowledge of its grammatical structure. We cannot call that man a skilful anatomist whose knowledge does not extend beyond the outward configuration of the human subject, and who is ignorant of those combinations of animal machinery which give life and action. So also the stringing together of certain set phrases and authorized expressions, with a correct ear for imitation, will often hide a multitude of infirmities which would soon become apparent in circumstances of difficulty, or under unusual tests. If a knowledge of the strict meaning of words, their arrangement in a sentence, and their relation to, and dependence upon each other, is requisite in any one kind of composition, more than in another, it is in the construction of *legal documents*. Property, character, life, and death hang upon their very syllables and letters; and yet one of the acutest lawyers of modern times has declared that he had never seen an act of parliament through which he would not drive a "coach and six;" that is, in less figurative language, in which there were not loopholes of very commodious dimensions. Surely such laxity, ambiguity, and confusion are altogether inconsistent with a strict knowledge of grammar, and an unambiguous arrangement of words.

If we look back to many of the standard authors even of the last century, we shall find that they abound in grammatical errors, in almost every conceivable form, and my object will be to show, by example and argument, that the statement is not overcharged. Nor do I wish to confine this charge to writers of the last, and of preceding centuries. It is applicable, in a very serious degree, to many of the most popular authors of the present age. "Hence," as observed by a writer in "Blackwood's Magazine," in an article entitled "Elements of Rhetoric,"—"hence an anomaly, not found, perhaps, in any literature but ours, that the most eminent English writers do not write their mother tongue without continual violations of propriety. With the single exception of Mr. Wordsworth, who has paid an honorable attention to the purity and accuracy of his English, we believe that there is not one celebrated author of this day who has written two pages consecutively without some flagrant impropriety in the grammar; such as the eternal confusion of the preterite with the past participle, confusion of verbs transitive with intransitive, &c. &c., or some violation, more or less, *with* the vernacular idiom." This is not only true as an assertion, but the writer has himself also inadvertently given us an example of that which he was in the very act of justly condemning; for it is not consistent with the English idiom to say a violation *with* a principle or a rule, but a violation *of* a principle or a rule. The author had previously said "violation *of* propriety." The observation, indeed, made by Swift, in a remonstrance addressed to the Earl of Oxford, is still applicable—that, "in many instances, it (the English language) offended against *every part* of grammar."

Much has been done of late years in cultivating the grammar of the English language. This, added to the more general diffusion of education, has banished some of those flagrant errors which were by no means uncommon in English composition; whilst our unbounded social intercourse, conversation, and collision of sentiment, together with the necessity of daily composition imposed upon public men, have given a facility of writing unknown to former times. The articles which appear in many of the leading public papers frequently afford the finest specimens of powerful and accurate composition. They constitute, in fact, an essential part of the literature of the day.

There are many to whom the observations which I

am about to offer may appear unnecessary; but such must bear in mind that there are others to whom those very observations may be both novel and useful. It must also be admitted that we require to be, now and then, reminded of that which was once familiar to us; and that a subject is sometimes presented in a new and a stronger light than that in which we have been accustomed to view it; and that some things worthy of attention may yet have altogether escaped our notice. In pursuing my object, I shall endeavor to give principles and reasons; for a principle once understood is never forgotten. It is, in grammar, what a physical principle is to the man of science—he never forgets it, and never misapplies it. A principle is a landmark, to which we can always look forward in doubt and perplexity. It is a pedestal on which we can take our stand prepared to climb higher and higher, but never to descend.

These pages, then, are offered as a small contribution to an object in which much still remains to be done. Too many persons are satisfied if they can but find a certain phrase absolutely in print; they are *more* than satisfied—they are *triumphant*, if they can appeal to an author of reputation. Such a practice must ever have a tendency to perpetuate error. That which is right is right, without any authority at all; and that which is wrong cannot be made right by any authority. If the following observations on the "Structure of the English Language" should attain no other object than that of shaking this misplaced confidence, they will not have been offered in vain.

I shall not enter into the vexed question as to the number of the "Parts of Speech" requisite for the expression of our ideas. Two thousand years have added nothing new to the subject; and though there may be much that is ingenious in such discussions, to the general reader there is not much that is practically useful. The Parts of Speech, as usually received, will be admitted without question; and the prominent properties and positions of each in the English Language as now constructed, will be briefly exhibited. The limited nature of this work will not admit of more. Under the general head of "Structure," I propose to explain the origin of the "Parts of Speech;" to give examples of false grammar, and the false position of terms, and to contrast them with sentences grammatically and properly constructed: to notice the effect of connecting particles when repeated, or omitted and understood; and cursorily to examine and discuss some of the unsettled idioms of the language.

CHAPTER II.

ORIGIN OF THE PARTS OF SPEECH.

All languages that ever existed are founded upon the same grammatical principles, in all their great essentials. He, therefore, who understands the philosophical principles on which any one language is founded, has got the substance of the grammar of every other, though he has not got the form. Before, therefore, we can show the peculiar characteristics of one language, it would be necessary to show in what respect it differs from other kindred languages, in particular; or even from more remote languages. All languages arrive at the same end, but by different forms, and in different degrees of perfection.

The Noun Substantive.

All languages must have terms to express *things*—they must have the *names* of things; for without these the first step to language would be wanting. This gives rise to the noun, or *name*—the corresponding term, in Greek and Latin, signifying simply *name*. As language advances, there must be terms expressive of the *state* or *condition* of things. This leads to the origin of the

Noun Adjective.

As the noun *substantive* simply expresses the substance or being of a thing, as *tree*, so the noun *adjective* expresses some attribute of the noun substantive, as *high* tree. The noun substantive, then, expresses the *being* of a thing only; the noun adjective, as the word implies, is a name added to express, either the essence of a thing, or some contingent quality belonging to it.

Pronoun.

But, as it would be inconvenient to repeat the name of a thing, over and over again, in a sentence, another part of speech has been invented, to supply its place, and this is called a *pronoun*—that is, something substituted for a noun—a *for-noun*. By the use of the pronoun the frequent repetition of the noun is avoided. How convenient the use of the pronoun is, may be seen from such a sentence as the following:—

"But think on *Joseph*, when it shall be well with thee (thee being used in the place of the butler's name), and show kindness, *Joseph* prays thee, unto *Joseph*, and make mention of *Joseph* unto Pharaoh, and bring *Joseph* out of this house, for indeed *Joseph* was stolen away from the land of the Hebrews, and here also *Joseph* has done nothing that they should put *Joseph* into the dungeon."

If we substitute the pronoun *I* for the nominative case of *Joseph*, and *me* for the objective, we avoid the frequent and inconvenient repetition of the noun *Joseph*.

The Article.

In modern languages, the article is considered a necessary part of speech. The Latin language is defective, on account of the want of the article, and is obliged to have recourse to the use of the demonstrative pronouns on occasions when a definite and specific designation is wanted. The Greek language would say οἱ δώδεκα; *the* English, the twelve; the Latin, *illi* duodecim, those twelve. When Virgil says, "*Fas odisse viros*," the word *viros*, signifying men, does not designate any particular men, though that designation is intended. In the Greek, indefinite signification was marked simply by the absence of the definite article. This is an economy of which the Greek is not often guilty; for it is in general the most prodigal of languages. Thus,

Κλῃαρχος would signify "one Clearchus," but ὁ Κλῃαρχος, *the* Clearchus, already mentioned: πασα αληθεια, all truth; ἡ πασα αληθεια, all *the* truth.

The Verb.

With the noun substantive, the noun adjective, and the article, we cannot, however, form a sentence, or even a simple proposition; because as yet we have no affirmation or negation, one of which is essential to a proposition. The word or part of speech which effects this is called *the verb*, or *the word*—the *word of words*. A *verb* is the *vital* principle of a sentence—it is the moving power. The Chinese most happily call verbs *live words*, nouns *dead words*, and all other parts of speech auxiliaries; and it is a singular coincidence that the Chinese should have hit precisely the notion of the Greek grammarians, who designated verbs τα εμψυχοτατα του λογου, the most animated parts of speech. A noun and a verb of themselves may constitute a perfect proposition; as, *man dies*. Here we have a subject, *man*, and we assign or attribute to man that he *dies*. We have, therefore, a subject and an attribute, with an affirmation, and the sentence is perfect. On this account, some of the ancient grammarians allowed only two parts of speech—*nouns* and *verbs*. All others they considered as *auxiliaries* only. There are, however, different kinds of verbs, as active transitive, active intransitive, and passive; active transitive, as, Cæsar *conquered* Britain; passive, as, Britain *was conquered* by Cæsar; active intransitive, that is, when the action of the verb does not fall on a noun, but is simply confined to the agent, as, *man thinks, birds fly*, or a verb may imply simple existence, and it is then denominated a *verb substantive*, that is, a verb implying the *substantia* or *being* of a thing.

The Participle.

Another part of speech is called a participle, that is, a *partaker*, inasmuch as it partakes of the nature of a verb, and also of a noun adjective; as, the mother *loving* her child. Here the word *loving* implies to *love*, and it also implies *time* or *tense*, indefinitely or definitely, according to circumstances. So far, it possesses the nature of a verb. But it also expresses an *attribute*—a capability of loving, and so far it partakes of the nature of an adjective: so do *having loved, being loved, having been loved, about to love, about to be loved*. This part of speech is, therefore, called a *participle*, or participator. In English, like the other parts of speech, it is very simple in form; in Greek, it is quite the contrary, running through a great variety of forms.

The remaining parts of speech—namely, Adverb, Conjunction, Preposition, and Interjection—in English never vary their form, however applied, and may be considered more than others as subsidiary parts of speech.

The Adverb.

An adverb, as its name implies, *ad verbum*, is generally joined to a verb, in order to indicate its mode, or its intensity of action; as, he behaved *unmercifully*, that is, in an unmerciful manner; the arrow flew *swiftly*:

or it is joined to an adjective, to qualify *its* signification; as, *simply* elegant, *incomparably* beautiful.

The Preposition.

A preposition, as the name implies, is something set before—that is, set before a word, as *to* him, *with* him, *by* him, *from* him, &c.; or it enters into composition with a noun, as abstinence—or with an adjective, as antediluvian—or with a participle, as, over-grown—or with a verb, as, distribute, over-rate. In English, the preposition is always followed by the objective case; but, the objective case being the same as the nominative, the distinction is not outwardly visible. If we use the pronoun after the preposition, the principle is immediately evident; as, to *him*, with *him*, by *him*, &c.; and to *he*, with *he*, by *he*.

The Conjunction.

Conjunctions are used to couple either words or sentences together, and are denominated copulative or disjunctive; as, John and Thomas, neither John nor Thomas; this and that, either this or that; *nor* being the correlative of *neither*, *or* of *either*. Conjunctions couple like cases of nouns and tenses of verbs; as, you neither respect *him* nor *me;* *him* and *me* being in the objective case. As both these words, *him* and *me*, essentially depend upon the verb respect, it is obvious that we cannot say respect *I*. In composition, much of the appropriateness and beauty of a sentence depends upon the repetition, or the entire absence, of the conjunction, according to the purport of the sentence.

The Interjection.

An interjection, as its name implies, is something thrown in—an ejaculation, in no way affecting the grammatical structure of a sentence; it falls neither under logical nor grammatical consideration; as, He, alas! perished, at an early age. Many interjections are inarticulate sounds, such as proceed from irrational creatures, and are merely symptomatic of pleasure or pain.

In English, then, we have ten parts of speech, all of which may occur in a single sentence, though the noun and the verb, of themselves, are capable of forming a perfect proposition; as, *man thinks*. Here we have a subject, *man*, to whom we attribute or assign the faculty of thinking. We have therefore a subject, of which we affirm something—that is, a perfect proposition. Or, again, a proposition contains a subject, an attribute, and an object; as, *vice produces misery*. Here vice is the subject of which we speak, and we predicate of it that it produces something, which something is misery. The term *misery* is the object. It is that to which the action of the verb *produces* is directed; it is the object on which it falls. By introducing other words, as auxiliaries, we may employ, in this one proposition, all the different parts of speech. We may say, "a gross vice produces misery." Here, then, we have the addition of an article and a noun adjective. We may go further, and we may say, "a gross vice, corrupting the reason and the heart, in the end, alas! certainly produces misery." Here the *framework* is vice produces misery. All the other parts of speech which enter into the composition of this sentence are subsidiary. In the construction of a sentence, then, the subject, the attribute, and the object should always be kept distinctly in view.

CHAPTER III.

GRAMMAR REGARDS CONSTRUCTION ONLY.

Now, Grammar strictly regards the construction of a sentence, and has nothing whatever to do *with the truth or falsehood of a proposition.* A proposition may be strictly grammatical and true; as, *man is* mortal; or false, as, *man is* a horse. Both sentences are grammatical; but the one true, the other false. If, however, a proposition is *un*grammatical, properly speaking, it has no meaning at all. We may guess at the author's or speaker's meaning; but, strictly considered, an ungrammatical, and therefore an incongruous and inconsistent sentence has no definite meaning. If we say, "*John were the persons who didst it,*" we have first a noun singular, and individual, John, joined to a verb, *were,* denoting plurality; and again, a plural noun, *persons,* having reference to a singular and individual noun, *John;* and again, a verb of the *second* person, *didst,* referring to a pronoun of the *third* person, the relative *who* being of course of the same person as the noun to which it relates. We may guess at the meaning intended; but, technically speaking, such a sentence has no meaning at all. Without rules of construction, therefore, to fix the meaning of language, the complicated affairs of civilized life could not be conducted. All would be error and uncertainty. Grammatical arrangement, then, has nothing to do with the *essential meaning* of words. As a matter of grammar, it is immaterial whether we say, *man is a vegetable,* or *man is an animal.*

SECTION II.

GRAMMATICAL CONSTRUCTION OF NOUNS.

CHAPTER I.

NUMBER OF NOUNS.

To begin with the *Noun.* Logically speaking, there is a variety of nouns; grammatically, all are looked upon as names; and, whether common or individual, are all subject to the same rules. First, then, let us consider nouns with respect to their unity and plurality. The Greek and some other languages have three numbers of nouns: the singular, speaking of *one;* the dual, of *two;* the plural, of any number *more* than *two.* This makes a language more complex, and uselessly so. The modern Greek has lost the dual number. The Gothic had the dual number; languages derived from it have lost the dual number. Faulkner, a Jesuit of Paraguay, states that the language of Patagonia has the dual number. The language of Lapland is said also to have it; and Crantz, one of the Moravian missionaries, says that the language of Greenland has a dual number. The English has but two numbers, the singular and the plural; the singular having reference to one, the plural to any number more than one. It will sometimes happen, however, that a term, from its ESSENTIAL signification, embraces more than one; but this plurality is comprehended in the mind as unity. As, corn *is* the staff of life, variety *is* pleasing, the multitude *was* innumerable; *corn, variety, multitude,* imply a plurality, but are comprehended in the mind as *unity.* Such words, then, though implying *many,* may have a verb of the singular number; each term being in itself a grammatical integrity or whole, composed of several parts. With respect, however, to nouns of multitude, we frequently meet with a confusion between nouns of *quantity* and nouns of *number.* Whatever cannot be conveniently numbered, and is not reckoned *numerically,* or *one* by *one,* we speak of as a *quantity;* as, a *quantity* of *corn,* of *sand,* of *leaves;* but not a *quantity* of *men,* or of *oxen,* because these are usually reckoned *numerically,* as four hundred men, five hundred oxen.

Examples.

"The congregation was almost exclusively of the people who had attended the execution, and *quantities* of men, as well as women, shrouded in their black silk faldettes, were listening to a tall, strong Capuchin friar."—*Head's Bubbles from the Brunnens of Nassau.*

"The deserts," says Adanson, "are entirely barren, except where they are found to produce serpents, and in such *quantities,* that some extensive plains are almost entirely covered with them."—*Paley's Quotation from Adanson.*

Numbers in both cases, though neither in number nor quantity would serpents constitute fertility; nor is abundance of serpents the opposite of barrenness, when speaking of the absence of vegetable productions.

"Such a result is a demonstration that no such law has ever been established in human nature, because nothing like even a millionth part of such a *quantity* has been produced in our world."—*Sharon Turner's Sacred History.*

Again, *number* of people, and not quantity. We do not say, How *much* men had Napoleon at Waterloo, as if speaking of quantity; but how *many*, as speaking of number.

Nouns of Multitude.

Nouns of multitude sometimes imply a *generality* only, and not a collective unity. In such a case, a plural verb is necessary; as, in the following example from Lawrence's "Lectures:"—

"It has generally been observed, that the European population of the United States *is* tall, and characterized by a pale and sallow countenance."

Now the tallness of the population cannot be universal, though it may be general. We cannot speak of it as *unity*, but as plurality. We can say, with propriety, the population is *great*, because each individual, whatever may be his physical or mental peculiarities, is a constituent part of its greatness; but each individual of a whole population is not necessarily a constituent part of their tallness. The population does not constitute a *tall* unity. So also we can say, there *is* a great variety of flowers, because *each* flower constitutes a part of that variety.

"That people," says Herodotus, "*rejects* the use of temples, of altars, and of statues, and smiles at the folly of those nations who imagine that the Gods are sprung from, or bear any affinity with, the human nature."—*Gibbon*, c. viii.

A *universality* of smiling is not necessarily implied, nor would the implication of such a universality be necessarily true, though the implication of a *generality* might be so; a *generality* is all that is wanted. We do not, in this case, comprehend the whole Persian nation as a collective whole. They are spoken of *distributively*, and not collectively. We therefore expect *reject* and *smile*, not *rejects* and *smiles*.

It sometimes happens that a noun of the plural number is used simply with reference to a space of time, taken collectively. In such a case, it will admit of a pronoun being joined to it, though of the singular number; as,

"I have ventured,
Like little wanton boys, that swim on bladders,
This many summers, on a sea of glory." SHAKSPEARE.

As a general rule, a noun of the singular number must be followed by a verb of the singular number; a noun of the plural number by a verb of the plural number; two or more nouns of the singular number, coupled by a copulative conjunction, by a verb of the plural number. There are, however, exceptions to this rule, the force of which we are disposed to allow; as when two nouns have an *indivisibility*, or *concentration* of meaning. Virgil is considered one of the most elegant, as well as one of the most correct writers in the Latin language; yet we find:—

"*Exoritur* clamorque virûm, clangorque tubarum."
Æneid, lib. ii. 313.

Again:—

"Omnis spes Danaum, et cœpti fiducia belli
Palladis auxiliis semper ste*tit*."   *Æneid*, lib. ii. 162.

This may, perhaps, be accounted for on the principle that the verb, though not expressed, must be applied to the first noun separately. The second noun would then stand alone, and require a verb of the singular number. Again, Phædrus,

"Quia dolor et gaudium misc*et* totam vitam."

So in the New Testament, Matthew xxiv. 35.

Ὁ ουρανος και ἡ γη παρελευσεται.

Again, Matt. xvi. 17:—

Ὁτι σαρξ, και αἱμα ουκ απεκαλυψε σοι.

In St. Paul's Epistle to Titus, we find a similar passage in the English translation:—

"But even their mind and conscience *is* defiled."—Ch. i. v. 15.

And again, in the book of Proverbs:—

"When distress and anguish *cometh* upon you."—*Prov*. i. 27.

In the case of a verb of the singular number following the two nouns, ὁ ουρανος και ἡ γη, there is a peculiar propriety. The passing away of these two objects is represented as absolutely simultaneous—a diversity of objects, but a simultaneity of operation.

So, again, in the case of *flesh* and *blood;* in their natural state, they are co-existent, and in the passage quoted above they are taken together, as one indivisible subject, and followed by a verb of the singular number. So also *clamor* and *clangor, spes* and *fiducia, mind* and *conscience, distress* and *anguish,* are co-ordinates. There is a certain identity of meaning between the nouns thus coupled together; and even in the quotation from Phædrus, the inseparable mixture of grief and joy which is found in human life is forcibly expressed by a verb of the singular number, "dolor et gaudium *miscet.*" These are exceptions to the ordinary rule of grammar, that two or more nouns of the singular number shall be followed by a verb of the plural number; but the exceptions are founded on the peculiar signification of the terms.*

CHAPTER II.

CASES OF NOUNS.

The word *case* is derived from the Latin word casus, a fall, the Greek word used to denote a case having precisely the same meaning. Grammatically speaking,

---

* Some nouns, of foreign origin, form their plurals according to the principle of the languages from which they have been derived; as arcana, errata, data, genera, radii, vortices, from the Latin; automata, phenomena, criteria, theses, from the Greek; Cherubim, Seraphim, from the Hebrew; with some others. Custom authorizes *encomiums,* not encomia.

the word *case* is used to express the condition of a noun, the relation which it bears to some other word or words with which it is connected. It is obvious that such condition or relationship may undergo great variation, and that cases may be numerous, varying with every conceivable degree of relationship. Hence different languages have different numbers of cases. *In, with, from, by, within, without, above, beneath, beyond, &c.* might all have their respective cases. Such a principle would uselessly add to the complexity of language; and therefore the number of cases, in most languages, has been reduced within comparatively narrow bounds. The Hebrew had four, the Greek five, the Latin six, the Sanscrit eight, the Finnish and Laplandish fourteen. Fielstrom, as quoted by Bosworth, gives nine cases of the Laplandish language, expressed by variable terminations; as,

Nom. Joulke, a foot.
Gen. Joulken, of a foot.
Dat. Joulkas, to a foot.
Acc. Joulken, a foot.
Voc. Joulk, a foot.
Abl. Joulkest, from a foot.
Priv. Joulket, without a foot.
Med. Joulkin, with a foot.
Locat. Joulkesn, in a foot.

It is obvious that such a principle might be extended far beyond these limits.

The English has discarded all useless variations of the noun, and expresses the relationship of the noun to the word with which it stands connected by the use of prepositions. We have, in fact, but one case or variation in the English noun - the genitive or possessive case; for the objective case, though different in signification from the nominative, is yet the same in *form;*

CASES OF NOUNS. 143

and that difference in form becomes visible only when the pronoun is used, instead of the noun. As, Alexander conquered *Darius;* or, *Darius* was conquered by Alexander. Though the order is here reversed, and an interchange takes place between the nominative and the objective case of the two nouns, *Alexander* and *Darius*, yet there is no change of form. I respected *him*. He respected *me*. Here the pronouns *I* and *he* change their form according to their relationship to the verb respected.

Some of the ancient grammarians did not consider the nominative as a case at all. It is, in fact, the starting point. It is the noun in its primary and simple form, and cannot, therefore, be a case, or fall, from a given state. They represented the nominative case by a perpendicular line. Every variation from this line they considered as so many stages, or *falls*, downwards. Others considered the nominative as a case indicating the noun in that state in which it simply falls from the mind. This case they called the *upright* case. All other cases were called *oblique* cases.

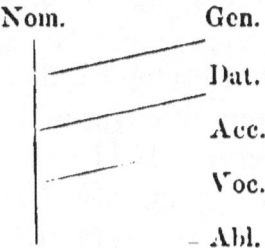

The oblique cases might be expressed indefinitely, according to the genius of any particular language.

The Hebrews used prefixes to denote the cases of nouns, and did not inflect the nouns themselves. This is the convenient and philosophical principle, which the English language has adopted.

The same prefixes, without any variation, in the Hebrew, serve to denote the cases of the plural number, a change taking place in the termination of the noun, to denote plurality. The Greek formed its cases, not by prefixes, but by varying the termination of the noun. These variations, being formed upon ten different declensions, five of simple, and five of contracted nouns, with their singular, dual, and plural number, together with an infinity of irregular, capricious, and anomalous nouns, form a labyrinth of variations to which no memory is adequate. The Latins formed their cases in a similar manner, though with less complexity. The modern Italian, derived from the Latin, has discarded these variations, and uses a prefix. The mixed Indian dialects form their cases not by *prepositions*, or variable terminations, but by *postpositions;* as, Ilhoda, a God; Ilhoda-ka, of a God; Ilhoda-ko, to a God. The French language denotes its cases by prepositions.

Languages that have adopted the principle of expressing cases by prepositions gain immensely in simplicity and convenience. It is true, by such means, they introduce a greater number of small words; but, in speaking a language, this is of trifling consequence, because words coalesce so much with each other in pronunciation that this imperceptible amalgamation forms one of our greatest difficulties in understanding a spoken language with which we are but imperfectly acquainted.

The form, then, of cases, and the number of cases, differ in different languages. The object of cases, however formed, is to express the different condition of the noun, or of its substitute the pronoun; and this may be effected by *variable terminations*, by *prepositions*, or by *post*positions. All cases in English are expressed by *pre*positions, except when the genitive case is expressed by 's following the noun with the apostrophe, which is nothing more than the old legitimate Saxon genitive case abbreviated.

CHAPTER III.

NOMINATIVE CASE.

The nominative case denotes the noun, as the subject of the verb, and every proposition must have a nominative case and a verb. The nominative case is generally expressed by a single word; as, *man* is mortal. Sometimes an infinitive mood performs the same office, as, "To err is human, to forgive divine." The infinitive mood in this case becomes virtually a noun, ονομα ῥηματικον, a verbal noun. The principle is much more palpable in Greek, when the verb is in the infinitive mood, and, undergoing no change itself, associates with the nominative, genitive, dative, or accusative case of the article. The infinitive mood of a Greek verb is sometimes coupled to a noun, as if it were a noun itself, as βουλη και μαχεσθαι (*Homer's Iliad*); literally, in counsel and to fight; in counsel and fight. The principle has been recognized in English, as far as the simplicity of our cases will permit.

Sometimes, an affair or circumstance, with concomitants or qualifications, forms the nominative case to the verb; as,

"Early to bed, and early to rise,
Makes a man healthy, wealthy, and wise."

What is it that makes a man healthy, wealthy, and wise? The fact of his going to bed early, and rising early. The sentence is a collective fact, though there are two members, viz. "early to bed, and early to rise;" yet if we write *make* instead of *makes*, would it not be a violation of grammar? because it is not asserted that going to bed early will produce this result, or that rising early will produce it, but both conjointly. They form a grammatical and a logical unity—*makes*, and not *make*, seems, therefore, to be required.

"That it should thus fail is contrary to the conceptions which reason teaches us to entertain of the wisdom, justice, and mercy of God."

"*That it should thus fail*" is the nominative case to the verb *is*.

A noun, then, cannot affirm or deny anything, whilst standing alone. It must be followed by a verb, which verb must agree with it in number. It sometimes happens, however, that the noun, after being expressed, is dropped, and a pronoun is substituted in its place, forming the legitimate nominative case to the verb. Thus:—

"Deborah, a prophetess, the wife of Lapidoth—*she* judged Israel at that time."—*Judges* iv. 4.

"The skipping king—*he* ambled up and down." SHAKSPEARE.

"But the Comforter, which is the Holy Ghost, whom the Father will send in my name, *he* shall teach you all things."—*New Test.*

Sometimes the objective case of the pronoun is substituted, and the noun left without grammatical government.

"For the Egyptians, whom ye have seen to day, ye shall see *them* no more, for ever."—*Old Test.*

At times no pronoun is substituted, nor does any verb follow the nominative case of the noun.

The ancient classics are full of examples of this kind of figure; but one of the most beautiful and striking modern instances of the kind is in the third book of Milton's "Paradise Lost:"—

> "No sooner had th' Almighty ceased, but all
> The multitude of angels, with a shout
> Loud, as from numbers without number, sweet
> As from blest voices uttering joy—Heaven rang
> With jubilee, and loud hosannahs filled
> The eternal regions."

The noun *multitude* is not followed by any verb, to which it can be applied. Bentley proposes to read, *gave a* shout, instead of *with a* shout. This alteration, it is true, would make the sentence conformable to the rules of grammar: but Milton, who so often constructs his sentences after the classical models, no doubt knew that he was supported by innumerable authorities in the use of this form of speech. If read with a pause after the word *joy*, the effect of the sentence is greatly increased, and we are ready to agree with Monboddo, when he says, "The lines are so wonderfully fine, that, if it were a real solecism, not to be justified by any ancient authority, I could excuse it." The poet, in fact, in the fervor of his imagination, seems carried up to the third heaven of inspiration, and there to stop and listen to the music of angels, and to the mellifluous rhythm of his own sweet numbers; he then collects himself, and gives this result of his impressions:—

"Heaven rang
With jubilee, and loud hosannahs filled
The Eternal regions."

But whilst the nominative case is thus sometimes left without a verb, it is, on some occasions, emphatically repeated before the verb, in order that attention may be more firmly fixed upon it:—

"Hell, at last,
Yawning receiv'd them whole, and on them closed—
Hell, their fit habitation, fraught with fire
Unquenchable, the house of woe, and pain." MILTON.

The examples of this description, already quoted, are to be looked upon as figures of speech, dictated by choice, and not the result of inadvertence. The following seems to arise from an oversight, and is not defensible on any grammatical principle, or figure of speech.

"Forasmuch as it hath pleased Almighty God, of his goodness, to give you safe deliverance, and *hath preserved** you in the great danger of child-birth."

The verb *hath preserved* has here no nominative case, for Almighty God occurs in the objective case after the verb hath pleased. The sentence ought to be, "Forasmuch as it hath pleased Almighty God, of his goodness, to give you safe deliverance, and *to preserve* you, or, *he hath preserved* you."

We often meet with a slovenly mode of expression, such as the following from Abernethy's "Lectures:"—

"It is *really curious, the course* which balls will sometimes take."

The noun *course* here stands without a verb. This awkward expression might have been avoided by saying, "The course which balls will sometimes take is really curious." Again, in an article from the "New Monthly," No. 103, we meet with the same form of expression, but with an aggravated aspect:—

"It is incredible, the number of apothecaries' shops, presenting themselves."

It would be quite as easy to say, "The number of apothecaries' shops, presenting themselves, is incredible."

---

* *To preserve*—in the Book of Common Prayer of the P. E. Church in the United States.—Am. Pub.

CHAPTER IV.

THE GENITIVE, OR POSSESSIVE CASE OF NOUNS.

The Genitive case is so called as denoting the source out of which something springs; as, the earth's fertility, or the fertility of the earth—fertility being traceable to earth, as being that out of which fertility springs. Cæsar's sword, or the sword of Cæsar; Cæsar being the person to whom the sword is traceable, in whose possession it is.

In the transition state of the Anglo-Saxon to the present English language, a grievous corruption of this case prevailed, which seems to have arisen from an ignorance of its true origin. The Anglo-Saxon had a regular possessive case, distinguished from the other cases by a diversity of termination. This possessive case, ending in *ys*, or *is*, or *es*, and sounding like the possessive pronoun *his*, was corrupted to *his*, forming a separate word. No such form existed, in the Anglo-Saxon, as the placing of *his* after a noun, to denote what we understand by the possessive or genitive case. It is a hideous solecism; and, if possible, to make matters worse, even *her* is added, in a similar way, showing an utter misconception of the whole principle. It is from about the end of the 14th century that we may date this corruption, and it has now totally disappeared from all modern English works. The following extracts will show that the legitimate Anglo-Saxon genitive case prevailed up to the beginning of the 15th century :—

In Alfred's will, "And ic bidde in *Godes* naman,"

and I bid in God's name; "*Godes* lufan," God's love; and many similar expressions occur.

In the parable of the Sower, from the "Northumbrian Gloss," or "Durham Book," written about the year 900, according to Mr. Bosworth, we meet with "Heanisse *eorthes*," highness (depth) of earth.

In a book called "Or molum," because written by one Orm, about 1180, being a metrical paraphrase of the Gospels and Acts, occur the following lines. He is speaking of the Marriage Feast:—

"And Cristess moder Marye was att tatt *bridalles* sæte."
"And Christ's mother, Mary, was at that bridal's feast (bridal-feast)."

In the laws of Ina, we find "Cunning*es* Huse," King's House, "Eoldermann*es* Huse," Elderman's House.

"The pope is to his chaumbre wende,
For dole he might ne speke na more,
And after cardinales he sende,
That much couthen of *Cristes* lore."
Elegy on the Death of Edward the First.

Chaucer, born 1328, perpetually uses the Anglo-Saxon genitive case:—

"And when he in his chambre was alone,
He down upon his *beddis* fete him sette."
Troilus and Cresseida.

"He was also a learned man, a clerk,
That *Christés* gospel woldè preche."
Canterbury Tales.

"Than if I win a *kinges* londe."   Gower (died 1408).

"As for the time, though I of *mirthis* food,
Might have no more, to look—it did me good."
James the First *of Scotland* (born 1395).

"Now was there made fast by the *touris* wall
A garden fair." JAMES THE FIRST *of Scotland*.

"Up-sprang the lark, the *hevenis* meustral syne."
DUNBAR (1465).

"And I ride with gold so red,
And I have to do with *landes* law."
DAME BERNERS (1496).

Again:—

"But I say if any such armys be borne, thoos armys be of no more auctorite than thoos armys be the wich be taken by a *mannys* awne auctorite."—*Dame Berners*.

In 1497, the following entry occurs in the Treasurer's book of James the Fourth of Scotland:—

"Item. To Roland Robison, for his *masteris* monethis pensioun."

Up to this period, then, and somewhat later, we find this form of the regular Saxon genitive case prevailing, without ever a trace of *his* as a substitute; and there can be no question that the introduction of *his* took place from its resemblance, in sound, to the termination *is*, or *ys*, or *es*, as cases gradually melted away from the old Anglo-Saxon.

In Drayton's "Polyolbion" (born 1563), we find the following sentence:—

"They afterwards were most willingly requested to multiply their number, by sending for more of their countrymen, to helpe King Vortigern, and under that colour, and by Ronix, *her* womanish subtlety, in greater number were here planted."

Here we have Ronix, *her* womanish subtlety, for Ronixis, Ronix's womanish subtlety.

GENITIVE CASE.

Even the plural *their* was used in the same manner as *his* and *her*, as in Welwood's "Memoirs:"—

"About the lawfulness of the Hollanders, *their* throwing off the monarchy of Spain."

The present form of the genitive case is simply an abbreviation of the Anglo-Saxon genitive, by the elision of *i* or *y* before *s*. Such expressions as the following are, therefore, unmitigated corruptions: as,

"Mars *his* idiot." SHAKSPEARE.

"Whereby I guessed that Ortelius did much incline unto Becanus *his* conceit."—*Verstegan*.

"If Socrates *his* free nature be not found, surely Socrates *his* slavish nature must be beaten, and that even by Socrates *his* own profession."—*Golden Grove*, book iii. 1608.

"My paper is the Ulysses *his* bow, in which every man of wit or learning may try his strength."—*Addison*.

"By young Telemachus *his* blooming years."
POPE, *Odyssey*.

It has been absurdly supposed that the same single letter *s*, on many occasions, does the office of a whole word, and represents the *his* or *her* of our forefathers. Were this the case, how should we deal with such expressions as the men's heads, the children's bread? As both these nouns are plural, on what principle can we say the men *his* heads, or the children *his* bread? It is in fact no such thing; it is a return from a gross solecism to the legitimate Anglo-Saxon genitive case, with the elision of *i* or *y* or *e*, which we still acknowledge by the use of the apostrophe in genitive cases ending in *s*; as, nom. man, gen. man*ys*, of a man. In English, nom. man, gen. *man's*.

Lowth supposes that the phrase Jesus Christ *his* sake, as we find in the "Book of Common Prayer," which used to be written Chris*tis* sake, was an oversight of the printers or compilers. The supposition is quite gratuitous by the side of "Mordecai *his* matters," "Asa *his* heart."

The error seems to have arisen from the similarity of sound between the real Anglo-Saxon genitive case of the noun, and the same noun with the addition of *his*, as Christ, Chris*tis* gospel, Christ, Christ *his* gospel.

The error would probably never have been introduced, had not this similarity existed; but, once admitted, it extended to words which did not end in *is*, or *ys*, in the genitive case, as in the case of "Asa his heart." The Anglo-Saxon nouns were finally reduced to three declensions, of which the genitive in *ys*, or *is*, or *es*, was one: as,

Singular.
Nom. Smith, a smith.
Gen. Smithes, of a smith.

Singular.
Nom. Witega, a prophet.
Gen. Witegan, of a prophet.

Singular.
Nom. Wilne, a maiden.
Gen. Wiln-e, of a maiden.

One form only, and that an abbreviated one, has survived. In the plural number, all Saxon genitives ended in *a*; as smitha, of smiths; Witegena, of prophets; Wilna, of maidens.

In the following sentence, the possessive case is improperly used:—

"And there went out with him all the land of Judea, and they of Jerusalem, and were all baptized of him, in the river *of Jordan*, confessing their sins."

The river is Jordan, and Jordan is the river. The terms are co-equal and identical, and reciprocal, and both ought to be in the same case, in the *river Jordan*, and not the *river of* Jordan. So also—

"The river *of Kishon* swept them away, that ancient river, the river *Kishon*."—*Judges* v. 21.

It is true we find examples of this kind in Latin, but then the expression is explained, as being elliptical, as in Virgil, "flumen Himellæ; the river of Himella; but the resemblance to the expression, the river *of Jordan*, is only in appearance. The sentence made out would be, flumen *cui nomen* erat Himellæ.

CHAPTER V.

COMPOUND TERMS JOINED BY HYPHEN.

WHEN two nouns come together, though *not* in apposition, the latter is not necessarily put in the *genitive* case. The English language admits of compound terms with great facility, many of which must be joined by the hyphen; and in such terms the sign of the genitive case must be omitted, as night-raven, not night's-raven, sun-beam, sea-nymph, ill-luck signs, yard-long tailed, the last epithet consisting of a noun, an adjective, and a participle, yet we feel that the combination is perfectly legitimate, and that it offers no violence to the English idiom. Compound words of this description require to be connected by the hyphen.

The following rules, applicable to the use of the hyphen, taken from a note appended to the 199th page of Dr. Carey's "English Prosody," are sufficient to meet the generality of cases in which there may be a doubt.

"1. When each of two contiguous substantives retains each its original accent, *omit* the hyphen, as, máster búilder. Where the latter loses, or alters its accent, *insert* the hyphen, as, ship-builder.

"2. When two substantives are in apposition, and either of the two is separately applicable to the person or thing designated, *omit* the hyphen; as, *lord chancellor*. When they are not in apposition, and only one of the two is separately applicable to the person or thing, *insert* the hyphen; as, a *horse-dealer*, who is a dealer, but not a horse.

"3. When the first substantive serves the purpose of an adjective, expressing the matter or substance of which the second consists, and may be placed after it with *of* (not denoting possession), *omit* the hyphen, as, *silk gown*, a gown of silk. When the first does not express the matter or substance of the second, and may be placed after it with *of* (denoting possession) or with *for*, or *belonging to*, *insert* the hyphen, as *school-master*, *play-time*, *cork-screw*, *laundry-maid*, i. e. the master of the school, time of play, screw for corks, maid belonging to the laundry.

"4. Between an adjective and its substantive (used as such in the sentence) *omit* the hyphen, as high sheriff, prime minister. When the adjective and its substantive are used as a kind of compound adjective to another substantive, *insert* the hyphen between the two former, as high-church doctrine.

"5. When an adjective, or an adverb, and a participle immediately following, are together used, as a kind of compound adjective, merely expressing an inherent quality without reference to immediate action, and (in order of syntax) precede the substantive to which they are joined, *insert* the hyphen, as, a *quick-sailing* vessel. When they imply immediate action, and (in order of syntax) follow the substantive, *omit* the hyphen, as, 'the ship *quick sailing* o'er the deep.'"

The accent, in every one of these cases, is a sure guide: that is, when the accent is thrown upon the first member of the compound, and lost on the second, the hyphen *is* to be used; when the accent is preserved on both, the hyphen is *not* to be used.

There are many other cases, no doubt, to which these rules will not strictly apply. As far as they go, they are sound and useful. To use a broad distinction, let us take a mílk-man, and a snów mán. Here the accent is upon *milk*, and the hyphen is used; but in the case of a snów mán, or a man made of snow, the accent is preserved in both terms, and we do not use the hyphen. So a *gláss-house* is a house for the manufacture of glass; a *gláss hoúse*, a house made of glass; a *gréen-house*, a house for the preservation of green plants; a *gréen hoúse*, a house of a green color. The compounding of terms may arise in a variety of ways, and out of this variety uncertainty may occur. Let us take, for instance, hórse-power. Without considering, we at once lay the accent on *hórse*, and properly so; because the horse is not the constituent material of the power, but only the instrument from which that material results. We use the phrase *hórse-power* as expressive of a certain intensity of power; and if to this we add number, we then throw the accent back upon the term *ten*, and constitute

14

a triple compound term, expressive of a definite quantity, and we see no impropriety in designating an engine as a *ten-horse-power* engine. Now, to show how far this is the case, we cannot say a ten horses' power engine, or *a* ten anything, except where a phrase is used collectively, as *a ten weeks' sickness*, for *a* and *ten* are numerically incompatible; yet we see no impropriety in designating an engine as a *one*-horse-power engine, or a *ten*-horse-power engine. Ought we then to say, how *much* horse-power engine, or how *many* horse-power engine? If we insist on *many*, we ought, in order to be consistent, to insist on how many *horses'* power. Either let us do this, or do that which is much better, namely, make the whole a compound term, and that, too, perfectly consistent with the genius of the English language. As, how *much* power engine? a *ten-horse*-power engine. Then (to work out the principle) we may *hope* to see the master builders, the ship-builders, the lord chancellors, the school-masters, the prime minister, the high-church-men, and the low-church-men, men-singers, and women-singers with silver-toned voices; together with the opera-dancers, and the horse-guards, and the foot-guards, the cow-keepers, the coal-porters, the lighter-men, the copper-smiths, the tin-men, the musical-instrument manufacturers, ladies in silk gowns, and water-men in cork jackets, and waiters with cork-screws and wine-coolers, even the anti-stay-and-corset-young-women-killing society, all in a quick-sailing vessel, going to see the snow man, made by the milk-man of Mary-le-bone, and then proceeding to view the "yard-long-tailed" monkey, and the elephant possessing the strength of a twenty-horse-power steam-engine, now exhibiting in Bishop-gate-street-without, a sight never-to-be-forgotten.

If these principles are correct, the following expression from Gibbon is erroneous:—

"The buckler was of an oblong and concave figure, four feet in length, and two and a half in breadth, framed of light wood, covered with *a bull's* hide, and strongly guarded with plates of brass."

If each shield was covered with one bull's hide, *a* bull's hide, the expression would be correct; though we cannot suppose that each shield or buckler would require the whole hide, and, according to the dimensions given, it certainly would not. But by bull's hide is probably meant simply the *material* with which the buckler was covered, without reference to any particular bull; and if so, the expression ought to be *bull*-hide, and not *bull's* hide. We say the chair was made of yew-tree, the cabinet was inlaid with box-wood, not yew's tree, box's wood. We say, also, the seat was stuffed with horse-hair, taking these terms as being expressive of particular materials, without any reference whatever to the individual source of production.

CHAPTER VI.

OBJECTIVE CASE.

As the objective case in English is the same as the nominative, it is impossible to err in point of form. Whether the noun depends upon an active transitive verb, or upon a preposition, the objective case, in English, is always the same as the nominative. Though not subject to a change of form, it is virtually in a different case. It is called the objective case, because it expresses the object upon which the action of a transitive verb falls. That a freedom from error in the use of the objective case very often depends upon the unchangeable nature of the noun, rather than upon a knowledge of the principles of grammar, is pretty obvious from the fact that errors are very frequently met with in the confusion of the nominative and objective cases of pronouns, though these have the very same grammatical construction as nouns. The cases of pronouns being varied, an opening is left for error, and errors we find in abundance, and those, too, in the most popular writers in the English language. Such will fall under consideration when treating of the pronoun.

An active transitive verb, then, requires the objective case, and so does a preposition; but the objective case, whether of noun or pronoun, does not necessarily follow the verb or preposition *in order*, though it must do so essentially, and according to grammatical government. The English language admits of a greater inversion of order than is generally supposed, and this we find carried to the greatest extent in the measured progression of blank verse. As—

"Now storming fury rose,
And clamor, such as heard in heaven, till now,
Was never;"

i. e. such as was never heard in heaven, till now.

"Orators such as Cicero and Demosthenes we have none."—*Blair's Rhetoric.*

The grammatical order would be, "We have no such orators as Cicero and Demosthenes were."

Sometimes a sentence forms the objective case after a verb grammatically, and yet precedes it in order, in the same manner as a simple noun might do. Thus, in "Paradise Lost:"—

"That thou art happy, owe to God;"

i. e. owe to God *the fact* or circumstance, "that thou art happy."

Again, from the same source:—

"For this fair earth I see.
Warm'd by the sun, producing every kind;
Them, nothing;"

i. e. For I see this fair earth, warmed by the sun, producing every kind. I see them producing nothing.

"And these *very thoughts*, these *very sources* of sentiment, this very *satiety*, this very *discontent*, this profound and melancholy *sentiment*, the result of certain social systems, the first two cantos of Childe Harold suddenly appeared to represent."—*Bulwer.*

Here we have four nouns in the objective case, all preceding the verb on which they depend, and that verb, namely, *represent*, placed at the very end of the sentence. In the following sentence, a verb in the infinitive mood fulfils the office of a noun in the objective case. As,

"Owe no man anything, but *to love* one another."—*New Test.*

"What went ye out *for to see*?"—*Ibid.*

"For *to provoke*."—*Ibid.*

CHAPTER VII.

GENDERS OF NOUNS.

Were any number of educated men required to form a new language, and fix its grammatical principles, they would, without doubt, distinguish all living creatures by masculine or by feminine nouns, according to their sex, and things without life by neuter nouns. In such a case, we should have a philosophical and an intelligible principle, founded on the very nature of things, adapting names to things and not things to names. But languages, being formed for the most part by men little removed from a state of savage nature, obtain certain intractable forms which will not admit of change even in a more advanced state of civilization. Hence the utter absurdity of classing nouns into masculine, feminine, and neuter, according to their *terminations.* Words are the mere arbitrary signs of things, and it cannot be of the least importance whether the name of a thing ends in one letter of the alphabet or in another, in one combination of letters or in another. The thing signified, under all names, remains the same. Hence, all languages which have attempted to form the genders of nouns on *termination* are full of inconsistency and absurdity, laying down rules apparently for the express purpose of annihilating them by innumerable exceptions; so that, both in the classics and in the modern continental languages, we are fully prepared to coincide with the candid remark of the author of a German grammar—

"But neither this rule, *nor any rules*, will be sufficient to distinguish the genders of nouns."—*Rawbotham.*

CHAPTER VIII.

PRINCIPLE OF GENDERS IN THE ENGLISH NOUN.

Now, the principle of genders in the English language is founded simply on the distinction of sex; that is, on a natural and unchangeable distinction. Where there is no sex, a distinction is made by the simple negation of sex; that is, by what is called the neuter gender, neither masculine nor feminine. This is instantly comprehended as a broad and important principle. In philosophical subjects, in plain narration, on all ordinary occasions, it is a principle from which the English language does not depart; but in oratory and poetry, it is not unusual for the name of inanimate things to be personified, and the masculine or feminine gender assigned; but always with reference to peculiar properties. This being done sparingly, and on peculiar occasions, adds greatly to the force or tenderness of description. The sun, for instance, which communicates light and heat, in poetry is frequently made masculine; not merely because the deity of the sun is represented as masculine in heathen literature, but because of the sun's inherent power and energy; whilst the *moon*, from her soft and chastened light, is denominated feminine. Thus Milton:—

> "As when the sun, new risen,
> Looks through the misty horizontal air,
> Shorn of *his* beams."

Thus Pope, "Homer:"—

> "And now from forth the chambers of the main,
> To shed *his* sacred light on earth again,
> Arose the golden chariot of the day,
> And tipt the mountains with a purple ray."

But speaking of the *moon*, the same author says:—

> "As when the moon, refulgent lamp of night,
> O'er heaven's clear azure sheds *her* sacred light."

We at once feel the propriety of this distinction. Speaking of either sun or moon philosophically, we should say *it;* speaking of them poetically, or rhetorically, we should say *he*, and *she*. Yet the Germans, running counter to the authority of antiquity and to our very innate feelings, make the sun feminine, and the moon masculine—the sun a *she*, and the moon a *he;* an act of violence and profanation against the majesty of the one, and the loveliness of the other. Neither gallantry, philosophy, nor poetical embellishment can have had any share in such an appointment. It is probable that the genders of the sun and moon, with other arbitrary and incongruous genders, were fixed in German, and in many other languages, at a time when they were the languages of barbarous hordes. The Anglo-Saxon of our forefathers was guilty of these incongruities in the application of genders. From such we are now happily released. We still, it is true, find traces of this capricious application of genders among a certain portion of our population; and agricultural implements, as harrows, and ploughs, and flails, and even measles, smallpox, or fever, are dignified with a *he* or a *she*, according to the taste of an individual, or of a district. This gives us a clue to the origin of the arbitrary and capricious genders of languages—barbarism rendered intractable by the force of custom. Some Indian nations make the sun and moon brothers. Euripides, on one occasion, calls them father and daughter. In Greek, the Furies—infernal goddesses—are *feminine;* but Lucan, as if to indicate their intense and powerful malignity, has made them *masculine:*—

"Terribilesque deos scelerum."

We must, however, bear in mind that θεος, a god, in Greek, and *deus*, in Latin, represented either gender. Euripides, speaking of Venus, says, την θεον; and Virgil, speaking of Venus, says, ducente *deo*. In speaking of children, as a family, without reference to sex, the Greek uses a neuter noun, τα τεκνα. The word *children* we consider, both masculine and feminine, of the common gender. When speaking of an infant, we say *it*. In Scripture the Deity is sometimes represented under the neuter gender:—

"Art thou not *it* that hath cut Rahab, and wounded the dragon? Art thou not *it* which hath dried the sea, and the waters of the great deep?"

There is a peculiar fitness in thus speaking of Deity, as

an abstraction, apart from all human distinctions. So, again, "Our Father, *which*," not *who*, "art in heaven," avoiding human personality and paternity.

Milton makes *thunder* of the masculine gender:—

> "And the thunder,
> Winged with red lightning, and impetuous rage,
> Perhaps hath spent *his* shafts."

The Greeks and Romans represented the impersonation of love under the masculine gender, as a mischievous and playful boy. English poets have followed their example. Thus Lodge, in "Rosalind's Madrigal:"—

> "Love in my bosom, like a bee,
> Doth suck *his* sweet;
> Now with *his* wings he plays with me,
> Now with *his* feet."

In English, we have lost some terminations, in themselves distinctive of masculine and feminine, the want of which we perceive in the following couplet from Crabbe's "Lover's Journey:"—

> "Gone to a friend, she tells me; I commend
> Her purpose—means she to a *f male* friend?"

If the word *friend* had retained its distinctive termination, it would not have been necessary to use the words *femal* friend. The old words were *freund*, a male friend, *freundinne*, a female friend.

As a general principle in the use of genders, whenever in poetry or oratory, we personify, we give the masculine gender to such inanimate things as are remarkable for strength, courage, majesty; and the feminine to such as are remarkable for gentleness and loveliness, or for which we cherish a tender affection. Thus, we speak of country under the feminine gender:—

"For thankless Greece such hardships have I brav'd,
Her wives, *her* infants, by my labor sav'd."
Pope's *Homer*.

We feel a peculiar fitness in representing justice, charity, mercy, as feminine; and night, with her soft and silent step, is aptly represented as feminine. Thus, in the Book of Wisdom xviii. 14:—

"For while all things were in quiet silence, and that night was in the midst of *her* swift course, thine almighty word leaped down from heaven, out of thy royal throne, like a fierce man of war, into a land of destruction."

The quiet and stealthy step of night, and the "almighty word, leaping down from heaven like a fierce man of war," may be ranked amongst the very sublimest conceptions of human genius.

SECTION III.

GRAMMATICAL CONSTRUCTION OF PRONOUNS.

CHAPTER I.

THEIR IRREGULARITIES.

The English pronoun, though not so complicated or irregular in form as the Anglo-Saxon pronoun, yet is necessarily so to a certain extent; and in that comparatively limited extent is the source of many grammatical errors—so much so, indeed, that the proper use of the pronoun, in its various forms, may, in a very considerable degree, be considered as the test of a grammatical education. We have no less than thirty pronouns, classified by different grammarians according to their supposed distinctive properties. It is not so much with these distinctive properties that we have to deal, as with the grammatical application of the pronouns themselves.

A personal pronoun is that which has reference to persons, or to things personified.

We have five personal pronouns, *I, thou, he, she, it,* with their plurals, *we, ye* or *you,* and *they.*

It is not necessary that the first person should be distinguished by any variation of gender; hence, whether male or female speaks, both would say, *I* give, or give it to *me;* the gender being marked by present personality. The same may be said of the plural of *I,* namely, *we* and *us.* So also the second person, whether singular or plural, has no variation of gender, because the persons are present when designated. As no ambiguity can arise, no distinction is necessary. In writing to an absent person, there is still a mental or implied presence. But as the third person of whom we speak is absent, or may be so, a distinctive term is necessary, and therefore we say, *he* or *she, him* or *her,* according to circumstances.

The personal and relative pronouns, admitting the greatest irregularities, are the most fruitful sources of error; and in the Latin and Greek languages, where cases and variations are much more numerous, the proper form of the relative pronoun always seems a matter of difficulty with the young student. All practical teachers know this by experience.

In treating of the grammatical application of the pronoun, the first object will be to point out that which is right by the exhibition of that which is wrong, and then to show how far the effect of a sentence, or of a paragraph, may be improved by the judicious repetition of the pronoun.

CHAPTER II.

PERSONAL PRONOUN.

To begin with the personal pronoun. We shall find that high authorities are no guarantee against the commission of flagrant error. There are facts in grammar, as well as facts in other matters; and against these no authority, however great, can contend; and as such errors may be quoted as authorities by those who never dream of subjecting them to grammatical scrutiny, it may not be a useless task to show that grammar has no aristocratic favorites—that there is no true standard except an impartial grammatical standard.

"Gentle reader, let you and *I*, in like manner, endeavor to improve the enclosure of the Carr."—*Southey, The Doctor.*

Let you and *me* (not *I*), both pronouns, you and me, depending upon the verb *let*. Mr. Southey would not have said, let *I* alone; yet this would be quite as correct as the *I* in the sentence here quoted.

> "And though, by Heaven's severe decree,
> She suffers hourly more than *me*." SWIFT *to Stella*.

Than *I*, that is, than *I do*; for *them*, in this position, is simply a conjunction. When followed by *whom*, and in no other case, is it a preposition; as, "Than *whom* (not than *who*) no better man exists."

> "At an hour
> When all slept sound, save *she*, who bore them both."
> ROGERS' *Italy*, p. 108.

Save *her*, that is, except *her*; and Rogers, in another passage, is inconsistent with himself; as,

> "I looked up,
> And all were gone, save *him*, who now kept guard."
> *Ibid.* p. 185.

> "Here is a pleasant place,
> And nothing wanting is, save *she*, alas!"
> DRUMMOND of Hawthorden.

"There was no stranger with us, in the house, save *we* two." 1 *Kings* iii. 18.

"All, *save I*, were at rest, and enjoyment."—*Frankenstein*.

In all these passages, *save* requires after it the objective case.

> "Nor hope to be myself less miserable
> By what I seek, but others to make such
> As *I*."   *Paradise Lost*, ix. 126.

Lowth quotes this passage, with Bentley's observation upon it, who says, "the syntax requires such *as me*."

Bentley was an acute classical critic; but his English is often perfectly childish, and betrays an utter ignorance of the commonest grammatical principles. Let us supply what is wanting, and the sentence will be quite clear:—

——"but others to make such
As I *am*."

Not as *me* am.

"But if there is one character more base, more infamous, and more shocking than another, it is *him* who," &c.—*Rev. Sydney Smith*, "*Trimmer and Lancaster.*"

It is *he*, not *him*.

Again:—

"When do we ever find a well-educated Englishman or Frenchman embarrassed by an ignorance of the grammar of *their* respective languages. *They* first learn it practically, and *unerringly*; and then, if *they* chose (choose) to look back, and smile at the idea of having proceeded by a number of rules, without knowing one of them by heart, or being conscious that they had any rule at all, this is a philosophical amusement; but *who* ever *thinks* of learning the grammar of *their* own tongue, before *they* are very good grammarians?"

"Whoever *thinks* of learning the grammar of *his* own tongue, before *he is* a very good grammarian?" The author surely meant to be facetious when he represented an English gentleman as learning his own language, practically and *unerringly*, without the knowledge of rules. There is much confusion, also, in the application of *their* and *they* to an Englishman *or* a Frenchman.

"The philosopher, who has spent a lifetime in laborious, but fruitless inquiry, does not enjoy the same reputation as *him* who, with less labor, and possibly less talent, has added something to the catalogue of discovery."—*Solitary Walks.*

As *he;* as *he* enjoys, not *him* enjoys.

"It is not fit for such as *us,* to sit with the rulers of the land."
—*Scott, Ivanhoe.*

Such as *we;* as *we* are.

Again:—

"Let *he* that looks after them, look on his hand;
And if there's blood on't, he's one of their band."
Scott, *Pirate.*

Let *him,* not let *he.*

Again:—

"I will be *her,* whose foot the waves wet not."

I will be *she.*

Perhaps, in these passages, Scott may be supposed to speak the language of the characters introduced.

"Now Margaret's curse is fallen upon our heads,
When she exclaimed on Hastings, you, and *I.*"
Shakspeare.

On *me,* not *I.*

"Ask the murderer, *he* who has steeped his hands in the blood of another—ask him who has terminated a life of iniquity by a death of infamy," &c.—*Dr. Rudge, Second Lecture.*

Ask the *murderer*—*him,* not *he,* him being put in apposition with *murderer,* which word is in the objective case; "Ask the murderer—ask *him,* who," &c.

"He that studies to represent one of known and eminent merit, to be a mere fool, and an ideot (id*i*ot), *he* gives himself the lie, and betrays he is (that he is) either *acted* by envy, or corrupted by a faction."—*Bentley.*

The pronoun *he* in the second place is superfluous, and the whole sentence insufferably faulty. Three of the phrases are not English, and *ideot* ought to be *idiot.**

"Sorrow not as *them* that have no hope."—1 *Thess.* iv. 13.

This sentence, made out, would be, sorrow not as *them* sorrow that have no hope.—As *they* sorrow, not as *them* sorrow.

"If he suffers, he suffers as *them* that have no hope."—*Maturin's Sermons.*

As *they* who, as *they* suffer, who, &c. The whole sentence ought to be, "If he *suffer*, he suffers as they that have no hope;" for the author is not speaking of time present, but of time future and indefinite. If, at any time, he *should* suffer.

"Holland and *thee* did each in other live."—DRYDEN.

"We are alone, here's none but *thee* and I."   *Idem.*

Each of these sentences exhibits a most incongruous and ungrammatical amalgamation of terms. They are absolutely ridiculous, as matters of grammar.

---

* Idiot is derived from ιδιωτης, a *private* person, in opposition to a *professional* one, the private or unprofessional person being supposed to be comparatively unskilful, ignorant, stupid, idiotic, ιδιωτικος.

Mr. Gilpin, in his "Remarks on Forest Scenery," says,

"I have, oftener than once, met with the following tender elegiacs in churchyards, in Hampshire:—

"*Him* shall never come again to *we;*
But we shall surely one day go to *he.*"

We may smile at this rustic simplicity, but there is certainly no reason why the Hampshire peasant should be entitled to our especial condescension. He goes, arm in arm, with the "*unerring* English gentleman," and may claim a personal companionship even with authors of the highest celebrity in the walks of English literature. Let *he*, then, hold up his head like a man, as *him* is.

"Her price is paid, and she is sold *like thou.*"
Milman's *Fall of Jerusalem.*

Like thou is not English; like *thee*, i. e. *to thee*, or, as *thou*, as thou art.

"He walks *like I* do," and such expressions are mere vulgarisms.

"Phalaris, who was much older than *her.*"—*Bentley's Diss.*
"There were thousands in the French army who could have done as well as *him.*"—*Napier's History of the French War.*

As well as *he* could, not as *him* could.

"He having none but *them*, they having none but *her.*"
Drayton's *Polyolbion.*

It is difficult to conceive how the author, who had just said *but them*, should immediately after say but *her*, both terms being subject to precisely the same grammatical government.

"They were more terrified than *us*."

Which, made out, runs, "they were more terrified than *us* were terrified."

"It was *thee* who peopled the confines of Asia, Sicily entire, and part of Italy."—*Monthly Mag.*

It was *thou*.

"I thought this a good occasion to ascertain how far my authority was nominal or real, and therefore insisted peremptorily upon their putting off again. 'Unless,' as I said, 'Messieurs, you are the masters, and not *me*.'"—*Basil Hall*.

"Unless you are the masters, and *I* am not;" not *me* am not.

"At the town we discovered that we had drawn up against peaceable travellers, who must have been as glad as *us* to escape."—*Burnes's Travels.*

As *we*.

"Stimulated, in turn, by their approbation and that of better judges than *them*, she turned to their literature with redoubled energy."—*Quarterly Review, Life of H. More.*

Better judges than *they* were, not than *them* were.

"And is this, thought we, in very deed the wife of poor Simon, the village lawyer, whose Burus was *him* of the justice and law ecclesiastical?"—*Blackwood's Magazine,* Article "*Very Odd.*"

Was *he*.

"There are the families of Muness Queendale, Thereliove, and I know not *whom* else are expected."—*Scott, Pirate.*

"The families of Muness Queendale, Thereliove, and I know not *who* else are expected." *Who* being the nominative before *are* expected.

"These are the men *who* are expected."

Not *whom* are expected.

"No one messmate of the round table was, than *him*, more fraught with manliness and beauty."

Than *he*.

"If thy hand or thy foot offend thee, cut *them* off and cast *them* from thee."—*Matt.* xviii. 8.

Cut *it* off, and cast *it* from thee, such being the grammatical effect of the conjunction *or*. Suppose the hand to offend, and the foot *not* to offend, surely the unoffending foot is not to be cut off. And again, suppose the foot to offend, and the hand *not* to offend, surely the unoffending hand is not to be cut off. *Or* is here necessarily disjunctive, and the nouns *hand* and *foot* must be taken separately, and each of them expressed by *it*.

Ambiguity in the Use of the Personal Pronoun.

"And it came to pass in those days, that Jesus came from Nazareth of Galilee, and was baptized of John in Jordan: and straightway coming up out of the water *he* saw the heavens opened, and the Spirit, like a dove, descending upon him."

"He saw." Who saw? Jesus, or John? The context requires that Jesus saw; that is, Jesus came, was baptized, and, coming up out of the water, saw the heavens opened, and the Spirit descending upon *him*, that is, upon *John*; whereas the meaning intended is, that John saw the heavens opened, and the spirit descending ἐπ' αὐτον on him, that is, on *Jesus*. The Greek text is also ambiguous, for the verb εἶδε will apply either to Jesus or to John; and, as Jesus occurs in the nominative case, in the preceding member of the sentence, we should certainly understand ιδε to be predicated of Jesus, and not of John. This ambiguity of the Greek is noted by Erasmus.

It may here be incidentally noticed, that there is another ambiguity in this passage, arising from the phrase *like a dove*. Like a dove conveys the notion of descending in the *similitude* of a dove; but the similitude was only a similitude in the descent, not a similitude of bodily form. If the phrase had been, "and the Spirit *descending like a dove* upon him," there would have been less chance of ambiguity than there is under the present arrangement of the phrase. "The Spirit descending like a dove;" as a dove would descend, ωσει περιστεραν.

"In his days Pharaoh-Nechoh, King of Egypt, went up against the King of Assyria, to the river Euphrates, and King Josiah went against him, and *he* slew *him* at Megiddo, when he had seen him."—2 *Kings* xxiii. 29.

From the confusion arising from the pronoun *him* in this sentence, it is not easy to understand whether Pharaoh-Nechoh slew Josiah, or Josiah slew Pharaoh-Nechoh, till we find, by what follows, that Josiah is dead and Pharaoh-Nechoh alive, and that this very Pharaoh-Nechoh makes Eliakim, the son of Josiah, king, in the place of Josiah his father.

"The Son of Man shall be delivered up to the chief priests and to the scribes, and they shall condemn him to death and deliver him to the Gentiles, and *they* shall mock him, and scourge him, and shall spit upon him, and shall kill him."

They, who? The Gentiles? or the chief priests and the scribes? The introduction of *who* after *Gentiles,* instead of *they,* would have rendered the sentence free from ambiguity; "shall deliver him to the Gentiles, *who* shall mock him."

As pronouns supply the place of nouns, it is, indeed, essentially necessary that they should distinctly point to the nouns which they represent; otherwise, confusion and ambiguity must necessarily be occasioned. Take the following sentence, from Goldsmith's "History of Greece:"—

"*He* wrote to that distinguished philosopher, in terms the most polite and flattering; begging of *him* to come and undertake *his* education, and to bestow on *him* those useful lessons of magnanimity and virtue which every great man ought to possess, and which *his* numerous avocations rendered impossible to *him*."

The pronoun *he* is introduced six times in this sentence, under different forms; and were it not that we are acquainted with the facts, the whole would be a mass of confusion. First it stands for Philip, then for Aristotle, then for Alexander, again for Alexander, and then twice for Philip. The sentence would have been rendered much clearer if the author had said, "undertake his son's education." And again, "his *own* numerous avocations."

In the following sentence, confusion arises from the indistinct use of the personal pronoun *they:*—

"And they did all eat and were filled, and *they* took up the fragment that remained, twelve baskets full."—*Matt.* xiv. 20.

Who took up? As the disciples placed the loaves

and the fishes before the multitude, and the multitude partook of them, it is not clear whether the disciples or the multitude took up the fragments.

'"When Diogenes was asked of what country he was, 'I am (said he) a citizen of the world.' The sentiment of this answer has been generally admired, although probably no person ever gave a more unamiable illustration of it, in his own life, than the Cynic in the tub *himself.*"—*Percy Anecdotes, Address.*

In this sentence, from the juxtaposition of the words *tub* and *himself*, the mind connects them together; so that *tub himself* seems intended, and not *cynic himself*. *Cynic himself* in the tub, or the *tub-cynic himself*.

CHAPTER III.

INCONSISTENCY OF NUMBER AND GENDER.

"During the discourse, upon every puncture he felt from his distemper, he smiled and cried out, Pain! pain! be as impertinent and troublesome as *you* please, I shall never own that *thou* art an evil."—*Spectator*, No. 312.

"On the other hand, the *Simiæ* cannot easily stand or walk upright; because *its* foot rests on the outer edge, the heel does not touch the ground, and the narrowness of the pelvis renders the trunk unsteady."—*Lawrence's Lectures.*

The *Simiæ*, being plural, required *their*, not *its.*

"We do not consider that *the wicked are* suffered to flourish till the sum of *his* iniquities is full."—*Cole's Sermons.*

His? their.

"Think me not lost, for *thee* I Heaven implore,
Thy guardian angel, though a wife no more,

> 1, when abstracted from the world *you* seem,
> Hint the pure thought, and frame the heavenly dream."
> SAVAGE, *Wanderer.*

> " Nor can the prison 'scape *your* searching eye,
> *Your* ear still opening to the captive's cry;
> Nor less was promised from *thy* early skill,
> Ere power enforced benevolence of will."
> SAVAGE, *Epist. to Walpole.*

" Yet *you*, my creator, detest and spurn me, *thy* creature, to whom *thou* art bound by ties only dissoluble by the annihilation of one of us."—*Frankenstein.*

" His design was to render Athens a maritime city, in which he followed a very different system of politics from *their* former governors."—*Goldsmith's Greece.*

From *that* of their former governors, otherwise, system is contrasted with governors, instead of the system of one governor with the system of other governors.

In the following passage, there is an incongruity between the number of the noun and that of the pronoun which refers to it.

" *Egypt* was glad at their departure, for *they* were afraid of them."—*Old. Test.*

Egypt, for the Egyptians, is a figure of speech quite justifiable.

The following passage presents a confusion of genders:—

" He that pricketh the ear maketh it to show *her* knowledge."—*Eccles.* xxi. 19.

We see no reason for *it* in one place, and *her* in the other.

The pronoun *he*, when standing for a noun substantive, or for a noun adjective, is indeclinable; it has no variation of case. As,

"Malevolti had noticed these splenetic efforts; but, though a man of fiery character, and proud enough to dare the proudest he who ruffled his self-complacency by a look," &c.

The proudest, *he*, that is, the proudest man. *He* is in this sense an indeclinable name, and in the objective case.

When standing in the place of an adjective, it again has no variation of case. As,

"I will take no bullock out of thy house, nor *he*-goat out of thy folds."—*Psalms.*

In this position *he* is an integral part of the term *goat*, and remains unchanged, though in the objective case. It would be rather odd to say, I will take no *him*-goat.

CHAPTER IV.

PROPER USE OF THE PERSONAL PRONOUN.

The following sentences present us with the *proper* use of the pronoun, contrasted with some of those errors which have already been given.

"Successful he might have been, had his horse been as ambitious as he."—*Goldsmith, Citizen of the World.*

That is, as *he* was.

"Surely there's not a dungeon-slave that's buried
In the high-way unshrouded and uncoffined,
But lies as soft and sleeps as sound as *he*."

BLAIR'S *Grave*.

That is, as *he* does.

"And let the king give her royal estate to another that is better than *she*."—*Esther* i. 15.

That is, than *she* is.

"For thou hast discovered thyself to another than *me*."—*Isaiah* lvii. 8.

That is, than to *me*.

The errors that have been pointed out, in the use of the personal pronoun, are but a few specimens out of hundreds, I might say thousands, which are scattered over our literature. It is the very fact of their perpetual recurrence that makes them a matter of consequence, and entitles them to notice; though individually, many of them are absolutely below criticism. They are of a character to which, perhaps, the language of no civilized people can afford a parallel. It is to be regretted that men of high literary reputation should, over and over again, be guilty of errors which must be glaring and obvious to every foreigner who applies himself to the study of the very first principles of the English language.

CHAPTER V.

ON THE USE OF YE, YOU, AND THOU.

CUSTOM has authorized that *ye* shall be used in the two extremes of *solemnity* and *familiarity;* whilst *you* is more properly confined to ordinary narrative and familiar occasions.

Solemnity.

" *Thou* hard firm earth, thou wilt not break before me,
And hide me in thy dark and secret bosom!
Ye burning towers, *ye* fall upon your children
With a compassionate ruin, not on me.
Ye spare me only. I alone am mark'd
And seal'd for life ; death cruelly seems to shun me,
Me, who am readiest, and most wish to die."
    MILMAN, *Fall of Jerusalem.*

" I speak to time and to eternity,
Of which I grow a portion—not to man.
Ye elements! in which to be resolved
I hasten, let my voice be as a spirit
Upon you! *Ye* blue waves, which bore my banner;
Ye winds, that fluttered o'er, as if *ye* loved it,
And filled my swelling sails, as they were wafted
To many a triumph! *Thou*, my native earth,
Which I have bled for, and *thou*, foreign earth,
Which drank [drank'st] this willing blood from many a wound!
Ye stones, in which my gore will not sink, but
Reek up to heaven! *Ye* skies, which will receive it!
Thou sun, which shin'st on these things! And *Thou*
Who kindlest and who quenchest suns! attest."
    BYRON, *Doge of Venice.*

Thou is used instead of *you*, in cases of marked personal appeal, or emphatic distinction.

> "Hail, horrors! hail,
> Infernal world! And *Thou!* profoundest hell,
> Receive thy new possessor."
> *Paradise Lost*, b. i.

> "*Thou* sun, said I, fair light!
> And *thou*, enlightened earth, so fresh and gay!
> Ye hills and dales! ye rivers, woods, and plains!
> And ye that live and move, fair creatures, tell—
> Tell if ye saw how I came thus, how here!"   *Ibid.*

There is an earnestness of appeal, and a sublimity, which rank these with the finest passages of English poetry. Let them be examined, and it will be seen how much of this effect is owing to the pointed and distinct personality expressed by *ye* and *thou*.

> "Clad in Achilles' arms if thou appear,
> Proud Troy may tremble and desist from war."
> POPE, *Iliad*.

> "Thy once proud hopes, presumptuous prince, are fled;
> This arm shall reach *thy* heart, and strike *thee* dead."   *Ibid.*

> "Ah, wretch! no father shall *thy* corpse compose,
> *Thy* dying eyes no tender mother close."   *Ibid.*

Change *ye* and *thou* into *you*, and *thine* into *yours*, and the earnestness, vigor, and solemnity of these passages will be destroyed. They will exhibit nothing but a mawkish and insipid conventionalism.

The following complet from Pope we cannot but dislike on these grounds: —

> "We then explained the cause on which we came,
> Urged *you* to arms, and found *you* fierce for fame."   *Ibid.*

The passage is offensive, because it is inconsistent with the language of the heroic age; and as the relation of a solemn appeal, is ridiculous. But when we pass from mere mortal subjects to the Deity, and the Redeemer, the term *you* in the place of *thou* becomes highly offensive.

What a grievous profanation would it be to substitute the *second* person plural for the *first*, and *your* for *thine*, in the Lord's Prayer! "Our Father, which art in heaven, hallowed be *your* name, *your* kingdom come," &c. All right feeling revolts against the impious familiarity.

The profanation is not much less, when the second person plural of the pronoun is applied to the Redeemer. As,

> "Jesus Christ! what great crime have I done? Who (whom) of those who believed in *you* have I ever treated so cruelly!"—*D'Israeli, Curiosities of Literature.*

In expressing contemptuous indignation, and withering scorn, the pronoun *thou* is used with great effect. As,

> "*Thou* elfish-mark'd abortive rooting hog!
> *Thou* that wast sealed in thy nativity
> The slave of nature, and the son of hell!
> *Thou* slander of thy mother's heavy womb!
> *Thou* rag of honor! thou detested!"
> SHAKSPEARE.

Substitute *you* for *thou*, and the passage becomes comparatively courteous.

Ye, used in cases of extreme familiarity.

"Love in my bosom, like a bee,
 Doth suck his sweet;
Now with his wings he plays with me,
 Now with his feet.
Within mine eyes he makes his nest,
His bed amidst my tender breast;
My kisses are his daily feast.
 Ah! wanton, will *ye!*"
       LODGE's *Rosalind's Madrigal.*

Drayton, in his Nymphidia, uses *ye* in the same familiar manner:—

"Come all into this nut, quoth she:
Come closely in—be ruled by me:
Each one may here a chooser be,
 For room *ye* need not wrestle;
Nor need *ye* be together heap'd:
So one by one therein they crept,
And lying down they soundly slept,
 And safe as in a castle."

"Show your small talents, and let that suffice *ye,*
 But grow not vain upon it, I advise *ye.*"   *Prologue.*

"Great critic in a 'noverint universi,'
Know all men, by these presents, how to curse *ye.*"
       BUTLER.

We sometimes find *ye* in the place of *you,* even in the objective case, and where the subject is of a solemn nature. Against this, Lowth strongly protests. "In the serious and solemn style," says he, "no authority is sufficient to justify so manifest a solecism."

EXAMPLES.
"God, therefore, cannot hurt *ye,* and be just."
       Paradise Lost, b. ix.

> "O Flowers,
> That never will in other climates grow,
> My early visitation and my last,
> At e'en, which I bred up with tender hand,
> From the first opening bud, and gave *ye* names,
> Who now shall rear *ye* ?"   *Paradise Lost*, b. xi.

> "Yet for my sons I thank *ye*, gods! 'Twas well,
> Well have they perish'd, for in fight they fell."
>   POPE, *Iliad*, b. xxii.

> "Be sad, as we would make *ye*."
>   SHAKSPEARE, *Henry VIII*.

> "Sparta! Sparta! why in slumbers
>   Lethargic dost thou lie?
> Awake and join thy numbers
>   To Athens, old ally;
> Leonidas recalling,
>   That chief of ancient song,
> Who sav'd *ye* once from falling,
>   The terrible—the strong."
>   BYRON, *Translation of War-Song*.

To say the least, no advantage seems to be gained by the use of *ye* in the place of *you*, in the five last-mentioned passages; nor can extensive custom be pleaded as an authority.

CHAPTER VI.

PRONOUNS ENCLITIC AND EMPHATIC.

AN enclitic pronoun is that which leans, or inclines, upon the word which immediately precedes it. It coalesces with it in pronunciation, so as to seem an integral part of that word.

An emphatic pronoun attaches to itself a distinct personality, claiming an uncombined enunciation.

Enclitic—as, *Give me* the book, *O spare me* a little, pronounced as if written, *giveme*, *spareme*.

The following sentence combines both the enclitic and the emphatic pronoun:—

"Who steals my purse, steals trash——
But he that filches from me my good name,
Robs *me* of that which not enriches *him*,
And makes *me* poor indeed." SHAKSPEARE.

Him and the latter *me* are in this case not only emphatic, but contradistinctive, antithetical.

So again:—

"Richmond is on the seas."
"There let him sink, and be the seas on *him!*"
SHAKSPEARE.

"Intendest thou to kill *me*, as thou killedst the Egyptian yesterday?"—*Exod.* ii. 14.

"Bless *me*, even *me* also, O my father!"—*Gen.* xxvii. 38.

"Oh, burst the harem—wrong not, on your lives,
One female form—remember *we* have wives."
Corsair, canto 2.

"Forgive *us* *our* trespasses, as we forgive *them* that trespass against *us*."

Us is here emphatic, and ought to be read as such; otherwise, the antithesis of the sentence is destroyed. So forgive us, when we trespass against *thee*, as we forgive *them* that trespass against *us*. *Them*, and *us*, and *our* are all emphatic.

Any man may have a defective voice; that is a natural defect, which he cannot remedy; at least, but partially; but nothing is so offensive, nothing shows so great an ignorance of the bearing of a sentence, as the confusion of enclitic and emphatic pronouns.

Instances of marked emphatic pronouns abound. To observe them requires nothing more than common sense and common apprehension. There is a *voice-grammar*, as well as a written grammar. In giving utterance to our own natural sentiments, voice-grammar is seldom violated. False emphasis and false intonation indicate the want of a distinct apprehension of an author's meaning, and virtually falsify his intentions.

Let us take the following sentence, and place upon the pronoun *him* a wrong emphasis :—

"And he said, Saddle me the ass, and they saddled *him*."

Him being pronounced without any emphasis, and enclitically. But place a strong emphasis on *him*, and the pronoun becomes antithetical. "And he said, Saddle me the ass;" and, instead of saddling the ass, they saddled *him*—the person who gave the order; *him* with the verbal emphasis being antithetical, and in fact changing the personality altogether. *Verbal* emphasis is an unchangeable principle, and in this respect differs from *syllabic* emphasis, which sometimes depends on the analogy of the language in question, and sometimes on custom.

Such words as *retinue* and *revenue*, *advertisement*, *committee*, and many others, have had a fluctuating syllabic emphasis. The general tendency of our pronunciation is, however, to throw the emphasis as far back as possible—that is, as near to the beginning of the word as possible. This is often done in the face of an increased difficulty of enunciation, as *cómmendable;* and even *irrefragable* has been attempted. The *syllabic* emphasis is, then, a fluctuating principle, and leads to error only when two words having different meanings are spelt alike; as, cónjure, conjúre, desért, désert. But, if a person clearly comprehends what he utters, he will, from mere natural impulse, use the *verbal* emphasis where it ought to be used; and it is in the pronoun where the most decided perversion of the meaning of a sentence is likely to take place by misplaced emphasis. A child would learn *syllabic* accent by *imitation;* *verbal* emphasis is the result of *natural feeling.* The merest child would say, "Give me that pretty thing," *give me* being enclitic; but if the same child were contending for the pretty thing with another child, it would say "Give it to *me,*" or "Give *me* that pretty thing." *me, me, me.*

CHAPTER VII.

THE RELATIVE PRONOUNS—WHO AND WHICH.

The use of the relative pronoun *who* and *whom,* as a general rule, seems to be confined to rational creatures; *which,* to the brute creation and inanimate things. In the violation of this rule, there is something offensive to our feelings. It is true we say the *men which,* because we mean the men, *which men:* and we say the *dogs which;* but we do not say the *dogs who.* Cats would not fare much better, in spite of the following authority:—

"This person informed me that he had the horror to see his own child dragged to the door by eight or ten cats, *whom* he with difficulty scared away."—*Barnes's Travels.*

Custom has, however, authorized the use of *whose* when we speak of men, brutes, or inanimate things. As, "The man *whose* peace you have destroyed;" "The wild beasts, *whose* roaring was dreadful;" "Virtue, *whose* form is lovely." The expression probably originated in the love of brevity. If we do not use *whose*, we must say, *of whom*, or *of which*. This in English was enough to decide the question. The principle is now fully sanctioned by general adoption. The same apology does not apply to *who* and *whom: who* and *whom* gain nothing in brevity over *which*.

"I shall, therefore, since the rules of style, like those of law, arise from precedents often repeated, collect the testimonies on both sides, and endeavor to discover and promulgate the decrees of custom, *who* has so long possessed, whether by right or usurpation, the sovereignty of words."

"Custom, *who*," cannot be tolerated.

"The olfactory nerves of the Cetacea, in *whom* the blowing holes occupy the place of the *nose*."—*Lawrence's Lectures.*

Though *whom*, as in the case of the *cats* already noticed, is here applied to living objects, yet we feel that the application is offensive and unnecessary.

"My lips will be fain when I sing unto thee, and so will my soul, *whom* thou hast delivered."—*Psalm* lxxi. 21.

The propriety of *whom*, in this situation, would depend upon the force and authority of custom at the time it was used.

"These considerations naturally lead to the consideration of a miracle, in which the kingdom of God is personally exalted over the powers of darkness, and which shows the superiority of faith, even when exerted over those principalities and thrones, *who*, by the first man's transgression, obtained," &c.—*Rennel.*

"I sailed along the ancient city of Priam, and then reached Tenedos, fifty miles north of it, where a Mahometan, Adun Oglou, was banished from Constantinople, on account of his riches, which had excited the jealousy of the Porte, *who* also compelled him to build a fortification for the defence of the former."—*Rae Wilson.*

In both these examples, personality ought to have merged in the terms *principalities*, and *thrones*, and *Porte*, as indicating the constituted powers of government in the abstract, and therefore we expect *which* instead of *who*.

Both sentences are altogether badly constructed. Again:—

"It is a kind of basin thirty feet in length, twelve in breadth, and fifteen in depth, enclosed by a wall, *which* comes from a distance of several miles, runs beneath Jerusalem, and is of a brackish, disagreeable taste."—*Ibid.*

In this passage, the relative *which* attaches itself to the immediate antecedent *wall*, and we do not discover our mistake till we find the wall running under Jerusalem, and having a brackish, disagreeable taste. Nothing, then, remains as an antecedent but the word basin. Then we have a basin enclosed by a wall, running, that is the basin, under Jerusalem, and having a brackish, disagreeable taste.

Mr. Rae Wilson is sometimes unfortunate both in his facts and in his mode of narrating. Take the following effort at chaotic sublimity. The view is from the summit of Mount Etna, and the description is at least curious.

"A *horizon* of *boundless* extent, *embracing* a *similar* tract of country, dotted with numerous villages, and showing the whole course of many rivers, from their *source* to their *estuary*, in their *serpentine directions*, through all their windings, *which* (what?) glittered in the beams of morning like silver threads, hoary mountains, like billows on a tempestuous ocean, and the smoke of mouldering (query? smouldering) volcanoes."

In this one sentence, there is food for an essay. It reels, and staggers, and talks inconsistent nonsense like a drunken Helot, and conveys the same moral. The subject is too great for the powers of the writer, and he sinks under a fruitless effort to give a description adequate to the object. A subject like this is a dangerous subject in ordinary hands. The fault is not so much in the failure as in the attempt.*

In the first clause of the Lord's Prayer, the Americans have changed *which* into *who*, as being more consonant to the rules of grammar.

"This" (justly observes the author of "Men and Manners in America") "is poor criticism; for it will scarcely be denied, that the use of the neuter pronoun carried with it a certain vagueness

---

* The same gentleman must pardon incredulity, when he says, "Etna, and the peak of Teneriffe, are estimated as *the most elevated* points on the earth." If he had said, are estimated at *half the height* of "the most elevated points on the earth," he would have been near the truth. Nor can we altogether believe that "the very *water* of the river (Guadalquiver) fattens horses more than the *barley* of other countries."

and sublimity, not inappropriate in reminding us that our worship is addressed to a Being, infinite and superior to all distinctions applicable to material objects."

"Jesus Christ! what great crime have I done? *who* of those who believed in you have I ever treated so cruelly?"—*Frankenstein.*

Whom of those? *Who* of those is grammatically as faulty as *he treated she* very badly.

"*Who* servest thou under?"   SHAKSPEARE.

Whom, that is, under *whom* servest thou?

"This, it seems, was proved by the report of Dr. Walter Baily, some time fellow of New College, then living in Oxford, and Professor of Physic in that University; *whom*, because he would not consent to take away her life by poison, the Earl endeavored to displace *him* at court."—*Ashmole's Antiquities.*

The word *him* is superfluous.

"He *whom* ye pretend reigns in heaven, is so far from protecting the miserable sons of men, that he perpetually delights to blast the sweetest flowers in the garden of hope."—*Spect.* No. 76.

"He *who* reigns in heaven, as ye pretend." *Ye pretend* is merely parenthetical, and has no influence whatever upon the relative *who*, and the verb *reigns*.

"If you were here, you would find three or four in the parlor after dinner, *whom* (you would say) passed their time agreeably."—*Locke, Letter to L. Molyneux.*

You would say is again parenthetical, and has no effect upon the grammatical construction of the rest of the sentence. Strike out the words *you would say*, and how transparent is a sentence like this. "You would find three or four there, in the parlor, after dinner, *who* passed their time agreeably

"On examining the above sum of 199*l*. 15*s*. 0*d*., it appears that the sum of 91*l*. 3*s*. 10*d*. was actually paid for subsistence to men with families, and single men, able to work, but could not obtain work."—*Appendix to the Report of Committee on the Poor Rate Returns.*

The relative *who* is wanting before the verb *could.*

"Breaking a constitution by the very same errors, *that* so many have been *broke* before."—*Swift, Contests and Dissensions.*

It seems incredible that a man of Swift's literary character should ever have written a sentence so faulty as this. Here is a sentence of fifteen words, with three grammatical errors, glaring and palpable. It is one which warns us against being led away by the mere authority of names. *By* is required before the relative, *that* ought to be *which*, and *broke broken*.

That, if ever proper, as including the relative *which*, has ceased to be so now. "We speak *that* we do know, and testify *that* we have seen" (John iii. 11), is a phrase not consistent with modern usage.

"Of a more serious kind are the injuries done to private individuals, which no one deplores more than I the cause of them."—*Article, Errors of the Press.*

Which, and *them*, in this sentence, are incompatible. *One* of them is useless. Thus, "of a more serious kind are the injuries done to private individuals; the innocent cause of which no one deplores more than I do."

"And I beg you not to think that this only applies to parents in a higher line of life than yours, and *are* therefore esteemed more learned, and more instructed than you are."—*Haggit's Sermons.*

The relative *who* is wanting before *are;* otherwise, the

verb *are* will have no nominative case; as the term *parents* occurs in the objective case in the preceding member of the sentence.

The following sentence is liable to the same objection. The relative *who* is wanting:—

"There is Miss Liddy, can dance a jig, raise paste, write a good hand, keep an account, give a reasonable answer, and do as she is bid."—*Spect.* 306.

"It has been remarked by some nice observers and critics, that there is nothing discovers the true temper of a person so much as his letters."—*Spect.*

That nothing discovers, or, "*that there is nothing which discovers,*" &c.

"There is nothing places religion in so disadvantageous a view."—*Sherlock's Sermons.*

There is nothing *that* places, &c.

"I have hardly seen a line from any of these gentlemen, *but spoke* them, as absent from what they were doing, as they profess they are, when they come into company."—*Spec.* 284.

But spoke—that or *which* did not speak them.

"We have thus gone through the art of poetry, which, as it is a work that required to be explained with particular exactness, I have enlarged the notes considerably."—*Watson's Translation of Horace's Art of Poetry.*

The relative *which* has here no grammatical connection with any other member or word of the sentence.

As improperly used for the Relative.

"As if there was no difference between Abraham's interceding for Sodom, for which he had no warrant, *as* we can find, and our asking those things which we are required to pray for."—*Spect.* 312.

If *as* supplies the place of the relative *that*, it is a mere vulgarism; if not, it alters the meaning of the sentence.

"The very night *as* would have suited a melancholic pensiveness."—*Clayton's Narrative.*

That.

"His work, in eight books, comprehends twenty years of the Peloponnesian war, and is written with a depth of reasoning, clearness of conception, and vigor, and dignity of language, as has not been equalled by any other Greek historian."—*Peithman on Latin Composition,* p. 130.

Not with "a depth of reasoning *as* has not been equalled:" either, "*such* a depth of reasoning *as* has not been equalled," or "a depth of reasoning *that* has not been equalled."

What do we think of "This is the man *as* I saw"—"This is the woman *as* is not to be equalled"—"This is the animal *as* chews the thistle?"

CHAPTER VIII.

RELATIVE PRONOUN OMITTED IDIOMATICALLY.

In common conversation, and familiar narrative, it is not usual to omit the relative pronoun altogether. This probably arises from that spirit of contraction which so generally pervades our language. As, *this is the man I spoke of,* that is, *of whom* I spoke: this is the house he built; that is, *which* he built. Use has sanctioned this elliptical mode of expression; but in serious and solemn subjects it ought to be avoided.

In the following sentence, the relative pronoun is three times omitted:—

"Is there a God to swear *by,* and is there none to believe *in,* none to trust *to ?*"--*Letters and Essays, Anonymous.*

By, in, and *to,* as prepositions, stand alone, denuded of the relatives to which they apply. The sentence presents no attractions worthy of imitation. It exhibits a license carried to the extreme point of endurance.

In that passage in the Bible in which Joseph is represented as inquiring affectionately after his father's welfare, the translators have not put this flippant phraseology into his mouth, but made him to express himself in more dignified and respectful language.

"Is your father well, the old man of *whom* ye spake?"--*Gen.* xliii. 27.

CHAPTER IX.

AMBIGUITY ARISING FROM THE PLURALITY OF ANTECEDENTS.

"There is among the people of all countries and all religions, a belief of immortality, arising from the natural desire of living, and strengthened by uniform tradition, *which* has certainly some influence upon practice, and some effect in fortifying the soul against the terrors of death." - *Lindsay's Sermons.*

The relative *which* is here too far separated from its

antecedent *belief*. The first impression made in reading the sentence is, that tradition is the antecedent. The intervening words almost obliterate the remembrance of the real antecedent *belief*. *Tradition* dwells upon the mind, as well as on the ear, and connects itself with the relative immediately following.

"For he hath made him to be sin for us, who knew no sin."— *New Testament*.

Here the meaning deduced from our own knowledge of the fact is at variance with that which is deducible from the strict grammatical arrangement of the sentence. Though the term *him* is the antecedent to the relative *who*, and required to be so by the facts of the case, yet *us*, from its juxtaposition with *who*, presents itself as the proper antecedent. By reason of the inflexion of the verb, in its grammatical concord with the relative, no mistake can arise in Latin or Greek; but in English the passage is ambiguous. If the passage had run, "For he hath made him, who knew no sin, to be sin for us" all ambiguity would have been avoided.

The following passage from Milton presents us with a peculiar construction, as respects the antecedent and the relative. A participle is thrown in between them. But, as no other word can be mistaken for the antecedent, no obscurity can arise from this construction, though singular in its kind.

"Nay, lady, sit : if I but wave this wand,
Your nerves are all chained up in alabaster.
And you a statue, or as Daphne was,
Root-*bound*, that fled Apollo."   MILTON.

CHAPTER X.

PRONOUN ADJECTIVES.

Aught.

THIS pronominal adjective is sometimes written *ought*, but erroneously so. Were it only for the sake of distinguishing it from the verb *ought*, it would be desirable that it should be written *aught*, and not *ought*, but it is derived from the Anglo-Saxon *aht*, written also *aught* and *awhit*, signifying anything; and therefore there can be no reason, either etymologically or otherwise, for writing *ought* and *nought*. Aht, aught; ne (not) aht, naht, naught, not anything.

"It is *naught*, it is *naught*, saith the buyer; but when he is gone his way, then he boasteth."—*Prov.* xx. 14.

"Nor aught avails him now,
To have built in heaven high towers." *Paradise Lost.*

Any.

Any is derived from the Anglo-Saxon *ænig, ullus*, any one. In the time of Henry the Third, it was written *oni*, masculine, *onie*, feminine.

"And gif oni, other onie cumen her ongenes."
"And if any man, or any woman come here against."
Pat. Rot. Henry III.

This distinction of gender is now lost.

In the following sentence, *any* is erroneously used for *all*:—

"Whatever be the motive, they are not only the most charitable of *any* other nation, but most judicious in distinguishing the properest objects of compassion."—*Goldsmith's Citizen of the World.*

The most charitable of *all* other nations, or more charitable *than any other* nation.

Either and Neither.

Either, Anglo-Saxon œgther, answers to the Latin term uter, which invariably refers to one of two things, and not one of a plurality. So also *neither* refers to two things only, and answers to neuter, neither of the two. But none, no one, refers to a plurality of objects, and is sometimes plural itself. As, "Two were invited, but *neither* of them came;" "I should have been satisfied, if *either* of the two had come;" "*Twenty* were invited, but *none, no one* (emphatically, and in the singular number), *not one* of them came." An illegitimate and ungrammatical use of these words, *either* and *neither*, has lately been creeping into the language, in the application of these terms to a plurality of objects; as, "*Twenty* ruffians broke into the house, but *neither* of them could be recognized." "Here are *fifty* pens, you will find that *either* of them will do."

"For injustice springs only from three causes; either because we have not the wisdom to perceive what is just, or the power to enforce it, or the benevolence to will it.—*Neither* of these causes for injustice can be found in a being wise, powerful, benevolent." —*New Monthly, Conversations with an Ambitious Student.*

None of these causes, *not one* of these causes.

"At last, a servant, who had lived with him, and knew the way of the house, plotted with one Cain a cooper, and one Digny a school-master, and a fellow of the name of M'Henry, to rob the house, on a Sabbath evening. *Neither* of them lived in that neighborhood."—*Life of Dr. Clarke.*

"*None*, or not one, of them lived in that neighborhood."

Either and *neither*, applied to any number more than one of *two* objects, is a mere solecism, and one of late introduction.

An Other, Another, the Other.

Another refers to one of many, *the other* to one of two; as, " Here are ten volumes of books; take this one, or *another*, if you please," speaking indefinitely. " Here are two books; take this, or *the other*, if you please," speaking definitely. " Two men were standing on the road; one walked away, *the other* remained." " Two men were standing on the road, and *another* came up." " Two women shall be grinding at the mill, *the one* shall be taken and *the other* left;" "una accipietur, *altera* relinquetur."

Confusion of Another with the Other.

" And they came into the house of Baal, and the house of Baal was full from one end to *another*."—*2 Kings x.*

If the house of Baal, like most houses, had only two ends, it might be full from one end to *the other*, not *another*, which implies one end of many.

" But, should he persist in refusing your daughter, then prepare the felek and the sticks, collect your strongest ferashes, and let them strike, till you cannot tell one foot from *another*."—*Zorab.*

As Zorab had, probably, only two feet, the expression ought to have been one from *the* other.

"These two kinds of diction, prose and poetry, are so different *one from another*, that the one will *hinder* more than *assist* the other."—*Peithman's Latin Composition.*

As the kinds of diction mentioned are but two, the writer ought to have said *from each other*, not one from *another*. Any number of objects above two might differ from *one another;* but two differ from *each other*. It may also be observed of this passage, that to "*hinder* more than *assist*" is nonsense. The terms are contrary, and do not admit of mixture. Where *hindrance* begins, there can be no *assistance*. We cannot depress an object two inches, and simultaneously raise it one inch. Hinder *rather* than assist.

"The reed grows to an amazing height, as the part the Indians use is from ten to eleven feet long, and no tapering can be perceived, one end being as thick as *another*."—*Wanderings in South America.*

Again: *the other.*

The Other in the Place of *Another.*

"On looking upwards, we saw them clinging by myriads to the roof, all in convulsive motion, with glittering eyes, open mouths, and hideous trembling wings, seeming, in their fear, to be hanging one to *the* other, tier below tier."—*St. John's Egypt*, vol. i. p. 147.

As there were myriads of bats, they must have hung one to *another*. They formed a concatenation of bats, and one bat hung to *another* bat throughout the whole series.

"Diodorus, whose design was to refer all occurrences to years, is of more credit in a point of chronology than Plutarch, or any other, who write lives by the lump."—*Bentley's Dissertation on Themist. Epistles.*

"Or any *others* who write."

Each.

Each is connected with *he, him, she, her, it*, and not with *they, them*.

"And they dreamed a dream, both of them, *each* man *his* dream in one night, *each* man according to the interpretation of *his* dream."—*Gen.* xl. 5.

"To each *his* proper phantom fell,
Whilst Cæsar reigned, the general care of hell."
—Rowe's Lucan's *Pharsalia.*

"*Each* had *his* place appointed, *each his* course."
—*Paradise Lost*, book iii.

His in all these cases is right. *Each* is always taken distributively, and is therefore necessarily of the singular number, and will therefore be connected grammatically with the personal pronoun of the singular number. *Every* is also distributive, and follows the same rule. The following passage has *their* improperly in the place of *his*, as the correlative of *every*.

"And the sea gave up the dead that were in it, and death and hell gave up the dead that were in them; and they were judged every man according to *their* works."—*Rev.* xx. 13.

His works.

Self.

Self is used in conjunction with the personal pronouns *I, thou, he;* and *selves* with the plurals of these, *we, ye,* and *they*. In the Anglo-Saxon, *self* was declinable; but about the time of Chaucer it shared the same fate as that which many other declinable words had undergone. Self varied in number, case, and gender, according to circumstances; and the language did not present the curious incongruity of such expressions as I *my*self, thou *thy*self, he *him*self, &c. Both the *pronoun* and *self* combined with it varied according to the case, gender, or number required. As—

Singular.		Plural.	
Icsylf,	I self.	Wesylfe,	We selves.
Minsylfes,	of myself.	Ureusylpha,	of our selves, &c.

Selves is the only variation of *self* now remaining. We now say—

Singular.	Plural.
I myself.	We ourselves.
Thou thyself.	Ye yourselves.
He himself.	They themselves.
She herself.	

So that *I* stands connected with its own *possessive* form in *my*self, *thou* also with *thy*self; whilst *he, she,* and *they* are connected with their own *objective* form in *him*self, *them*selves. These forms seem to have been regulated by euphony rather than grammar, for no grammatical principle can be recognized. I self, thou self, we selves, are objectionable as combinations of sound, though consistent with ancient authority, and with grammar.

In the present state of the English language, myself and thyself, and ourselves and yourselves, and himself and themselves, are not used alone, at least in the nominative case. We do not say "myself did it," "thyself did it," but *I myself, thou thyself,* &c., such expressions being strongly and distinctly personal.

Itself has no variation, though it is probable that the s, indicating the possessive case of this word, has been dropped, because self begins with an *s;* as self, *its* self, contracted to *itself*.

CHAPTER XI.

REPETITION OF THE PRONOUN—ITS EFFECT.

The frequent repetition of the pronoun in a sentence gives force, beauty, or tenderness, just as the nature of the subject may require. It is true, this is not strictly a question of grammar; still, it is one intimately connected with the vigor, the perspicuity, and the beauty of composition.

Take the following passage from the hymn of Adam and Eve, addressed to the Creator:—

> "His praise, ye winds, that from four quarters blow,
> Breathe soft or loud, and wave your tops, ye pines!
> With every plant, in sign of worship wave.
> Fountains, and ye that warble as ye flow,
> Melodious murmurs, warbling tune his praise.
> Join voices all, ye living souls, ye birds,

> That singing up to heaven-gate ascend,
> Bear on your wings, and in your notes his praise."
> *Paradise Lost*, b. v.

This principle is still more forcibly exemplified in the scene between Adam and Eve, after their fatal transgression. As she clasps his knees, and supplicates forgiveness, she never allows him one moment for reflection. She places her beloved image before him under every variety of condition, and mingles their past, present, and future destinies together in an overpowering flood of tenderness.

> "Forsake *me* not thus, Adam! Witness heaven!
> What love sincere, and reverence, in my heart,
> *I* bear thee, and unweeting have offended,
> Unhappily deceived! Thy suppliant,
> *I* beg, and clasp thy knees—bereave *me* not
> Whereon I live—thy gentle looks, thy aid,
> Thy counsel, in this uttermost distress,
> *My* only strength and stay! Forlorn of thee,
> Whither shall *I* betake me? where subsist?
> While yet we live—scarce one short hour perhaps—
> Between us two let there be peace, both joining,
> As joined in injuries, one enmity,
> Against a foe by doom express assigned us,
> That cruel serpent. On *me* exercise not
> Thy hatred, for this misery befallen,
> On *me* already lost—*me* than myself
> More miserable! Both have sinned, but thou
> Against God only—*I* against God and thee,
> And to the place of judgment will return,
> There with my cries importune heaven that all
> The sentence, from thy head removed, may light
> On *me*, sole cause to thee of all this woe.
> *Me, me*, only, just object of this ire."
> *Ibid.* b. x.

In this passage, the pronoun alternating between Adam

and Eve, as personal or possessive, is used no less than *thirty* times; and it is, in a great degree, to this circumstance, to the intense personality of the scene, that much of its beauty and inimitable tenderness is to be attributed. It rouses all the generous impulses of the soul, and,

>"As one disarmed, his anger all he lost."

Heaven had given Eve as a help-meet to Adam, and he now feels the full force of a former acknowledgment:—

>"How can I live without *thee*! How forego
>*Thy* sweet convérse, and love so dearly join'd,
>To live in these *wild woods* forlorn!"*

We see the same principle running through Eve's farewell address to Paradise, when the archangel commanded them to leave the blissful abode:—

>"Oh unexpected stroke, worse than of death!
>Must I thus leave *thee*, Paradise! thus leave
>Thee, native soil! *These* happy walks and shades,
>Fit haunt of gods, where I had hope to spend,
>Quiet, though sad, the respite of that day
>That must be mortal to us both. O flowers!

---

* Though foreign to the immediate purpose, it would be difficult to pass unnoticed the profound melancholy expressed by the very construction of this concluding line

>"To live in these *wild woods* forlorn."

Milman, in the "Fall of Jerusalem," uses a similar construction of the verse, and one equally true to nature,

>"Bless thee! but we may meet again, e'en here.
>Thou look'st content, I see it through thy tears,
>Yet, once again, that *cold, sad word*—farewell."

That never will in other climate grow,
My early visitation, and my last
At e'en, which I bred up with tender hand,
From the first opening bud, and gave *ye* names;
Who now shall rear *ye* to the sun, or rank
Your tribes, or water from the ambrosial font?
Thee lastly, nuptial bower, by me adorn'd
With what to sight or smell was sweet, from *thee*
How shall I part, and whither wander down
Into a lower world, to this obscure,
And wild? how shall we breathe in other air,
Less pure, accustomed to immortal fruit?"
Paradise Lost, b. xi.

The language of Adam on the prospect of leaving Paradise, and of being deprived of the visible and immediate communion with God, is of the same character:—

"Here I would frequent
With worship place by place, when he vouchsafed
Presence divine, and to my woes relate—
On *this* mount he appeared, under *this* tree
Stood visible—among *these* pines his voice
I heard; here, with him, at *this* fountain talk'd."
Ibid. b. xi.

Unquestionably this is the language of strong feeling and personal attachment to a beloved object. The repetition of the pronoun exhibits the mind as impatient of interruption, and falling back again and again upon that object, at one moment collectively, at another individually, and dwelling with a lingering fondness on each of its separate parts.

Corresponding with this principle, is the following passage from the "Noctes Ambrosianæ:"—

"Nae thou't so unsupportable as that o' entire, blank forgetfulness. .... When she, the cretur that once laucht, and sang, and wept to us, close to our side, or in our varra arms, is as if her smiles, her voice, her tears, her kisses had never been."

Every touch of this passage points directly to the heart.

So also Milman. On the night in which Jerusalem was taken, Salone had been married to Amariah. Her sister Mariam, when the city was in flames, goes to seek her, and finds that Amariah had stabbed her, in order to prevent her from falling into the hands of the enemy; Salone is dying, and her intellects are wandering. She tells the following tale:—

> "He came back, and kiss'd me, and he said,
> I know not what he said—but there was something
> Of Gentile ravisher, and his beauteous bride.
> Me, me, he meant, he called me beauteous bride,
> And he stood o'er me with a sword so bright,
> My dazzled eyes did close. And presently
> Methought he smote me with the sword—but then
> He fell upon my neck, and wept upon me,
> And I felt nothing but his burning kisses."
>
> *Fall of Jerusalem.*

This passage owes its beauty to the strange bewilderment and the intense personality that pervade it. The pronoun, personal or possessive, is *twenty-two* times repeated in eight lines and a half.

Affectionate Entreaty.

Hector feels himself called to the field of battle by honor, duty, and the cause of his country, though at the same time with a firm conviction that there he must perish. Hecuba, with earnest prayer and maternal tenderness, beseeches him to remain within the walls:—

> "*Her* zone unbraced, *her* bosom *she* display'd,
> And thus, fast falling the salt tears, *she* said,
> Have mercy on *me!* O *my* son!
> If ever *thee* in *these* fond arms I press'd,
> Or still'd *thy* infant clamors at *this* breast,
> Ah, do not thus *our* helpless years forego,
> But by our walls secured repel the foe."
>
> <div align="right">POPE, <i>Iliad</i>, b. xxii.</div>

So also Priam:—

> " Then wept the sage;
> *He* strikes his reverend head, now white with age,
> *He* lifts his wither'd arms—obtests the skies,
> *He* calls his much-lov'd son, with feeble cries.
> 'Ah, stay not, stay not guardless and alone,
> Hector, *my* lov'd, *my* dearest, bravest son!
> Methinks already I behold *thee* slain,
> And stretch'd beneath that fury of the plain.'"
>
> <div align="right"><i>Ibid.</i> b. xxii.</div>

Intense Personal Hatred.

> "A plague upon them, wherefore should I curse them?
> Would curses kill, as doth the mandrake's groan,
> I could invent as bitter, searching terms,
> As curs'd and harsh, and horrible to hear,
> Deliver'd strongly through my fixed teeth,
> With full as many signs of deadly hate,
> As lean-fac'd Envy in her deadly cave.
> *My* tongue shall stumble in *mine* earnest words,
> *Mine* eyes should sparkle, like the beaten flint,
> *My* hair be fix'd on end, as one distract,
> Ay, every joint should seem to curse and ban.
> And even now, my burden'd heart would break,
> Should I not curse them — poison be *their* drink,

Gall—worse than gall, the dainties that *they* taste!
Their sweetest shade—a grove of cypress trees!
Their chiefest prospect—murdering basilisks!
Their softest touch—as smart as lizards' stings!
Their music—frightful as the serpent's hiss!
And boding screech-owls make the concert full!
All the foul terrors of dark-seated hell!"

Shakspeare, *Henry VI.*

In this passage hatred, withering, scorching, burning, pursues like a stanch bloodhound, and never quits the personal order of its object.

Contemptuous Indignation.

" *Thou* liest, *thou* thread, *thou* thimble,
Thou yard, three-quarters, half-yard, quarter, nail,
Thou flea, *thou* nit, *thou* winter-cricket—*thou*."

Taming of a *Shrew*, act 4, sc. 2.

See the life and energy given to a contest by the repetition of the pronoun.

"As on the confines of adjoining ground,
Two stubborn swains with blows dispute the ground,
They tug, *they* sweat, but neither gain nor yield
One foot, one inch of the contested field.
Thus obstinate to death, *they* fight, *they* fall,
Nor *these* can keep, nor *those* can win the wall."

Pope, *Iliad.*

It is questionable whether any modern fraternal appeal can equal that of young Harry to his comrades on the field of battle; and yet the most powerful instrument in that appeal is simply the personal pronoun *we*. It combines and condenses the destinies of all into one firm and indissoluble mass. The meanest soldier, in life or death, shares in the glory, or mingles his blood with that of his indomitable chief:—

> "This story shall the good man teach his son,
> And Crispin Crispian shall ne'er go by,
> From this day, to the ending of the world,
> But *we*, in it, shall be remembered.
> We few—*we* happy few—*we* band of brothers!
> For he to-day that sheds his blood with me,
> Shall be my brother; be he ne'er so vile,
> This day shall gentle his condition."
>
> SHAKSPEARE, *Henry V.*

It would be easy to multiply examples of a similar kind. In reading such passages, a deep interest and sympathy are excited; and, if we investigate the ground of this feeling, we shall find that it mainly consists in the frequent recurrence of their *personality*. Dry, abstract reasoning may convince the understanding, but it is feeble in exciting human sympathies and affections. It is just so in the practical scenes of life. The dumb appeal of the wounded, helpless traveller, laid by the road side, is far more eloquent than the most forcible exhortation to relieve the distressed. It is personality, whether in real or descriptive life, that makes its way to the heart, and it is to this principle, properly applied, that many of the finest passages, whether of poetry or of prose, owe their energy, or tenderness—their power of exciting the deepest sympathies of our nature.

SECTION IV.

ARTICLE.

CHAPTER I.

ANGLO-SAXON ARTICLE.

The Anglo-Saxon *an, aen, ain,* was seldom used as an indefinite article. It had the signification of the Latin *unus,* one. Where an indefinite signification was required, no article was prefixed, and the sentence followed the Latin construction; as, "Deodric was Cristen," Theodoricus fuit Christianus. Theodoric was a Christian; as we should now express it. This particle, originally the numeral one, became the indefinite article *a* or *an,* with no other variation.

The Anglo-Saxon definite article passed through several inflexions, all which have been discarded. It had four cases in the singular number, and was inflected in the masculine, feminine, and neuter gender of the nominative and accusative cases. It had four cases in the plural number, the accusative, in form, however, being the same as the nominative. In the plural number, there was no variation of gender. The present English definite article has no variation in number, case, or gender. If any error, therefore, should ever occur in the use of the definite article, it must be an error of application, not of form.

CHAPTER II.

DISTINCTION OF ARTICLES.

The indefinite article *a*, before a word beginning with a consonant, and *an* before a word beginning with a vowel or *h* mute, is applied to anything not before mentioned or known. When no article at all is used, the sense is still less definite. The following sentences from the second chapter of Genesis introduce the different applications of the indefinite and the definite article, and also illustrate the principle upon which the absence of the article is founded.

"And the Lord God formed *man* of the dust of the earth."

Man not having previously existed.

"Therefore shall *a* man leave his father and mother."

Any man at any future time.

"And the Lord planted a garden eastward, in Eden, and there he put *the* man (before mentioned) whom he had formed."

"And the Lord God said, it is not good that *the* man should be alone; I will make him *an* help-meet."

These sentences exemplify the use of the present English article, whether definite or indefinite, whilst the absence of the article altogether before the term *man* denotes species at large.

"Which in time past were not *a* people, but are now *the* people of God."

Here, also, we have a marked distinction between the indefinite and the definite article.

If Pilate had said, "Behold *a* man," the observation would not have had either point or specific application. If Peter had said, "I know not *a* man," instead of *the* man, the observation would have been false, as a matter of course, and not merely as a matter of distinct application. If it had been stated, that any two sides of a triangle are greater than *a* third side, the position might have been either true or false, but not necessarily either; *a* third side would allow us to fix upon *some other* triangle, and so to compare two sides of *one* triangle with one side of *another* triangle. But, when it is stated that any two sides of *a* triangle are greater than *the* third side, the position is confined to *the third* or remaining side of the triangle in question, and is either necessarily true, or necessarily false.

Again:—

"In every parallelogram any of the parallelograms about *a* diameter, together with the two complements, is called a gnomon."—*Simpson's Euclid. Def.* 2, b. ii.

If the expression *a* diameter had been *the* diameter, the position would have assumed that a parallelogram could have *one* diameter only.

By the proper use of the articles in the English language, we obviously gain great precision of meaning, and such as is not attainable in Latin. As an illustration of this, let us take the phrase "Amicus Imperatoris" propounded by Mr. Grant, which in Latin is susceptible of four different significations, compressed and undistinguished. Now in English each signification would be perfectly defined, as "*a* friend of an emperor, *the* friend of *an* emperor, *a* friend of *the* emperor, *the* friend of *the* emperor."

DISTINCTION OF ARTICLES. 217

So, also, in the "Fas odisse *viros*" of Virgil, and

"Obstupuit primò aspectu Sidonia Dido
Casu deinde *viri* tanto,"

we feel the want of definition.

The following passage will show how frequently the definite article may enter into the composition of a single sentence, and that necessarily.

"But when the military order had levelled, in wild anarchy, the power of the prince, the laws of the senate, and even the discipline of the camp, the barbarians of the North, and of the East, who had long hovered on the frontier, boldly attacked the provinces of a declining monarchy."—*Gibbon's Decline*, c. viii.

Here the definite article occurs eleven times, and the indefinite once.
Again:—

"'Tis not the balm, the sceptre, and the ball,
The sword, the mace, the crown imperial,
The enter-tissued robe of gold and pearl,
The farced title running 'fore the king,
The throne he sits on, nor the tide of pomp,
That beats upon the high shore of this world,
No!"   SHAKSPEARE.

Here, again, the indefinite article occurs twelve times in six lines. The distinct properties and the correct application of the English articles become, therefore, a matter of the greatest moment.

CHAPTER III.

ENGLISH ARTICLE COMPARED WITH THE GREEK ARTICLE.

The English definite article, in its general use, corresponds with the Greek article; but every language has its own peculiar idioms, which refuse to bend to any foreign authority. Thus, the Greeks used the definite article before *abstract* nouns; as, ἡ ἀρετή, ἡ κακία, virtue, vice. If we prefix the article in English, we confine the terms to some particular virtue and vice already specified, or to be specified. The French, in this respect, follow the Greek form; as, la vertu, le vice.

Again, the Greeks used the definite article before a proper name in the singular number; as, ὁ Σωκράτης, Socrates, whereas in English we use it only before the plural of proper names; as, "the Johnsons," "the Addisons," except in a case of marked distinction, such as can seldom occur:—

"Go to *the* Douglas, and deliver him
Up to his pleasure, ransomless and free."
Shakspeare.

"I do no injustice to the Red Rover, when I say he is too slight to be weighed with *the* Douglas."—*Scott, Chronicles of Canongate.*

We have also a peculiar use of the indefinite article, as applied to nouns of the singular number.

"From liberty each nobler science sprung,
A Bacon brightened, and *a* Spenser sung."
Savage: *Epistle to Walpole.*

CHAPTER IV.

IRREGULAR USE OF THE DEFINITE ARTICLE.

A VARIETY of examples, both in Scripture and in some writers of the same and even of later date, sanction the use of the definite article before the word *death* when that term has nothing more than a general signification, and when no reference is made to any particular form of death; thus:—

"Jeoparded their lives unto *the* death."—*Judges* v. 10.
"Let him die *the* death."—*Matt.* xv. 4.

"Bear Worcester to *the* death."   SHAKSPEARE.

"True to *the* death."   COWPER'S *Task*.

"It shall not save him from *the* death."   BYRON.

Nor is this form of expression confined to the phrase "*the* death." The article is, on some other occasions, placed before the noun in a manner not recognized by modern custom; as,

"They lie in *the* hell like sheep."—*Psalms*.

As *hell* is, however, probably derived from Halla or Walhalla, the phrase may be accepted as signifying *the* abode of the dead. They lie in *the* place of the dead.

"O that *the* salvation were given unto Israel."—*Psalms*.

Phrases of this description seem to be founded upon Greek rather than English construction. They are certainly inconsistent with our modern idiom.

The use of the definite article before the relative *which* has now become obsolete.

"Where there was a garden, into *the* which he entered."— *John* xviii. 1.

We have also an anomalous use of the article before adjectives, or rather adverbs of the comparative and superlative degree: as, "I like this *the* better;" "I like this *the* best." If, in such cases, we leave out the article, and take *better* and *best* adverbially, there is no difficulty. "I like A. well, B. better, but C. best." Must we then treat the phrases *the better* and *the best* as stiff-necked vulgarisms, rendered intractable; or must we look upon them as elliptical expressions used in the place of *in the best way, in the best manner?*

Again, what can we make of the phrase "I saw him *the other* day?" meaning a short time ago; the definite *the*, in the interpretation of the phrase, becoming the indefinite *a*; I saw him *the* other day, that is, a short time ago.

CHAPTER V.

ENGLISH ARTICLE COMPARED WITH THE GERMAN ARTICLE.

In German, the article is repeated before nouns of different genders: as, "*der vater, die mutter, und das kind;*" the father, the mother, and the child. When nouns are of the same gender and number, the article is required before the first only, as "*der rock und hut,*" the coat and hat.

As the English article has no inflexion, but is used under the same form to signify masculine, feminine, or neuter, it might be argued that, on this principle, it is necessary to place the article before the first of a series of nouns *only*, as "the men, women, and baggage." It is not, however, a proper view of the English definite article to suppose that it is masculine, feminine, and neuter at *the same time*. The English article is masculine when applied to a masculine noun, feminine when applied to a feminine noun, and neuter when applied to a neuter noun. Its want of inflexion is a mere matter of form; and the same article which is applied to a masculine noun, and therefore of itself masculine, cannot at the same time be applied to a feminine noun, and be at the same time feminine. It cannot be two different things at the same time; and the repetition of the article in English, when applied to objects differing in gender, number, or condition, is just as necessary for the sake of definite meaning as the German article would be in German under similar circumstances. The English adjective has no inflexion as to gender, number, or case; yet in the phrase *a tall man* it is masculine, in *a tall woman* it is feminine, and in *a tall tree* it is neuter. In signification as to gender and number, it is just as mutable as alt*us*, alt*a*, alt*um*; though its form may not be altered. So also in the verb, we say, I *love*, thou *lovest*, he *loves;* yet we say, we *love*, ye *love*, they *love*, so that the same form, *love*, is first person singular, first, second, and third persons plural; yet the invariable form of the verb in the plural number expresses the meaning just as well as its variable form in the singular number—I *love*, thou *lovest*, he *loves;* we *love*, ye *love*, they *love*.

In the case of the article, its immutable form has nothing to do with the question. The question is, can that which is masculine define that which is feminine, and that which is neuter, all at the same time; or, that which is singular, and that which is plural, at the same time? Logically and grammatically, it cannot, whatever custom, or negligence, or ignorance, may sanction to the contrary. The Greek and German articles have their fixed principles; but scores of passages might be adduced from the Old and the New Testament, in English, in which the sense is essentially changed by the omission of the definite article, where that article is clearly and distinctly applied in the original for the express purpose of definition. It is an easy matter to propound phrases in the English language, which custom has sanctioned and which militate against this principle; but, on examination, we shall find such examples either obviously unjustifiable, and dependent solely on the *tyranny* of custom and the tenacity of error, or upon some peculiar modification generally overlooked. Examples of the former kind are painfully numerous. Of the latter, take such an example as the following: "*I met a man and horse.*" Now it is so customary for man and horse to be associated, that we look upon them as forming a compound animal—a kind of Centaur. But who would think of saying, "I met a man and crocodile," or, "a woman and Ornithorhynchus paradoxus!" The association is very improbable, and requires distinct specification—a man and *a* crocodile, *a* woman and *an* Ornithorhynchus paradoxus. But if we speak of a man as well known—as having made himself notorious by his exhibition of a crocodile, and both are conjointly celebrated, we then say, "*Have you seen the man and crocodile?*" for there is in this case a logical association of objects, in fact, a unity. To pass to the definite article, to the question, "*Have you seen the man and crocodile?*" It might be answered, "*There are several men exhibiting crocodiles.*" I answer, "So there may; but the others are not worth looking at. I mean *the* man and *the* crocodile," emphatically and contradistinctively. The justice of these distinctions will, I think, be acknowledged; yet they are not the more necessary here than they are in a thousand instances in which they are neglected. A grammatical principle is either right or not right; it cannot be right by halves.

We say, "*I saw the father and mother of the child,*" because we recognize parental *association* in the phrase; but I cannot with the same propriety say, "*I saw the General and Adjutant,*" because there is no association of office. I speak of two distinct persons, and two distinct conditions, and I ought to say, "*I saw the General and the Adjutant.*" On what principle, then, do we say, The Pharisees, and scribes, and chief officers, each class being distinct? We do it in direct violation of principle.

The same rule is applicable to adjectives. When two epithets involving distinct and incompatible properties are applied to a noun, the definite article, where used before the first, must be repeated before the second: as, "*The Lords Spiritual and Temporal.*" As the *Spiritual Lords* are not *Temporal Lords*, nor the *Temporal Lords Spiritual Lords*, they ought to be distinguished, and not combined as a unity. The Spiritual and *the* Temporal Lords, or the Spiritual Lords and *the* Temporal.

CHAPTER VI.

THE DEFINITE ARTICLE IMPROPERLY OMITTED.

"Howbeit, when the Spirit of truth is come, he will guide you into *all* truth."

The passage should have run all *the truth*, that is, *the* truth as far as it respected the Christian religion, and so it is expressed in the original Greek, εἰς πᾶσαν τὴν ἀλήθειαν, into all the truth. We cannot suppose that Jesus meant that the Holy Spirit should lead the disciples into the knowledge of *all* truth, scientific, &c. &c. As well might the 33d verse of the 5th chapter of St. Mark be translated in the same way, *all* truth, instead of all *the* truth.

"But the woman, fearing and trembling, and knowing what was done in her, came, and fell down before him, and told him *all* truth."

The passage is properly translated, all *the* truth.

"Thou art my beloved son." Σὺ εἶ ὁ υἱός μου ὁ ἀγαπητός.

Which does not mean "thou art my beloved son," but "thou art my son, *the* beloved." The article, which is here so emphatic in the Greek, is lost sight of in our translation. In the Latin, the sense is preserved by the substitution of the demonstrative and personal pronoun *ille*, the Latin having no article. "Tu es filius meus, *ille* dilectus." But the ὁ ἀγαπητός, the "ille dilectus" is not expressed in the English version. Nor does "I am the good shepherd" come up to ἐγὼ εἰμὶ ὁ ποιμὴν ὁ καλός.

"When the morning was come, all *the* chief priests, and *elders* of the people, took counsel against Jesus to put him to death."

In cases of this kind, attention to the original text, in the use of the article, would keep us from error. In the Greek, we have οἱ πρεσβύτεροι, and in the English we ought to have had *the* elders. The term elders, in this passage, without having the definite article prefixed, according to the plainest idiom of our language, has a very different meaning from that which it is here intended to convey; for, if we say that *elders* of the people took counsel, we mean that *certain* elders, or *some* elders, took counsel, which might be five out of five hundred; but when we say *the* elders, we mean *the elders* as a body, a class, and this is the meaning required; οἱ πρεσβύτεροι.

"When, therefore, the chief priests and officers saw him." &c.

Though the term *chief* is applied to priests, it is not intended that it should apply to officers; nor is there a mutual community of signification between the terms "priests and officers." The definite article ought, therefore, to have been repeated: οἱ ἀρχιερεῖς, καὶ οἱ ὑπηρέται.

"When the morning was come, all the chief priests and elders," &c.

Priests and elders being distinct, the article ought to have been repeated before the latter, according to the original. Elsewhere, we have *the* chief priests and *the* scribes.

"And they continued stedfastly in the apostles' doctrine and fellowship, and in breaking of bread, and in prayers."—*Acts* ii. 42.

A strange inaccuracy and carelessness characterize the whole of this passage. In the first place, there is an ambiguity in the *sound* of the apostles' doctrine, which might mean the doctrine of one particular apostle, or of all the apostles. This might have been avoided by saying the doctrine of the apostles. Secondly, there is a grammatical error in the phrase, in *breaking of* bread. Thirdly, there is a total perversion of the meaning in the omission of the definite article before *fellowship*, before *breaking*, before *bread*, and before *prayers;* for the definite article is used before each of these terms in the original, and is absolutely necessary for a proper understanding of the passage, either in Greek or English. The whole passage, translated according to the original, would run thus:—

"And they continued stedfastly in the doctrine and the fellowship of the apostles, and in the breaking of *the* bread and in *the* prayers."

Now, as we understand the doctrine and the fellowship of the apostles to be a specific doctrine, and a specific fellowship; and, as the act of breaking this bread was not an ordinary act of breaking bread, but *the* act of breaking bread for a specific purpose; and, as *the* bread was not ordinary bread, to be used as food merely, but *the sacramental* bread; and as the prayers were not accidental prayers, but *the* prayers used by the Christian converts at that time, and so expressed in the original, it will be obvious that the whole passage is lamentably deficient in accuracy of expression.

"That thy power, thy glory, and mightiness of thy kingdom might be known unto men."—*Psalm* xiv. 12.

The mightiness.

"And are choked with cares and riches and pleasures of this life."—*Luke* xviii. 14.

The cares—the specific cares that belong to this life.

We should not say, "I saw beauty of his face," "I admired strength of his arm," but *the* beauty, *the* strength; so also *the* "mightiness of thy kingdom," "*the* cares," &c.

"While unfortunate gloomy Dust, who came whipping behind, was cheered by the encouragement of some, and pity of all."— *Goldsmith's Citizen of the World.*

Both grammar and euphony require *the* pity.

"Some of the most sacred festivals in the Roman ritual were destined to salute the new calends of January with vows of public and private felicity, to indulge the pious remembrance of the dead and living."—*Gibbon's Decline,* c. xv.

Though the dead and the living are perfectly distinct classes, yet here is an operation comprehending both indiscriminately, as if they were dead and alive at the same time. The blind and lame form one class laboring under the infirmities of blindness and lameness;

the blind and the lame form two classes, each laboring under one distinct infirmity: so the living form one class, and the dead another; but neither class can be both living and dead.

CHAPTER VII.

THE DEFINITE ARTICLE NOT ONLY SUPERFLUOUS, BUT MISCHIEVOUS.

"For as the lightning that lighteneth out of the one part under heaven, shineth unto *the* other part under heaven."—*Luke* xii. 24.

If there had been only two parts under heaven, then the definite article would have been required; but as the parts are indefinite, it is improper to limit them to *the* one, and *the* other, as if there were but two parts only.

"Even Terah, the father of Abraham, and the father of Nachor."

As Terah was the father of Abraham, and the father of Nachor, the phrase ought to have been, "the father of Abraham and *of Nachor;*" otherwise, some other person might be meant as the father of Nachor.

"There are few words in the English language which are employed in a more loose and uncircumscribed sense than those of *the* fancy and *the* imagination." *Spectator.*

The author does not here mean the words *of the* fancy and the imagination, but the words *fancy* and *imagination* themselves. The words *those of the* are worse than superfluous.

We do not say this is *the* man *of* John, but this is

the man John. Here the man is John, and John is the man; so the words are the *imagination and the fancy*, and *the imagination and the fancy* are *the words*.

CHAPTER VIII.

THE DEFINITE ARTICLE PROPERLY REPEATED.

"And he stood between the dead and *the* living, and the plague was stayed."—*Numbers* xvi. 48.

If, in this passage, we strike out the definite article before the term *living*, the beauty and the distinctness of the passage are destroyed. Aaron stood between *the* dead on one side, and *the* living on the other. *Dead and living* would present to the eye nothing but an indiscriminate mass, where a marked distinction is peculiarly necessary.

In the Creed, the same distinction is properly observed:—

"And he shall come again with glory, to judge both *the* quick and *the* dead."

Again, Matt. v. 45, the same form of expression is correctly introduced:—

"For he maketh his sun to rise on *the* evil, and on *the* good, and sendeth rain on *the* just and on *the* unjust."

Evil and *good, just*, and *unjust*, are so totally distinct, that nothing could warrant a confusion of the terms.

"The Lord hath caused the solemn feasts and Sabbaths to be
20

forgotten in Zion, and hath despised, in the indignation of his anger, *the* king and *the* priest."—*Jeremiah's Lamentations* ii. 6.

The offices of *king* and *priest* being distinct, the article is properly repeated.

"For they shall fall by *the* sword, by *the* famine, and by *the* pestilence."—*Ezekiel* vi. 11.

"How much more, when I send my four sore judgments upon Jerusalem, *the* sword, and *the* famine, and *the* noisome beast, and *the* pestilence, to cut off from it man and beast."

In both these passages, a distinct instrumentality is here properly marked by the repetition of the definite article before each noun. As a matter of grammar, the principle is perfectly just, for, when there is no community of meaning in a sequence of nouns, there ought to be no community of article; at the same time, the force of the passage is wonderfully increased by the repetition of the article and the conjunction before each noun. The agents of destruction seem multiplied, and each of them seems to labor with individual energy in the work of death.

"And immediately while yet he spake, cometh Judas, one of the twelve, and with him a great multitude, with swords and staves, from *the* chief priests, and *the* scribes, and *the* elders."

The article is here properly repeated before the three last nouns of this sentence, because *the* chief priests, *the* scribes, and *the* elders were distinct classes.

"From the reign of Augustus to the time of Alexander Severus, the enemies of Rome were in her bosom—*the* tyrants, and *the* soldiers."—*Gibbon*, c. viii.

i. e. the emperors as tyrants, the soldiers as mercenary and tumultuous instruments of tyranny, both parties acting on their own individual impulses, and both, too, often the enemies of Rome. The definite article was required before the noun soldiers, because they were a distinct cause of tyranny.

> "By their tumultuous election, a Syrian, a Goth, or an Arab was exalted to the throne of Rome, and was invested with despotic power over *the* conquests, and over *the* country of the Scipios."—*Gibbon*, c. vii.

If the definite article had not been repeated before the noun *country*, the conquests and the country of the Scipios would have been identified; whereas the conquests of the Scipios were not their country, nor their country their conquests.

> "A chorus of twenty-seven youths, and as many virgins of noble families, whose parents were both alive, implored the propitious gods in favor of the present, and for the hope of the rising, generation; requesting in religious hymns that, according to the faith of their ancient oracles, they would still maintain *the* virtue, *the* felicity, and *the* empire of the Roman people."—*Gibbon*, c. vii.

Virtue, felicity, and empire are all distinct objects, marked as such.

> "The life of the former was almost a perpetual journey; and as he possessed the various talents of *the* soldier, *the* statesman, and *the* scholar, he gratified his curiosity in the discharge of his duty."—*Gibbon*, c. i.

Sentences like these have not merely the merit of grammatical accuracy in the use of the article; they also exhibit a refined taste in the construction and the harmony of a sentence.

> "From the beginning of the world an uninterrupted series of predictions had announced and prepared the long-expected com-

ing of the Messiah, who in compliance with the gross apprehensions of the Jews, had been more frequently represented under the character of a king and conqueror, than under that of *a prophet, a martyr,* or *the son of God.*"

Mark here the nice discrimination in the use of the definite and the indefinite article. In consequence of the near affinity between *king* and *conqueror*, not merely in the abstract, but more particularly with reference to the expectations of the Jews, who imagined that he would come in the character of both, the author does not repeat the article before *conqueror;* but there being no affinity, either absolute or relative, between prophet and martyr, the article is properly repeated before the term martyr. Again, the indefinite article is properly changed for the definite before the words *son of God,* indicating that he was the sole and only son of God, and not *a* son of many sons. This one sentence is, in fact, a lecture on the use of the article.

> "If I but stretch this hand,
> I heave *the* gods, *the* ocean, and *the* land."
>   POPE's *Iliad*, viii.

All the objects are here perfectly distinct, and are properly and grammatically marked as such, by the repetition of the definite article before each of them.

"For this cause came I into the world, that I should bear witness unto *the* truth. Every one that is of *the* truth, heareth my voice. Pilate saith unto him, What is truth?"—*John* xviii.

Christ here speaks of the specific spiritual truth which he came to establish. Pilate not seeing the drift of our Lord's observations, speaks of truth generally; the article is therefore properly prefixed to the noun *truth* in the two former cases, and as properly omitted in the latter case.

"His purpose was to infuse literary curiosity, by gentle and unsuspected conveyance, into *the* gay, *the* idle, and *the* wealthy."—*Johnson's Life of Addison.*

"Behold, I will bring them from the north country, and gather them from the coasts of the earth, and with them the blind and *the* lame."—*Jer.* xxxi. 8.

If the definite article had not been repeated before the term *lame*, one class of persons only would have been designated, and that class both *blind and lame;* whereas, by the repetition of the article *the* before the term *lame*, two distinct classes are pointed out—those that were blind and those that were lame. The blind might not be also lame, or the lame blind.

When, however, there is a community of signification between two nouns or epithets, there is no impropriety in leaving out the definite article; as,

"Now I Paul beseech you by the *meekness* and *gentleness* of Christ."—2 *Cor.* x. 1.

Meekness and gentleness are inseparably connected, and therefore the repetition of the definite article before the latter was not required.

"Yea, a *joyful* and *pleasant* thing it is to be thankful."

The epithets have a necessary connection. Again:—

"He had compassion on the *poor* and *needy.*"

Now a poor man being, in the ordinary acceptation of the terms, a needy man, and a needy man a poor man, the definite article was not required.

20*

"Blessed be the man that provideth for the sick and needy."—
Psalm xii. 1.

A sick man is not necessarily a needy man, in the usual acceptation of the term *needy*, nor is a *needy* man necessarily a *sick* man. The benediction, therefore, only applies to those who provide for the wants of such as labor under the *combined* infirmities of sickness and poverty. Allowing that one class of persons only is here meant, under the terms *sick* and *needy*, the sentence is right; if two, it is wrong. Suppose I say, "he selected all the black and white cattle for himself, and left the rest." Grammatically, this sentence means that he selected those individual beasts that were black and white, partly black and partly white. But place the definite article before white, as well as before black, and then it means that he selected all the black cattle and all the white cattle, and left the rest; which, for anything that is implied to the contrary, might be all black and white, that is, combining the two colors of black and white.

This rule depends upon the obvious principle that a particle, applied to some particular word to define and limit its signification, cannot, at the same time, have a community of application to some other word, when that other word has no community of import with the word to which that particle was in the first place applied. Generally in this, as well as many other cases, we feel obliged to follow in the wake of custom; but in all cases where the sense is manifestly falsified by such a compliance, surely we are justified in following that course which grammar and sense conjointly demand.

CHAPTER IX.

THE INDEFINITE ARTICLE PROPERLY REPEATED.

"*A* cool head, *an* unfeeling heart, and *a* cowardly disposition, prompted him, at the age of nineteen, to assume the mask of hypocrisy, which he never after laid aside."—*Gibbon's Decline*, c. iii.

The author's object in repeating the article before *cool head, unfeeling heart,* and *cowardly disposition* is to mark distinctly the three properties of Augustus.

"As they prevailed [curiosity and vanity], and as they were attracted by different objects, Hadrian was, by turns, *an* excellent prince, *a* ridiculous sophist, and *a* jealous tyrant."—*Gibbon*, c. iii.

The indefinite article again properly repeated.

"Just balances, just weights, *a* just ephah, and *a* just hin shall ye have."—*Lev.* xix. 36.

"This earth, *a* spot, *a* grain,
An atom."   Milton.

The repetition of the article marks a distinct descent.

These examples are sufficient to show the propriety of repeating the indefinite article where the things or qualities specified are in themselves distinct. Yet Gibbon occasionally deviates from this rule, and is inconsistent with himself.

CHAPTER X.

THE INDEFINITE ARTICLE IMPROPERLY OMITTED.

"A FEEBLE senate and enervated people."—*Gibbon* c. iii.

Again:—

"His rise, from so obscure a station, to the first dignities of the empire, seems to prove that he was a bold and able leader."—*Decline*, c. vii.

A leader may be bold, though not able. Inconsiderate boldness may involve a leader in fatal difficulties. In such a case, he could not be characterized as an able leader. Callicratidas, rather than sheer off, fought the Athenians when he had no chance. As boldness and ability may be distinct qualifications, they ought to be marked as such, according to Gibbon's usual practice.

"But the great triumphs of modern ingenuity and art are those astronomical clocks and watches in which the counted equal vibrations of a *pendulum or balance-wheel* have detected periodical inequalities even in the motion of the earth itself."—*Arnott's Physics*, p. 60.

A pendulum is not a balance-wheel; the terms are not convertible. I cannot say this is a *pendulum or balance-wheel*, meaning that it may be designated by either term; because the instruments are distinct - a pendulum or *a* balance-wheel marks the distinction. If I say a *pendulum or balance-wheel*, the latter member of the sentence is a mere exposition or definition of the former. I can say with propriety, "He was a *Georgian or Circassian*," "he was a *Negro or Ethiopian*," because the individual might be designated by either term; but I cannot with propriety say, he was a Negro or Laplander, but a Negro or *a* Laplander, the former phrase marking community; the latter, distinction.

CHAPTER XI.

CONFUSION OF ARTICLES.

An in the Place of *The.*

"AND the contention was so great among them, that they departed asunder, one from *another*."—*Acts* xv. 39.

As Paul and Barnabas only are here spoken of, they departed one from *the* other, not from one *another*; the said Paul went this way, and the said Barnabas that. When we say they departed one from *another*, we at once plunge into plurality; and there might have been five hundred, or five thousand persons departing asunder, one from another: but one from *the* other, or *the* one from *the* other, would limit the expression to the two persons previously mentioned.

"Therefore said the disciples (the disciples being many) one to *another*."—*John* iv. 33.

The in the Place of *A* or *An.*

Αληθως Θεου υιος ην ουτος. "Truly this was the Son of God."

The centurion was a heathen, and either believed, or affected to believe, in a plurality of gods—in gods many; and therefore, with the common heathen notion of the existence of demigods, on seeing the supernatural appearances that attended the crucifixion of our Lord, exclaims, "Truly, this was *a* son of *a* god;" and not, as we render it, "*the* Son of God;" in which there are two errors—the first in the words *the* son, which expression is definite and emphatic, when it ought to have been indefinite and indifferent; the second, in the words "of God," which again, according to our idiom and notion of the unity of the godhead, is definite; when, according to the real words, and the meaning of the centurion, it ought to have been indefinite, the word θεου never being used in Scripture without the article του when God, *the* God, is spoken of. In this case, the article is wanting before θεου. Pilate, as a heathen, believed that such things existed as men descended of gods, and he expressed himself according to this belief. It would not have been in character for a Jew to express himself as Pilate did, or for Pilate to express himself as a believer in the unity of the Godhead would have done.

Again; in the case of Shadrach, Meshach, and Abednego, we ought to have "the fourth is like a son of a god," not "the Son of God."

SECTION V.

ADJECTIVE.

CHAPTER I.

THE ADJECTIVE—ITS PROPERTIES.

An adjective is a term adjected or added to a noun, and is expressive of its quality, or dimensions; as, good, least. In this respect, it bears the same relation to the noun as the adverb does to the verb. It expresses some attribute of the noun, either essential or contingent, absolute or relative. It is capable, therefore, of expressing the attributes of nouns under different modifications and intensities. The English adjective has no variation in number, case, or gender. In this respect, it differs from most other languages, and from the Greek in particular, which riots in contractions, evolutions, involutions, and inflexions of case, gender, and number. With whatever letter, or whatever combination of letters the English adjective may terminate, it is immutable. The terminations of adjectives are on this very account various, because they are not subject to restraint. They are not cast in any particular mould. They have no artificial paces. They at once say what they mean; and the same adjective, under the same form, is applicable to any object in creation, supposing the quality which it expresses to belong to that object, either accidentally or essentially. With respect to the signification of adjectives, one broad distinction is to be found in words ending in *ful*, and those ending in *less;* the former denoting *possession of*, the other *absence of.* Adjectives of this description are of extensive and easy application; and, when a foreigner is told that the English adjective has no variation whatever, and that, as a general principle, adjectives ending in *ful* denote the *possession of*, and adjectives ending in *less, absence of*, what a gigantic step is here made into the properties of this part of speech! With what facility are adjectives of this description (numerous as they are) formed out of nouns; as hope, *hopeful;* power, *powerful;* scorn, *scornful!* Again; in the case of adjectives ending in *less*, the coalition of *less* with a noun is so easy, natural, and expressive, that we at once acquiesce in the formation of adjectives of this description, though such formation may individually be entirely novel.

> "The world was void;
> The population and the powerful was a lump
> Seasonless, herbless, treeless, manless, lifeless
> A lump of death—a chaos of hard clay."   BYRON.

Its Position.

As, then, the adjective in English has no variation, undergoes no change of form, it is obvious that its proper place must be such as not to run the chance of ambiguity by a false position. The process must be one of agglutination, adhesion. The general position of the English adjective is, therefore, immediately before the noun to which it belongs; as, "a *wise* man," "a *blind* man." But, if the adjective should be qualified, or affected by something which follows, then its proper position will be after the noun; as, "a man *wise* in his own conceit." Such is the general principle in the use of the English adjective; and the following passage, which deviates from this principle, is inconsistent with the English idiom:—

"For a great door and *effectual* is opened unto me."—1 Cor. xvi. 9.

CHAPTER II.

CONFUSION OF PRONOMINAL ADJECTIVES.

THERE is so strong an instinctive abhorrence of grammatical inflexions in the English character everywhere manifested in the present structure of the language, that the adjective is fortunate indeed in thus escaping the possibility of mutilation. We have, however, certain terms which may be looked upon as *pronominal adjectives*, inasmuch as they are added to nouns, as demonstrative, distributive, alternative, collective; and these, being subject either to a variation of form, or to a restrictive application, meet very often with unceremonious and irrespective treatment. Thus, we find *this*, of the singular number, joined to *means* of the plural; whilst *those*, of the plural number, is joined to *kind* and *sort* of the singular number: as, "Those kind of things" (*Swift*); "Those kind of gods" (*Addison*); "These kind of sufferings" (*Sherlock*). Such expressions exact a humble resignation to the tyranny of custom.

Collective numbers, however, will admit of *this* being

used before nouns of the plural number; as, "*This* forty summers" (*Shakspeare*); "This nineteen years" (*Ibid.*).

Even a numeral adjective denoting plurality is sometimes joined to a noun of the singular number, as in Chaucer's "Canterbury Tales:"—

"In *twenty* manere con'd he trip and dance."

This form of expression would not, however, be tolerated now.

Each.

The pronominal adjective *each* is distributive, and has reference to individual objects only. Here we take advantage of its immutable form, and apply it often in a collective sense, when it ought to be applied in a distributive and restrictive sense; as,

"It is observable that *each* one of the letters bear date after his banishment."—*Bentley.*

To this might be added innumerable examples.

Either.

Again; *either* is sometimes used in the place of *each*. *Either* gives simply an alternative; as, "Place them on *either* side," that is, on one side *or* the other, but not on both: whilst *each* signifies *both* taken distributively; as, "Place them on each side," that is, on both sides apart. Thus:—

"They crucified two others with him, on *either* side one, and Jesus in the midst."

An expression which does not meet the case; for it is not meant to assert that, if you do not find that a thief was crucified on *this* side, he was crucified on *that;* but that two thieves were crucified, one on each side, on this side and on that; not this *or* that, ἐντεῦθεν καὶ ἐντεῦθεν. So, also,

"On *either* side of the river was the tree of life."—*Rev.* xxi. 2.

On *each* side.

Every, Any.

Whilst, in the two preceding examples, the alternative pronominal adjective *either* is used in the place of the distributive pronoun adjective *each*, we have, in the following example, the distributive *every* used in the place of *any;* the former implying all *distributively*, the other all *electively*.

"The warriors, on the contrary, represented the powers of the neighboring kings, the combinations formed against their state, and the weakness of their wall, which *every* earthquake might overthrow."—*Goldsmith, Citizen of the World,* Letter 25.

In this passage, *every* ought to be *any;* for, when once the wall should be overthrown, it was not in the power of any other earthquake to overthrow it. Twenty earthquakes in succession could not all overthrow the wall, when the first of the series had already done it, unless one and the same thing could be done at different times, which is absurd.

None.

We have, again, an irregular and capricious use of *none*, which is a contraction of no one, and therefore improperly used to express plurality.

All.

All, which is a collective adjective, is sometimes used for *every*, which is distributive.

"Hence, to use the preceding examples, it is evident that the idea tree is applicable to a laurel or to a plane-tree, to a lofty tree or to a low one, to a fruit tree or to one of the forest; it may, therefore, be regarded as one nature common to *all* individual trees."—*Note to Translation of Aldrich's Logic.*

All trees, both here and elsewhere, means all trees *collectively,* whilst *individual* trees means each tree taken separately—something incapable of division—*individual.* There is, therefore, an incongruity of terms. We can say *each* individual, and *every* individual, but not *all* individuals; for, whilst one of the terms embraces community, the other is antagonistic.

When we seem so incapable of managing our pronouns and the pronominal adjectives which we possess; mingling indiscriminately collectives, distributives, alternatives; confounding the singular with the plural number, and the nominative with the objective case; what havoc must have taken place if our simple adjectives had not happily been denuded of all their variations!

In the following passage, the pronominal adjective *all* is beautifully, and with great propriety, used in the place of the copulative conjunction:—

> "*All* heart they live, *all* head, *all* eye, *all* ear,
> *All* intellect, *all* sense."   *Paradise Lost*, book vi.

The meaning of this could not have been given but by a repetition of the word *all* in each member of the sentence. The copulative conjunction would not have served the purpose intended. Raphael, in this passage, is describing to Adam the nature of

> "Spirits that live throughout,
> Vital in every part—that
> Cannot, but by annihilating, die."

He affirms, therefore, that spirits do not, like men, depend upon the functions of particular organs, but that in every part they possess all the essentials of vitality; and that, though one or more organs should receive injury, still the principle and use of that organ, or organs, are to be found in each of the other organs. They are not *all* heart, *and* head, *and* eye, *and* ear, *and* intellect, *and* sense. That is, these are not the qualities which collectively constitute a spirit; but its having every one of these attributes, in every one of its separate organs, so that the destruction of the eye would not affect the faculty of sight, or the destruction of the ear the faculty of hearing.

CHAPTER III.

ADJECTIVE IN THE PLACE OF THE ADVERB.

In poetic diction, we very frequently meet with the adjective in the place of the adverb. This principle is by no means peculiar to the English language. In Latin, indeed, its use, in this respect, has a wider range than the idiom of the English language will allow.

> "So *swift* through æther the shrill harpy springs,
> The wide air floating to her ample wings."
> POPE, *Iliad*, xix.

> "The charioteer then whirled the lash around,
> And *swift* ascended at one active bound."   *Ibid.* xix.

> "As when the sun, now risen,
> Looks through the misty horizontal air,
> Shorn of his beams."   *Paradise Lost*, book i.

> "Cross æther *swift* glance the vivid fires,
> As *swift* again each pointed flame retires."
> POPE, *Iliad*.

The difference in the meaning conveyed by the adjective *swift*, from that which would be conveyed by the adverb *swiftly*, is that, in cases of this kind, the adjective denotes some qualification, or *habitual* property; whereas the adverb, which qualifies the verb, applies only to the individual action then expressed by the verb. For instance: though Achilles might ascend his chariot *slowly*, yet he was not the less, on that account πόδας ὠκύς, swift of foot; and, though another hero might ascend his chariot *swiftly*, still he might not be entitled to the general character of *swift of foot;* the adjective, in such a case, denoting the quality of the *noun;* the adverb qualifying simply the particular action or state expressed by the *verb.* The signification of the adjective is *permanent*, that of the adverb *transitory*.

The genius of the English language, as it has been

observed, is not always compatible with that of the Latin, in the use of the adjective in the place of the adverb. As in the example given in the Eton Grammar, we can say, "Pii orant *taciti*," and the pious pray *silent;* yet, as Mr. Edwards has justly observed, there are many examples at variance with the idiom of our language, as taceo mul*tus*, loquor *frequens*, scribo epistolas rarissi*mus*.

When an adjective is not an epithet of the noun, but simply qualifies the action of the verb, its usurpation of the place of the adverb is not altogether consistent with grammatical propriety. It must, however, be acknowledged that it adds greater force to the passage into which it is introduced. As:

"Science by thee flows *soft*, in social ease,
And virtue losing rigor learns to please."
Savage, *Verses to Viscount Tyrconnel.*

"In still descent she melts on opening flowers,
And *deep* impregnates plants with genial showers." *Ibid.*

In the following passage from Savage, "Wanderer," canto 5, the use of the adjective for the adverb has not even the merit of conveying the meaning intended by the author:—

"He weeps, stamps wild, and to and fro now flies,
Now wrings his hands, and sends unmanly cries,
Arraigns his judge, affirms *unjust* he bleeds,
And now recants, and now for mercy pleads."

The grammatical meaning is here the reverse of that which the poet intends. Were the adverb used in this place *unjustly*, instead of *unjust*, the sense would be that he bleeds—suffers unjustly, or by an unjust sentence; and this is the meaning obviously intended, the term unjust having reference to the verb *bleeds*, and not to the *man:* but when we say that *unjust* he bleeds, the affirmation is, that he bleeds or suffers as an unjust man. In the one case, the man affirms that his punishment is not just: in the other that he, being a guilty man, is punished. Whatever may be the poet's intention, this difference of meaning would arise out of a confusion of the adjective with the adverb.

The old form of using the adjective in the place of the adverb, to qualify the meaning of another adjective, is now generally exploded. Such phrases as "*marvellous* white," "*indifferent* well," of Shakspeare, "*wonderful* silly," of Butler, &c., are not, or at least ought not, to be found in modern authorities.

CHAPTER IV.

ADJECTIVE IN THE PLACE OF THE NOUN.

MILTON frequently uses the adjective in the place of the noun substantive; as,

> "So much of death her thoughts
> Had entertain'd, as dyed her cheeks with *pale.*"
> *Paradise Lost,* book i.

> "I by conversing cannot these erect
> From *prone.*" *Ibid.* book ix.

> "From strength, from truth divided, and from *just.*"
> *Ibid.* book vi.

> "Tending to *wild.*" *Ibid.*

> "What heaven's lord had *powerfullest* to send." *Ibid.*

With all due deference to the authority of Milton, the effect is not agreeable.

In the following passage from Ezekiel xxviii. 7, the noun is elegantly understood, the adjective standing alone:—

> "Behold, therefore, I will bring upon thee the *terrible* of the nations"—

the term *terrible* being here taken in a partitive sense, and quite justifiable.

CHAPTER V.

PREVENTIVE.—PARTICULAR.—PECULIAR.

THERE is a word in our language, a participle adjective, which is frequently written and spoken improperly; the term *preventive*, which is made *preventative*. It is almost needless to say that the word preventive is derived from two Latin words, *præ* before, and *venio* to come; and is used to signify something coming before a certain thing, which otherwise would happen, and thus hindering or preventing it from happening. In one of our collects, *prevent* is used in its simple and original meaning—*go before* us, and so make way for us. "Prevent us, O Lord, in all our doings." Now *venio* makes *veni* and *ventum*, from which we have *ventive, præ ventive*—not *ventitive* or *ventative*—preventive.

Savage properly writes—

"*Preventive* of thy call, behold my haste,
(He says) nor let warm thanks thy spirits waste." *Wanderer.*

Again:—

"I spring *preventive*, and unbar the way." *Ibid.*

Yet in Brewster's "Natural Magic," page 305, we find,

"And it has been plausibly conjectured by Beckman that, during the fir t three days, the *preventative* was applied to those whom they wi hed to acquit."

Amo makes *amatum*, from which we have, *amative*, not *amatative*; inveho, *invectum*, *invective*; affligo, *afflic-*

tum, afflictive; dono, *donatum, donative. Preventative* may, therefore, be looked upon as a prodigal son who has wandered out of the family circle, and ought to be brought back as a penitent, and resume the family features and habiliments.

Particular and *Peculiar.*

Particular relates to that which is possessed in common; *peculiar* to that which is exclusive. The style of singing might be the same in two parties, yet one of them might be distinguished from the other, as singing *particularly* well. But should one singer differ from every other singer in his style of execution, then he might not only sing *particularly* well, but in a style *peculiar* to himself.

CHAPTER VI.

COMPARISON OF ADJECTIVES.

Things in their *essences* do not admit of comparison. A mouse is just as much an animal as an elephant is. They both come under the generic term animal; both possess the same principle of animation. They possess this principle in common. Whether mouse, elephant, or man, all are equally animals.

Again; an animula miscrula, an infinitesimal fraction of humanity as far as magnitude is concerned, is "every inch a man," and possesses all the essential qualities of the species, as much as a man of the most gigantic proportions.

Comparison begins where *unessential* properties only are designated. This man possesses the attribute of strength; that man possesses it in a *greater* degree; he is more strong than the other. A third is not only *stronger* than the first; he is *stronger* than the second; he is the *strongest* of the three. As men, they do not differ; but they differ in the gradations of non-essential attributes: and these attributes are denoted by the adjective, either absolutely or relatively.

It is, however, a question, whether any *absolute* quality can exist, and whether any epithet, which we can apply to a noun, has not reference to something either expressed or understood. If I say "this material is coarse," "this man is tall," in the first case the coarseness of the material has reference to the *general* condition of materials of a certain kind. In the second case, the tallness of a particular man has reference to the general stature of men; and though, in such cases, there is no immediate comparison between individual things or persons, there is a reference to a general standard. A learned man is so termed with reference to some general standard of intelligence; and were the term *learned* used *absolutely* and *without reference* to a tacit standard, it might be applied indifferently to a scientific European, or to a luminous Hottentot. It is with reference to a general though local standard, then, that we call a man *good*, or *tall*, or *learned*; so far, those terms which we term *positive*, and *absolute*, are comparative. Amongst a certain class, one man ranks as *learned*; he is above the general condition. Another is *more learned* than this man; and another is the *most learned* of all. Thus, a general standard is the basis. A *learned* man is the first gradation of comparison, *more learned* the second, and *most learned* the third gradation.

The comparative degree relates to two objects, or two parties only, one of which may be taller, shorter, thicker, thinner, than the other. The superlative degree relates to any number more than two. It is the third gradation, and stands above all competition. A man may be the tallest of three, or of three thousand. He oversteps all subordinate gradations of stature. Hence we say the *taller* of two, but the *tallest* of three, or of many.

CHAPTER VII.

ADJECTIVES NOT ADMITTING COMPARISON.

Some adjectives do not admit of comparison. Their inherent signification admits neither increase nor diminution, intensity nor remission. Among these are reckoned definite quantity, as a *hundred*. A *hundred*, whether applied to things small or great, is still a hundred. Definite property, arising from figure, admits of no comparison. One circle cannot be more of a circle than any other circle. Circles may differ in magnitude, which is an accidental property; but they cannot differ in the essential property of figure. One figure cannot be more circular than another, for every figure is either circular or not circular at all. There can be no comparison between a property that exists in one thing, and which does not exist at all in another.

A quadrangle must have four angles. If we take away one angle, it ceases to be a quadrangular figure; if we add one, it ceases to be quadrangular. It cannot be made more or less quadrangular. It admits of no intension—no remission.

Dr. Andrews gives a list of adjectives which do not admit of degrees; as,

Almighty.	Free.	Reverend.
Certain.	Full.	Right.
Chief.	Godly.	Royal.
Circular.	Golden.	Safe.
Conscious.	Gratuitous.	Serene.
Continual.	Heavenly.	Solid.
Dead.	Human.	Sound.
Earthly.	Infinite.	Square.
Empty.	Lawful.	Subject.
Extreme.	Leaden.	Supreme.
External.	Living.	Triangular.
Everlasting.	Natural.	True.
False.	Paternal.	Universal.
Filial.	Perfect.	Void.
Fluid.	Perpetual.	

We frequently, however, meet with some of these adjectives in a comparative or superlative form; as,

"But first and *chiefest* with thee bring."
MILTON, Il Penseroso.

"That on the sea's *extremest* border stood." ADDISON.

Again: we have gradations of the superlative degree. That which is infinite cannot, in the nature of things, be more or less infinite; yet we say infinitesimal, and not only great, greater, greatest, but by far the greater and far greatest. We even qualify the positive form of an adjective, as, "He is *tallish;*" "The taste of it is *bitterish.*" Such expressions denote an approximation only to the positive form of the adjective. We also qualify comparatives by such terms as *somewhat little, still, almost, much, so, exceedingly.* In particular cases, a double superlative is admitted; as when applied to the Deity, as *Most Highest.* Shakspeare uses it in an ordinary case; as,

"This was the *most unkindest* cut of all." *Julius Cæsar.*

Another mode of comparison, which in its nature is eminently superlative, is to select a certain class out of numbers, and to make that class which, as a whole, is superior to the common herd, the starting-point of comparison; as, "Lord of lords;" "King of kings;" "The bravest of the brave." As all men are not *brave, brave* is in itself comparative in such a situation; and if the brave exceed the common herd, much more does the bravest exceed the common herd.

The mind readily acquiesces, too, in the sublime conception of Milton:—

"And in the *lowest* deep, a *lower* deep
Still threatening to devour me opens wide."
Paradise Lost, book iv.

In the following passage, a progressive increase in the comparison is effected by the addition of *yet* after a comparative adjective; as,

"*Short, shorter, shorter yet* my breath I drew."
SAVAGE. *Wanderer.*

Though custom, and even the nature of things, admit of graduated comparatives, custom and propriety have ceased to recognize double comparatives. They were common in a former age; but not having necessity as their foundation, they have deservedly fallen into disuse, and are now looked upon as mere vulgarisms.

"Which title had been *more* truer, if the dictionary had been in Latin and Welsh."—*Verstegan, Epistle to our Nation.*

"The waters are *more* sooner and harder frozen, than *more* further upward, within the inlands."—*Verstegan.*

"Where he shall find
Th' unkindest beast *more* kinder than mankind."
SHAKSPEARE. *Timon.*

Lesser and *worser* have also fallen into disuse; in the age of Shakspeare, they were very common.

"I wish your grandam had a *worser* march." *Richard III.*

"There is ne'er a man in Christendom
Can *lesser* hide his love or hate than he." *Ibid.*

"*Lesser* muse." ADDISON.

"*Worser* far." DRYDEN.

"*More* sorer punishments." *Hebrews* x. 29.

CHAPTER VIII.

CONFUSION OF COMPARATIVES.

SEE what confusion arises in the following sentence from Lawrence's "Lectures on Physiology," page 168, from inattention to the laws of comparison:—

"For, allowing one grain of encephalon to a hundred fibrils, the brain which is *absolutely the least* will have an overplus of two drams, while the larger *has only one.*"

The author is here speaking of two brains, and, in instituting a comparison between the two, properly calls one of them the *larger;* but why not the other the *less* or *smaller,* and not *least,* for *least* would have reference to more brains than two? Then would not one of them be *comparatively* less, not *absolutely* so? for, standing *absolutely,* the term *less* would have no reference to any other brain at all. Then another important error is couched in the phrase, "while *the larger has only one.*" The author really means, while the larger has an *overplus of one dram only.* To have only one dram, and to have an overplus of one dram only, are very different things generally; and so they are here; yet the elucidation is introduced with, "in order that my ideas may be better understood."

Butler, in his characters, Small Poet, sarcastically observes of *obscure* illustrations:—

"A man is sure to gain by an illustration of this kind, for the darker and more unintelligible the illustration, the clearer and more comprehensible will the position to be illustrated become *comparatively;* for, as ladies wear black patches to make their complexions seem fairer than they are, so, when an illustration is more obscure than the sense that went before it, it must of necessity make it appear clearer than it did, for contraries are best set off by contraries."

In the following passage, the position of the comparative adjective is wrong:—

"Whereas the more *mild* and *gentle* they are treated, the *greater* is there a chance of their recovery."—*Rae Wilson.*

"The *greater* chance is there for their recovery," to say nothing of *mild* and *gentle*.

> "From my knowledge of astronomy, navigation, and astrology, the former of which I have professionally studied above twenty-four years, and the latter art for my own amusement during more than seven years, I have no hesitation in saying that the principle of your inventions and discoveries, now published, may be applied with infinite advantage by all persons who practice one or other of the above arts."—*Morrison's Recommendation of Oxley's Planisphere.*

Former and *latter*, as applied to three thing distributed, are nonsense. This error might have been avoided by saying the *two former* of which, &c.

> "The question is not whether a good Indian or bad (a bad) Englishman be *most* happy, but which state is *most* desirable, supposing virtue and reason to be the same in both."—*Johnson, Life of Sir F. Drake.*

In this sentence, the indefinite article should have been repeated before the term bad. Besides, there are two errors arising from the use of the superlative degree in the place of the comparative. If we use the superlative degree in this case, the comparison instituted is not between the happiness of a good Indian and a bad Englishman, but between the happiness of a good Indian and that of all mankind, and the happiness of a bad Englishman and that of all mankind; the question thus being whether a good Indian is the happiest of all mankind, or a bad Englishman the happiest of all mankind,—the happiest of men; but the question intended is, whether a good Indian is, or is not, happier than a bad Englishman. It does not follow that either one or the other should be the happiest of men, but one of them may be happier than the other.

SECTION VI.

THE VERB.

CHAPTER I.

ITS MOODS AND TENSES.

The *Verb*, by way of pre-eminence, *the word*, is the vital principle of every sentence. Without it, no sentence, either affirmative or negative, can exist. It has reference to time present, past, and future; and that, too, under various modifications. These properties of the verb give rise to tenses and modes, or moods. The verb thus becomes more varied and complex than any other part of speech. Languages differ in the number of moods and tenses; and grammarians differ in the classification of moods and tenses in one and the same language. Moods representing the condition, or affections, of the mind would be as varied and extended as those affections. Hence we might have Indicative, Imperative, Potential, Optative, Subjunctive, Infinitive, Vocative, Precative, Interrogative, Causal, Reflective, &c. Then, again, verbs have respect to different persons, and are distinguished by inflexions, as relating to the first, second, or third persons, and to the singular or plural number. The English Language, by prefixing the pronoun to the verb, obviates the necessity of inflecting the verb in many of its persons. Thus we say, I *love*, we *love*, ye *love*, they *love* (the old plural form *loven* having become obsolete), and I *loved*, he *loved*, we *loved*, ye *loved*, they *loved*. In this case, the distinction between the singular and the plural number of the verb, as also the distinction of persons, as far as the verb itself is concerned, is mental, but not visible. Instances, however, may occur, in which the verb may become ambiguous from the want of inflexion; as, "On these two commandments *hang* all the law and the prophets," *hang* being either indicative or imperative.

Then we have verbs Active, Passive, and Neuter, Active Transitive and Active Intransitive, Irregular, Defective, Impersonal, Auxiliary. Amidst all these complexities, we need not be surprised that many errors should exist in the diversified application of the verb to varied times, conditions, and contingencies.

The subtle and logical Harris considers twelve tenses requisite to form a perfect system; three indefinite, that is, marking present, past, and future time, without reference to a beginning; and nine, as marking present, past, and future time, *with* reference to a beginning.

Indefinite or Aorist of the Present, I write.
of the Past, I wrote.
of the Future, I shall write.

Inceptive Present, I am going to write.
Extended Present, I am writing.
Completive Present, I have written.

Inceptive Past, I was beginning to write.
Extended Past, I was writing.
Completive Past, I had done writing.

Inceptive Future, I shall be beginning to write.
Extended Future, I shall be writing.
Completive Future, I shall have done writing.

"It is not to be expected," says Harris, "that the above hypothesis should be justified, through all instances, in every language. It fares with tenses as with other affections of speech: be the language, on the whole, ever so perfect, much must be left, in defiance of analogy, to the harsh laws of mere authority and chance."

Though the English language, in its system of tenses does not follow this classification and denomination, yet it is by no means useless to have these philosophical and explanatory principles of the tenses placed before us.

Moods or modes are defined by Priscian, "Modi sunt diversæ inclinationes animi, quas varia consequuntur declinatio verbi." Modes or moods represent the different feelings of the mind, to which feelings the varied inflexions of the verb are adapted. According to Dr. Andrews, the Arabic has thirteen moods, the Sanscrit six, the Russian seven. These are the greatest numbers of modes, or moods, out of twenty-eight European and Asiatic languages. The number of moods is obviously, therefore, a matter of uncertainty, depending upon the peculiar genius and construction of a language.

CHAPTER II.

THE AUXILIARY VERB.

The auxiliary verb in English simplifies the inflexions of the principal verb, by its being prefixed to the present or past participle; as, I am loving, I am loved, I was loving, I had loved, I shall be loving, I shall have loved. Here we have but two terminations of the principal verb, and yet in all these cases the action of the verb is clearly defined with reference to time. By means of this simple contrivance, the inflexions of a *regular* English verb are reduced to six, including its participial terminations, love, lovest, lovedst, loveth (or loves), loved, loving. An irregular verb has one more variation, as drive, drivest, drives, drivedst, drove, driving, driven; an extraordinary fact, when compared with the manifold windings and diversities of the Greek verb, and traceable perhaps to the genius and character of a people who are prone to set aside all useless incumbrances and appendages in the business of life, and to effect their purpose by the simplest means.

The auxiliaries be, do, have, let, may, can, shall, will, might, would, should, ought, must, are the exponents of our moods and tenses. They determine the time and mode of the verb's action; they express the perceptions and volitions of the mind.

To Be.

Be, in the sense of *am*, as I be, is now obsolete, though still in use amongst our peasantry of the south. The verb *to be* is also a principal, as well as an auxiliary; and, in this case, has the sense of exists, and stands separately—"God *is;*" "There is a God;" "Honesty *is* the best policy." In these cases, the verb *is* expresses a general proposition, having reference to present, past, and future time—on eternal truth—a variable, everlasting now.

Am and *Was.*

Lowth doubts of the propriety of such expressions as the following, though doubt seems too modest a term:—

"The rules of our holy religion, from which we *are* infinitely swerved."—*Tillotson.*

"*Have* infinitely swerved."

"*Was* also ceased."—*Tillotson.*

"Whose number *was now amounted* to three hundred."—*Swift.*

"This mareschal, on some discontent, *was entered* into a conspiracy against his master."—*Addison.*

"At the end of the campaign, when half the men *are deserted* or killed."—*Ibid.*

The principle upon which the propriety of using *am* and *was* as auxiliaries is this; *am* and *was* may be applied to verbs as auxiliaries, when the principal verb implies *motion*, or a *change of* condition; as, "I *am come;*" "I *was gone;*" "I *was fallen;*" "They *are waxen* fat;" "Israel *is fled.*" We find the same principle in French, "*Il a venu,*" he is come; "*Il est tombé,*" he is fallen. But, if we take the phrase, "when *half the men are* deserted, *or killed,*" we then place *are deserted* in the same category as *are killed;* "are deserted and are killed." Both are the passive forms of the verb. In both cases, *passion* is understood. Both verbs express something acted upon. Both forms are precisely alike. Both are derived from the active verbs to desert, to kill; yet in the first case the verb expresses voluntary action, in the second sufferance. *Are deserted* signifies properly are deserted by something; and *are killed* signifies *are killed by something.* But this is not the author's meaning, nor will the sense bear it. The sentence is, in fact, nonsense.

Am and *was* may then be used, with propriety, as auxiliaries, when, in conjunction with the *principal* verb, they simply express the *time* of an action, but not when they *affect the action itself.* This is Lowth's view of the principle involved in the use of these auxiliaries, and it seems to be the right one.

There is, however, a much more palpable violation of grammar in the use of the verb *was.* It falls upon a grammatical ear like a hideous discord. In weighing such expressions, we must divest ourselves of every vestige of reverence for mere names. Poets, orators, historians, critics, when thrown into the grammatical crucible, come out simply as men, stripped of all adventitious ornaments. *You was,* instead of you *were,* in point of propriety stands on a par with *thou were.* The authority of Addison in matters of grammar; of Bentley,[*] who evidently never made the English grammar

---

[*] This great critic is now rather lightly spoken of, even in his stronghold classical criticism. The following observation occurs in the advertisement to the first edition to "Tate's Introduc-

his study; of Bolingbroke, Pope, and others, is as nothing. Nothing short of universal adoption, before which all must bow, can ever sanction the expression *you was*. It can find no refuge but in ignorance or silly affectation.

"Knowing that *you was* my old master's good friend."—*Spectator*, 517.

"The account *you was* pleased to send me."—*Bentley.*

"Would to God you *was* within her reach."—*Bolingbroke.*

"I am just now as well as when you *was* here."—*Pope.*

Lowth justly calls this expression "an *enormous* solecism." But this is not all, in the case of Bentley; he even uses the verb *was* in connection with a plural noun of the third person.

"As one would think *there was* more *sophists* than one had (who had) a finger in this volume of letters."—*Bentley's Discourse on Socrates' Epistles.*

A specimen of mere nursery English, in a very short space embracing two vile errors.

The auxiliary verb joined to the participle, as *he is drinking*, in some instances does not convey the same meaning as *he drinks*. He *is drinking* indicates a present action; *he drinks* may indicate a habit. Thus, *he drinks wine at dinner* means that he does so habitually: whilst *he is drinking wine at dinner* confines the act of drinking wine to that particular occasion. *Boys play*, that is, it is the nature of boys to play. The Esqui-

---

tion to the principal Tragic and Comic Metres:" "Many things now familiar to *young academics*, thanks to the labors of Dawes and Burney, and Parr and Porson, and Elmsley, were utterly unknown to scholars like Bentley, and to Scaliger before him."

maux eats raw fish, and drinks whale oil; *i. e.* these are the habits of his life. A habit is also expressed by the simple verb *to be* used in the present tense, which could not be expressed in any other mood; as,

"I knew thou *art* a hard man."—*Matt.* xxv. 24.

That is, I knew thee *to be* a hard man generally. If we say *wert*, the hardness would refer to a particular occasion, and not express a habit.

An unwarrantable expression has of late years been creeping into the language, more particularly in light dialogue. It is the omission of the adverb *there* after *have been.*

"Seriously, though," continued Lady Bab, "you must, and shall go, and buy some of Fanny's flowers. I need only tell you, it will be the greatest charity you ever did, and then I know you won't rest till you *have been.*"

Have been (*there*).

In the following sentence from Rae Wilson's "Travels in the Holy Land," *had been* is omitted altogether:—

"No respite was given; but, whenever the operation ceased, the whole table was covered, and appeared perfectly black, as if so much soot *thrown* upon it."

Had been thrown upon it.

Do.

The verb *do* occurs both as a principal and an auxiliary. When used as a principal, it is usual to write *doest*, and not *dost;* as,

"If thou *doest* well, shalt thou not be accepted? and if thou *doest* not well, sin lieth at the door."—*Gen.* iv. 7.

"Which *doest* great things past finding out."

Sometimes the auxiliary *do* stands in the place of the principal verb, to which it has reference, rendering the repetition of that verb unnecessary; as,

> "He loves not plays
> As thou *dost*."   SHAKSPEARE.

On some occasions, *do* and *didst* are strikingly emphatic; as,

> "Perdition catch my soul,
> But I *do* love thee."   *Ibid.*

> "Nay, but thou *didst* call me."

Having reference to an expressed or silent negation, as the case may be.

Don't is a contraction of *do not*, and not of *does not*. *Don't* for *does not* is a mere vulgarism.

"The clock don't tick as it goes."—*Bulwer's England and the English.*

"It *were* an intolerable spectacle, even to the inmates of a felon's cell, *did* they behold one of their fellows in the agonies of death."—*Chalmers' Bridgewater Treatise.*

It *would* be an intolerable spectacle, even to the inmates of a felon's cell, *should* they behold, or were they to behold, one of their fellows in the agonies of death.

Have.

The variations of the auxiliary verb *to have* are *have*, *hast*, *hath* or *has*, and *hadst*. *Doth* and *hath*, in the place of *does* and *has*, are associated with serious and solemn subjects, more particularly of a religious kind. They accord with the date and character of Scripture phraseology. Independent of their use on solemn occasions, there are a peculiar softness and tenderness in the use of *th* in the place of *s*, whether in the auxiliary or principal verb. *Doth* and *hath* are sometimes used in the place of *does* and *has*, in order to avoid the hissing sound arising from the too frequent repetition of the letter *s*.

In the following sentence from Dr. Chalmers' "Bridgewater Treatise," *hath* and *has* are used in the same sentence without any reason for the distinction:—

"It is for their sake that human law *hath* interposed in some countries of the world, and by creating and ordaining a right for them, *has* endeavored to make good the deficiency of nature."

Shakspeare, "Richard II.," even uses *has* in the second person singular:—

"Why, uncle, *thou has* many years to live."

An expression, at all events, not to be tolerated now.

The verb *to have* has no distinctive form whatever in the plural number. The first, second, and third persons are all alike in the several tenses. The following sentence affords a curious example of "confusion worse confounded" in the use of this verb:—

"The events which he narrates are authentic, but the subject could have been better chosen, and *have* more unity."—*Pailhman on Latin Composition*, p. 132.

Might have been better chosen, and have *had* more unity. Again; the word *better* ought to qualify the subject, and not the act of choice. The author probably means to say, that, in his opinion, "a better subject, and one possessing more unity, might have been chosen."

I'd rather is frequently used in familiar discourse for *I would* rather, and not for *I had rather*. I *had rather* is a mere corruption, arising from the letter *d* forming the final sound of *would* and *had*.

In the following example from Coleridge, "On the Constitution of Church and State," page 68, confusion arises from a want of the application of the auxiliary verb *be:*—

"I do assert that the nationality cannot rightfully, and that without foul wrong to the nation, it never has been alienated from its original purposes."

It is evident that the verb *be* is here wanting, and that the word *has been* cannot grammatically be applied both to a thing past and a thing future: to that of which it is declared that it cannot *be alienated;* and that of which it is declared that it never *has been* alienated, without foul wrong to the nation. "I do assert that the nationality cannot rightfully be alienated from its original purposes, and that, without foul wrong to the nation, it never has been so."

Whenever an ellipsis takes place, that which is expressed should never be incongruous with that which is not expressed. The phrase *never has been* in this case is incongruous with *cannot rightfully be.* "*I am,* and *always have taken, great pains;*" that is, "I am *taking,* and *have* always *taken* great pains." Here is a transition from the present to a past time; and *am* and *have,* present and past, are auxiliaries in common of the verb to take—a manifest incongruity.

It is not easy to see upon what principle Harris constructed the following sentence:—

"Now, as all these several contacts, unless some opening of the mouth either immediately precede, or immediately follow, would rather *occasion* silence, than *to produce* a voice," &c.

Why not "rather occasion silence than *produce* a voice?" The incongruity arising from the transition from one tense to another is remarkable, and, one would suppose, must have been overlooked.

Shall and *Will.*

In a review of Justice Brenan's "Foreigner's English Conjugator," contained in the Atlas newspaper of Jan. 23d, 1831, the following observations are made on the subject of *shall* and *will:*—

"He (Brenan), however, has not removed the difficulty. There is no general rule to be drawn from his work. In the case of *shall* and *will* (says the reviewer), let us try to supply this deficiency. *Will* is the sign of resolution, *may* of possibility, *can* of ability, *must* of necessity, *ought* of propriety; these have all a view to the future, without contingency. *Shall* supplies the place of either (any one) of these signs, when the future involves a doubt, or a contingency, especially when it regards the first person. Its comparative power is simple, and is never abused; its contingent force alone creates the difficulty. With respect to human life and purpose, doubt is the very essence of futurity. The vivacity of the southern nations confounds *will* and *shall*, because they determine, in the levity of their minds, without doubt or dread. The cautious Englishman doubts ever; he sees contingency in the future; and from this peculiarity of the national mind comes a delicacy of expression which has no equivalent in any other language."

This is rather a *moral* than a *grammatical* disquisition, and leaves the subject very much in the same state as we found it.

Though the auxiliaries *shall* and *will*, in certain

positions, are very different in their meaning, yet they are frequently used the one for the other, as exemplified in the trite but forcible case of the drowning Irishman; "I *will* be drowned and nobody *shall* help me;" and it is a common expression used by an Irish servant, "*Shall* you take tea to-night, and *will* I bring it in?"

The Scotch are also apt to confound the use of *shall* and *will;* as,

"Without having attended to this, we *will* be at a loss, in understanding several passages in the classics, which relate to public speaking and the theatrical entertainments of the ancients."—*Blair's Lectures.*

"In the Latin language there are no two words we *would* more readily take to be synonymous than *amare* and *diligere.*"—*Ibid.*

Shall and *should* are required.

"Think what reflection *shall* most probably arise."—*Ibid.*

Will is here required.

"If I draw a catgut, or any other cord, to a great length between my fingers, I *will* make it smaller than it was before."—*Goldsmith.*

Shall.

"There is not a girl in town, but let her, in going to a mask, and she *shall* dress as a shepherdess."—*Spectator.*

Will.

A well-educated Englishman, however, seldom makes a mistake in the application of *shall* and *will*, though it may sometimes be necessary to feel the way, as it were, by a delicate touch. There *must* be, and *is*, a broad principle of distinction. In the modest language of the reviewer just referred to, let us try to find it. From example, let us endeavor to work out the principle.

I *shall go* to town to-morrow. Here simply the intention of doing a certain thing is expressed, without any anticipation of, or reference to, hinderance. But when I say I *will* go to town to-morrow, I declare my resolution to do so, in spite of all opposition. I *must* and *will* go to town to-morrow. Now, we must bear in mind that, in both these cases, the *person that speaks* is also the *person that is about to act*. He, therefore, at pleasure, expresses an act of *simple volition*, or of *fixed purpose*, according to circumstances. Both are at his own option; he has the control of both in his own mind. But, when we pass to the *second person, thou shalt or will*, it is to be borne in mind that, though the *second person is the actor, the first is still the speaker*. If, therefore, the acting of the *second* person is dependent upon the will of the *first*, the *first* person says to the *second, thou shalt*, and not *thou will*, for the willing rests with the *first;* but if the *first* leaves the *second* to act as he may think proper, he says *thou will*, and thus claims no control over that *willing*. Again; in the third person, *he shall* or *he will*, we still see the same principle. When the first says *he shall*, he deprives the third of the exercise of his own *will;* but when he says *he will*, he leaves him the exercise of that *will*, and simply expresses his belief that it is the intention or *will* of the third person to do this or that.

The principle to be borne in mind in the distinction of *shall* and *will* is, that it is *always* the first person that speaks; and that, in the first *person of the verb, the speaker is also the agent;* but that in the second and third, the *first* person is *the speaker, but the second or third the agent.* Hence, as volition is allowed to the second or third person, or control exercised over that volition, the use of *will* and *shall* must vary in passing from the first to the second and third persons.

When, however, we pass to the interrogative forms of *shall* and *will*, the case is reversed. In the second person of the verb, we simply inquire what the will of that person is, the act of volition remaining in the breast of that person, and not being subject to the control of the person asking. We therefore say, *wilt* thou? or *will* you? In the third person of the verb, again, the act of willing remains with that person, and we simply ask for an enunciation of that *will;* as, *will* he? if plural, *will* they? Thus: *Shall* I go to London? *wilt* thou go? *will* he go? *shall* we go? *will* you go? *will* they go?

This distinction of *shall* and *will* does not form a part of the system of a Latin or a Greek verb.

The verb *will* is also a *principal,* as well as an auxiliary. As, *I will, thou willest, he wills, we will, ye* or *you will, they will.* A confusion of *will* as a principal and an auxiliary occurs in the following passage from Atterbury's "Sermons:"—

"Thou that art the author and bestower of life canst doubtless restore it also if thou *will'st,* and when thou *will'st;* but whether thou *will'st* please to restore it, or not, thou alone knowest."

Here *will'st* in the two former cases is a principal, in the last *an auxiliary,* and ought to be *will,* and not *will'st* or *willest:* that is, but whether thou *will restore* them or not, &c.

Would and Should.

Would expresses volition, and has reference either to time past, or present. "*I* would do it, were I in your situation," expresses a present inclination with reference to a future action, the pronoun *I* being emphatic and contradistinctive. "I *would* do it," with the emphasis on *would*, expresses a present feeling and determination to have done a thing with reference to a particular time passed; that is, I *would*, at that time, do it—I was *determined* to do it.

Should expresses duty, a sense of obligation; "I *should* do it," i. e., all things considered, I feel that it is my duty to do it. In the same sense also we use I *should* have done it, *ought* to have done it. *Should*, with a future subjunctive signification, expresses a *simple* contingency: as, "If he *should* do it, that will be sufficient:" whereas the expression, if he *would* do it, has a stringent reference to volition, as well as to contingency; as, "if he *would* but do it, I should be satisfied," the term *would* being expressive of a supposed aversion on his part. The operations of the mind, as far as the use of these auxiliaries is concerned, are generally expressed with sufficient accuracy, according to the drift of the sentence, and the intentions of the speaker.

Either, however, *should* and *would* have changed their meaning in the following passages from the Psalms, or their application is erroneous:—

"If I *would* declare them, and speak of them, they are more than can be numbered."— *Bible version*, *Psalm* xl. 5.

"If I *should* declare them, and speak of them, they *should* be more than I am able to express."—*Prayer Book*, *Psalm* xl. 6.

The sense required in the first case is that of a simple contingency, without any express volition. We therefore expect, "*If I should declare them,*" and not "*If I would declare them.*" Again: "If I *should* declare them, and speak of them, they *should* be more than I am able to express." *They would be* more, and not *should*, because *should* in this case would indicate a latent reason why they should be more, instead of a simple contingency. If I *should* declare them, and speak of them, *they should*, that is, *ought*, according to all reasonable calculation, to be more than I am able to express. But this is not what is meant. Let us take the following example: "Were he to do such a thing in England, he *would* be hanged." *Would* be hanged here indicates a necessary result, without assigning or implying any reason for such a result. But if I say, "Were he to do such a thing in England, he *should* be hanged," we see that a reason is implied why he should be hanged. He *should* be hanged, that is, *ought* to be hanged, either because it is an aggravation of the offence that it is committed in England, or because, according to the scale of punishment in England, the offence *ought* to be punished by hanging.

"In judging only from the nature of things, and without the surer aid of Revelation, one *should* be apt to embrace the opinion of Diodorus Siculus."—*Warburton's Divine Legation*.

Would.

"This man was taken of the Jews, and *should* have been killed of them."—*Acts* xxiii. 27.

Should in this situation would now mean *ought*,—*ought to have been killed;* in modern phraseology, *would have been killed by* them.

> "O had it been a stranger, not my child,
> To smooth his fault, I *should* have been more mild."
>
> SHAKSPEARE.

Would have been more kind is the signification which first presents itself; but *should* is defensible, as bearing a signification different from *would*. *Would*, in this case, would express resolution; i. e. though a stranger and not my child, still in spite of *that* I *would* have been more mild. *Should*, on the other hand, would express a simple intention.

The following sentence from Psalm cvi. 23, is a good example of the proper use of *would* and *should:*—

"So he said he *would* have destroyed them, had not Moses his chosen stood before him in the gap to turn away his wrathful indignation, lest he *should* destroy them."

So he said, after the occasion had passed away, that he *would* on that occasion have destroyed them, had not Moses stood before him, lest he *should* destroy them; not, should have destroyed them, an expression which would place the prevention *subsequent* to the supposed act.

"This was a thing deeply resented; and to have spoken to me about the manuscripts *had* been to lose a plausible occasion of taking revenge." *Bentley, Preface to Dissertation on Epistle of Phalaris.*

Would have been.

"If he had writ me word the very next post * *, this *had* been just and civil."—*Ibid.*

Would have been.

Might.

May refers to a *present* or a *future* privilege, *might* to a *past* one. As, he *is* attentive in order that he *may* learn; he *will* be attentive in order that he *may* learn; he *was* attentive in order that he *might* learn.

"Let us therefore reflect how a serious and attentive study of the books of the Old Testament best *answer* the great end for which they were written, namely, that we, through patience and comfort of the Holy Scriptures, *might* have hope."—*Rennel's Sermons*.

There are, in this sentence, three grammatical errors, two of which are chargeable upon the author, and one on the quotation. The first is of minor importance, and occurs so frequently in various authors, as to have some claim to justification—"a serious and attentive," instead of a serious and *an* attentive. The second is *answer* instead of *answers*; a serious and an attentive study *answers*, not *answer*. The third error consists in the use of *might* instead of *may*. The Scriptures were written that we, through patience and comfort of those Holy Scriptures, *may* have hope. They were written, *that ages that have preceded* us *might* have hope, that *we may* have hope, that future generations *may* have hope. Speaking of the past, we should say *might;* of the present, or the future, *may*.

"And Jesus answered and said, What wilt thou that I should do unto thee? The blind man said unto him, Lord, that I *might* receive my sight."—*Mark* x. 51.

May receive.

Can and Must.

The auxiliary verb *can*, under its different forms,

is seldom misapplied; and *must* affords the curious grammatical phenomenon of a verb without a single variation.

Ought.

Ought is not an auxiliary, but a *primary* verb. We cannot connect it with another verb simply; as, I *ought* go, I *ought* write, in the same way as we can say, I *should* go, I *should* write. It must be connected with the verb that follows in the same way as any other principal verb must be, by the particle *to*;—I ought *to* go; I ought *to write*.

CHAPTER III.

GENERAL REMARKS ON THE AUXILIARIES.

In English, we have as many moods as we have auxiliary verbs, allowing these verbs to be *auxiliaries*, and not *principals*; for every auxiliary verb in the language expresses some modification of action, or volition, or condition, which cannot be so well expressed in any other way, and thus constitutes a separate mode or mood. For instance, I *write verses* is an indefinite aorist of the present time, and implies a habit; I *do* write verses is a *decisive assertion* in opposition to an expressed or latent doubt; I *am writing* verses is a present imperfect tense; I am now in the act of writing verses. Now we have here three distinct significations, all included under the indicative mood present tense; and distinct as they are, there is but one word in Latin to express the indicative mood present tense, namely, *scribo*, which falls far short of the nice discriminations of the English auxiliaries. The auxiliaries *may, can, might, would, could, should, ought, have, had, shall, will*, &c., afford greater precision in the expression of various shades of meaning than is attainable by the use of single and unaided terms. They possess an elasticity which adapts itself with ease to the extension or contraction of our ideas, and the varied modifications under which they present themselves. How shall we translate into Latin, and by one word only, *I have been going to write?* As, I am glad I have met you, for *I have been going to write* to you for some time past; or, *I have been writing;* or, *I had been writing;* or, *I shall or will have been writing.* Such expressions may seem encumbered with expletives; nevertheless, these expletives clearly and definitely express our meaning, when properly applied. Mr. Pickbourn has pointed out that we have no less than eight future tenses or forms of expressing future time; four of these express time simply; as, I shall write, I will write, I shall be writing, I will be writing. In each of these forms of expression, we clearly recognize a distinction of meaning; yet their equivalent in Latin is simply *scribam*—a poor equivalent, it must be confessed. The other four, I shall have been writing, I will have been writing, I shall have written, I will have written, express future time in a more complex manner, as antecedent to some definite future period, pointed out by some other word or member of the sentence. The English language is often blamed for want of definiteness. Let us first learn to make a proper use of our tools before we complain of their inapplicability to the work which we have in hand.

CHAPTER IV.

THE NEUTER VERB.

By a neuter verb is meant a verb that has *neither an active* nor *a passive signification*. The action of the verb is not transitive. It does not pass on to the following noun, unless that noun has an identity of meaning with the verb itself, or unless the expression may be grammatically resolved into a verb, preposition and noun. To *dream a dream* would be an example of the first case; *to walk a mile* of the second, that is, over the space of a mile. This, in fact, is a mere elliptical expression. The neuter verb properly has no object, the action of the verb being limited to itself. It cannot, therefore, be followed by the objective case. The child *cries*, gives us an example of a simple neuter verb. The sense is complete. But, if we say the child *destroys*, we necessarily suppose something destroyed, that something being the object upon which the action of the verb or the destructive agency falls, and therefore in the objective case. As, the child destroys *his playthings*. A neuter verb, then, has no transitive signification, and its character is happily designated in Greek by the word αυτοπαθια, autopathy.

Neuter verbs have the same construction as verbs

which simply indicate a state of being. Cæsar is Emperor, or the Emperor is Cæsar, are convertible propositions, and both the nouns are in the same case.

"While *his lovelocks* descended a *golden-shower.*"
Savage, *Wanderer*, canto iv.
"*Which* rose a *stately colonnade.*" *Ibid.*

His lovelocks, as they descended, were a golden shower.

The building, as it rose, was a stately colonnade.

Neuter Verbs improperly used actively.

Pope claims an unwarrantable license when he converts the neuter verb *success* into an active one:—

"How would the gods my righteous toils *succeed!*"
Odyssey, xiv. 447.
"If Jove this arm *succeed.*" *Iliad.*
"The heroes pray'd, and Pallas from the skies
  Records their vows—*succeeds* their enterprise."
Iliad, x. 351.

That is, makes it to succeed. *Succeed*, as an active verb, is utterly unwarrantable.

Equally unwarrantable is the term *approaches*, used actively by Bulwer:—

"This is true power, it *approaches* men to gods."—*England and the English.*

What do we think of *approach the candle to me?*

"You *rejoice* me."—*Dr. Wharton.*

"He *retired* the army behind the river."

"Me of these
Not skill'd or studious higher argument
Remains."   *Paradise Lost*, book ix.

That is, higher argument *remains* me—*to* me surely.

If we do not consider the expression "*remains me*" as elliptical, and standing in the place of *remains to me*, it is a liberty which even Milton was not justified in taking. When large fishes break through the meshes of the net, we need not be surprised that the small fry should follow them.

Active Verbs improperly used as Neuter.

" I must *premise with* three circumstances."—*Swift.*
"Those that think to *ingratiate* with him by calumniating me."
—*Bentley.*

Premise *three* circumstances. Ingratitate *themselves.*

Neuter Verb To Lie.

There is, perhaps, no verb in the English language, in the use of which so much ignorance is manifested, as in the confusion of the active verb *to lay* with the neuter verb *to lie*. "He *lays* this book down on the table, and then the book *lies* on the table;" *lay* being an active transitive verb, and the object on which that action falls, or to which it extends, being the word *book*. *Lies*, on the other hand, being a neuter *intransitive* verb, simply expresses a condition. *Lies*, the neuter verb, in the imperfect past tense makes *lay:* as when I saw the book, it *lay* on the table. The following examples embrace the difference in the signification of these two words:—

Present Tense of Lie.

" Eight forky arrows from his hand have fled,
And eight bold heroes by their points *lie* dead."
Iliad, viii. 361.

"When Jesus saw him *lie*."—*John* v. 6.

That is, to lie.

"And seeth the linen clothes *lie*."—*John* xxii. 6.

Again, to lie; elliptical.

> "Though now they *lie*
> Grovelling and prostrate on yon lake of fire."
> *Paradise Lost.*

These are examples of the *present tense* of the neuter verb *to lie*.

Past Tense.

"Then the king arose and tore his garments, and *lay* on the earth."—2 *Samuel* xiii. 2.

> "Nine times the space, that measured day and night
> To mortal man, he with his horrid crew
> *Lay* vanquish'd."   *Paradise Lost*, book i.

> "Unwept, unhonor'd, on the plain he *lay*,
> While the proud victor bore his arms away."
> POPE, *Iliad.*

These are examples of the *past tense* of the neuter verb *to lie*.

Participle of the Neuter Verb To Lie.

He *lies* upon straw now, he *lay* upon straw last night, he is said to have *lien*, or *lain*, upon straw last night.

"For now would I have *lain* still, and been quiet."—*Job* iii. 13.
"Though ye have *lien* among the pots."—*Psalm* lxviii. 13.
"See where thou hast been *lien* with."—*Jer.* iii. 2.

Lien with, a passive participle of a *neuter* verb, effected by the conjoint efficacy of the preposition *with*.

Active Verb To Lay.

"No more with presents her embraces meet,
Or *lay* the spoils of conquest at her feet."
Iliad, xi. 3.

The active verb *to lay* admits a passive form. As *I lay* the book down, the book is *layed* or *laid* down, the book has been *layed* or *laid* down.

"O that my griefs were weighed, and my calamity *laid* in the balances together?"—*Job.*

CHAPTER V.

IRREGULAR VERBS.

THE whole number of verbs in the English language, regular and irregular, simple and compound, is estimated at about 4,300. The whole number of irregular verbs, defective included, is about 177. The ungrammatical use of some of the most striking of these will here be noticed. Irregular verbs are such as *draw,* drew, drawn; *fall,* fell, fallen; *take,* took, taken; *sit,* sate, sitten; *begin,* began, begun, &c. Defective, such as *may, might, can, could, shall, should, must.* The past tenses of these verbs, and the passive participles, are so perpetually confounded and mutilated, that they exhibit a perfect grammatical slaughter-house. Shakspeare, Addison, Swift, Pope, Milton, Dryden, and Atterbury, Prior, Gay, Sterne, Gibbon, Byron, and a host of others, up to the present day, violate a principle which is obvious to the merest school-boy in writing any other language than his own. The man of vegetables says, "Potatoes *is rose* or *riz,* and turnips *is fell.*" The language serves his purpose, and more is not expected; but men of high literary character should take care not to mislead by corrupt example. There is not one iota of difference between I had *drank*, and I had *knew,* I had *rode,* and I had *blew,* I have *sat,* and I have *gave,* a web was *wove,* and a stone was *threw.* In such cases as these, the error may be more palpable than in ordinary cases; but there is not the slightest difference in degree. In prose composition, there can be no excuse. It is, perhaps, to the poets that we in some degree owe these solecisms; for the perfect tense of the verb in the place of the participle frequently offers a convenient rhyme, which the particle would not supply. As Pope:—

"Rapt into future times, the bard *begun,*
A virgin shall conceive, a virgin bear a son."
Messiah.

"At length he roll'd in dust, and thus *begun,*
Imploring all, and naming one by one." *Iliad,* xxii.

"Doom'd from the hour his luckless life *begun,*
To dogs and vultures, and to Peleus' son." *Ibid.*

"In the fat age of pleasure, wealth, and ease,
Sprung the rank weed, and thriv'd (throve) with large increase."
POPE, *Essay on Criticism.*

Not satisfied with using the participle in the place of the verb, Pope also uses the verb in the place of the participle:—

"And now the years a numerous train have *ran,*
The blooming boy is ripen'd into man." *Odyssey.*

In the following couplet, grammar and rhyme fortunately coincide:—

> "Near as he drew, the warrior thus *began*,
> O great Ulysses! much-enduring man."   *Iliad.*

We see, in these examples, how unscrupulously grammar is sacrificed to rhyme:—

> "From liberty each nobler science *sprung* (sprang),
> A Bacon brighten'd and a Spenser *sung* (sang)."
>   SAVAGE, *Wanderer.*

> "And with my years my soul *begun* (began) to pant
> With feeling of strange tumult, and soft pain."
>   BYRON, *Lament of Tasso.*

Without the apology of rhyme, Dryden says, "have *sang*" (sung); Montgomery, "could he not have *sang*" (sung); Rowe, "since time *begun*" (began). Yet a few lines further on, he says:—

> "From hills they taught how melting currents *ran*,
> When the first swelling of the flood *began*." (right)
>   *Pharsalia.*

Here it is obvious that no grammatical principle has been kept in view.

> "And all the city was moved, and the people *ran* together."— *Acts* xxi. 30.

> "He *began* to curse and swear."

> "Now the first man who *began* to speak."—*Monboddo, Origin and Progress of Language.*

In these examples, the imperfect tense of the verb is of course used with propriety.

> "At the close of such a folio as this, *wrote* (written) for their sake."—*Sterne.*

"I satisfied the cravings of hunger with bread and water, which, I may add, was *ate* in a filthy stable."—*Burnes's Travels.*

This is gross indeed. *Was ate!* I *eat* now, I *ate* yesterday, the dinner "was *eaten* in a filthy stable." So I *sit* now, I *sate* yesterday, I had *sitten* down.

"The Queen, bound with love's powerful charm,
Sate with Pigwiggen, arm in arm."
Drayton's *Polyolbion.*

"Many a time
On holidays we rambled through the woods,
We *sate*—we walk'd." Wordsworth, *Wanderer.*

Right in both examples. Sit, *sate*, sitten; bid, *bade*, bidden.

"A certain man made a great supper, and *bade* many, and sent his servant at supper time to say to them that were *bidden.*"—*Luke* xiv. 17.

Dr. Thirlwall, Bishop of St. David's (History of Greece), uses *bad* falsely in the place of *bade.*

"I, like the arch-fiend, bore a hell within me, and finding myself unsympathized with, wished to tear up the trees, and spread havoc and destruction along with me, and then to *have sat* down and enjoyed the ruin."—*Frankenstein.*

"To *have sat*" is here doubly wrong. Grammatically, *sat* ought to be sitten. As a matter of sense, this also would be wrong; for the fiend wished to tear up the trees, to spread havoc and destruction around him, and then to do what? *to sit* down and enjoy the ruin; for the act of sitting down and enjoying the ruin was posterior to the other acts, and certainly posterior to the wish. As well might we say, "I wished to have gone to London," which means I wished to do something anterior to my wish to do it. But were we to assimilate this expression to the one in question, we must say, "I wished to *have went* to London."

"In the middle of one night in September, I awoke from sleep, in a breathless and burning heat, though I was conscious that I had neither *ate* nor *drunk* anything that ought to have fevered me."—*Campbell's Letters from the South*, vol. i. p. 182.

"Neither *eaten* nor *drunk*."

"In the ways hast thou *sat* for them, as the Arabian in the wilderness."—*Jer.* iii. 2.

Sitten.

Lowth gives some examples of the proper use of *sitten* instead of *sat*:—

"The army *having sitten* there so long."—*Raleigh.*

"Which was enough to make *him* stir that would not *have sitten* still."—*Raleigh.*

"That no parliament should be dissolved till it *had sitten* five months."—*Hobbes.*

"To *have sitten* on the heads of the apostles— to *have sitten* upon each of them."—*Dr. Middleton.*

He at the same time points out the impropriety of using *set* in the place of *sit*, the former being an *active* verb signifying to *place*, the latter a *neuter* verb simply expressive of condition. To *set*, or to be *set*, or was *set*, is not in any way expressive of posture. A person set down might *stand* or *lie*, or *sit;* and, as καθισαντος αυτου expresses a particular posture, namely, that of *sitting*, was *set*, is *set*, or any other form of the verb to *set*, cannot be a correct translation of the terms καθισαντος αυτου.

> "Full in their eyes the dazzling flashes broke,
> And with amaze their troubled senses *stroke*."
> Rowe's *Translation of* Lucan's *Pharsalia*,
> b. vii. l. 237.

There can be no doubt that *stroke* is here used in the sense of struck—that is, *struck their* senses with amaze—an expression which violates sense and grammar. We cannot suppose that the poet means stroke in the sense of *to stroke*, but in the sense of *to strike*. Stroke is, therefore, ambiguous, at the same time that it is ungrammatical. It ought to be *struck*, which would have been somewhat injurious to the rhyme.

These corruptions, arising out of the use of the perfect tense of the verb in the place of the participle, are as "plentiful as leaves in Vallambrose." They are profusely scattered over our literature, and, with various other blunders, show that men of great ability, and great critical attainments in the classics, had never paid a proper attention to the grammatical structure of their mother-tongue. A few out of thousands may be given:—

"But at the close of such a folio as this, *wrote* for their sakes."—*Sterne*.

> "That cracks, as if the axis of the world
> Was *broke*." Blackmore.

> "That no part useless, none misplaced we see,
> None are *forgot*." *Ibid*.

> "Lo! Pan himself, beneath the blasted oak,
> Dejected lies, his pipe in pieces *broke*." Congreve.

"The camp was almost immediately *broke* up."—*Gibbon*.

Milton uses have *spoke*, words *interwove*, have *chose*,

hath *bore*, had *stole*, had *rode*, was *took;* Addison, had *drank*, has *wrote*, was *broke;* Swift, had *rose*, have *stole*, have *mistook;* Bolingbroke, has been *shook;* Atterbury, to be *shook;* Prior, have *fell;* Gray, has *befell;* Bentley, have *wrote*, (though in another place have *written*,) and has *rose*. Atterbury says, have *sprang*, instead of *sprung;* Clarendon, had *spoke*, had *began;* Shakspeare, have *swam*.

Some of our verbs, which terminate alike in the present tense, are extremely arbitrary in the formation of the other tenses and of the participle; as, *spit, spat, spitten; sit, sat, sitten;* yet we say, *fit, fitted, fitted; hit, hit, hit;* as, I *hit* the mark, he *hit* the mark, the mark was *hit*, and he had *hit* the mark. There are a few verbs of this kind which never vary in form, whether in the present or past tense, or in the participle; as, *read, read, read*, in the past tense and participle pronounced *red, red* contracted from *readed; let, let, let; rid, rid, rid; set, set, set; shut, shut, shut; shred, shred, shred; cut, cut, cut; cast, cast, cast; split, split, split.* In the present state of the language, these verbs do not vary, though, in the case of *cast* and *split*, Shakspeare uses *casted* and *splitted;* as,

"And newly mown.
With *casted* slough, and fresh celerity." *Henry V.*

"*Splitted* the heart itself." *Antony and Cleopatra.*

It is probable that the national spirit of verbal contraction has come over such words as these, and cut off the final syllable. He *lighted* the candle, has been pruned down to *lit;* he *lit* the candle, leaving nothing but the bare stem. In all such cases, submission is mercilessly exacted by custom, "penes quem jus et norma loquendi." Few men would now venture to write "it *snewed;*" yet Chaucer says:—

> "It *snewed* in his house of mete and drinke,
> Of all daintees that men could of thinke."
>
> *Canterbury Tales.*

Or, *clomb:*—

> "So *clomb* the first grand thief into his fold."
>
> MILTON, *Paradise Lost,* book iv.

There are, however, no two words in the English language used so vaguely, uncertainly, or so erroneously, as the forms arising out of the commonest of all terms, namely, to *eat* and to *drink*. At the expense of a little repetition, it may, therefore, be necessary to draw attention to the use of these two words.

Eat, ate, eaten; I *eat,* I *ate,* I had *eaten;* the dinner was *eaten; drink, drank, drunk—drunk* being a contraction of the participle *drunken;* I *drink,* I *drank,* I had *drunken,* or *drunk;* the wine was *drunken* or *drunk*—not I had *drank,* or the wine was *drank,* both of which are sheer nonsense. The following passages from the Bible, 1 Kings i. 13, are rich in the *proper* use of the words:—

> "So he went back with him, and did eat bread (or ate bread) and *drunk* water."

Not *drunk* water.

Again:—

> "But camest back, and hast *eaten* bread and *drunk* water."

Again:—

"After he had *eaten* bread, and after he *had drunk*."
"It shall be *eaten* the same day ye offer it."—*Lev.* xix. 6.
"They did *eat*, they *drank*."—*Luke.*

The Bible, with a few exceptions, which may perhaps be admitted as contractions, makes a proper distinction between the past tense of the verb and the participle. In the case of *drunken*, it is now generally contracted to *drunk;* as, the wine was *drunk:* but no man having but the slenderest pretensions to grammatical knowledge would even write or use the expression had *drunk*. Let "*beer* to be *drank on the premises*," be confined to the sign-board, where no man ever looks for a grammatical guide. *Bound* retains its proper form, *bounden,* as our *bounden* duty; and with propriety we still say a drunken beast, though the fastidious delicacy of the age would perhaps denominate him an *intoxicated individual*.

We often hear a confused use of the verb to *swim*. Its form is *swim, swam, swum:* I *swim* over the river, I *swam* over the river, I had *swum* over the river.

The verb *cleave,* to stick to, and *cleave,* to split, are both the same in the present tense, but differ in the past tense and the participle. *Cleave,* to stick to, to adhere, makes *cleave, clave, cleaved:* I *cleave* to him, I *clave* to him, I had *cleaved* to him. *Cleave,* to split, makes *cleave, clove, cloven,* and *cleft:* I *cleave* the wood, I *clove* the wood, I had *cloven* the wood, the wood was *cloven,* or *cleft.*

The verbs *fly* and *flee* are sometimes confounded. *Fly* denotes the act of flying, without reference to a particular cause or object. As, "the eagle *flies* through the air." *Flees* denotes the act of escaping from a threatened danger to a place of refuge. "The pigeon *flees* from the hawk, the pigeon *fled* or *fleed* from the hawk."

Again, *flown* and *flowed* are sometimes confounded. "The birds had *flown* or were *flown*," "the meadows were over*flowed*," not over*flown*, which would mean that birds had *flown* over them, not that water had over*flowed* them.

CHAPTER VI.

THE SUBJUNCTIVE MOOD.

WE now come to the consideration of a part of English grammar, in which we shall look in vain for anything bordering upon a principle, even in authors of the highest authority in English literature, namely, the *use of the subjunctive mood.* It would be folly to suppose that there is not a principle—the question is, how that principle is to be investigated and developed. It is no uncommon thing to find two hypothetical members of a sentence both placed under the same circumstances, yet one of them shall be in the indicative, the other in the subjunctive mood. Throughout a whole work, we shall find these moods used indiscriminately and promiscuously.

"There are few or no English writers who seem to have adhered uniformly to any rule in the use of the verbs after the conjunctions. In consequence either of ignorance or inattention, the most correct writers have *fallen* into inconsistencies even in the same sentence."—*Noah Webster's Dissertation.*

It signifies nothing that this or that expression has been used by Johnson, or Addison, or Swift, or Pope, or any other author whatsoever. All of these, whose names I have mentioned, and innumerable others, have written incorrectly, and their authority will go just so far as it can be supported by grammatical principle, and no farther. The mere *ipse dixit* of any man, in a case of this kind, is not worth a rush. Time and space, tenses and moods, possess principles which bend not before authority. It is not a question of genius and utility, but simply a question of *syntax;* and, as authors of the highest reputation in English literature are, over and over again, inconsistent with themselves, it is impossible that in all cases they can be right, unless a sentence, which is indicative and declarative, can be equally hypothetical and subjunctive, and in many cases unless past, present, and future time should be so accommodating as to be capable of being expressed by the same form of the verb.

We are told that the subjunctive mood is required when a contingency is implied. Now, contingency has respect to that which is *past*, that which is *present*, or that which is to *come*. But with respect to that which is *past*, and that which is *present*, there can be no contingency of *fact*. In both cases, a thing either *has been* or *has not* been; either *is* or *is not*. The contingency exists nowhere but in the mind of the speaker. But when we come to a consideration of a thing that, as yet, *exists not at all*, but which is future, we then have a contingency of *fact* added to the uncertainty of the speaker's mind. In the very nature of things, then, we speak declaratively and indicatively of that which is *past* or *present*, but *hypothetically* of that which is *contingent as a fact*. Let us, then, try this principle by supposed examples, and then by existing examples, as they occur in various authors. "Is Thomas able to repeat his grammar this morning?" "No, he is not, because he *was* ill last night." "If he *was* ill, that is enough." "Has Thomas come to repeat his grammar?" "No, he *has* not, because his head *aches*." "*If* his head *aches*, that is enough." In neither of these cases is there any contingency of the *fact*, and therefore we say if he *was* ill at that time, and if his head *aches* at this time. But, if we pass on to a future time, we then put the case *hypothetically*. As, "Will Thomas come up to repeat his grammar to-morrow?" "Yes, if his head *do* not ache,"—if he *be* better, that is, should it so happen, *should* his head not ache, *should* he be better. "Did you take a walk yesterday?" "No, I did not, because it was wet." "If it *was* wet (not if it *were*) you were better at home." "Will you walk *now?*" "Yes, if it *does* not rain." "If it *rains now*, will you take a walk an hour hence?" "Yes, if in the mean time it *clear* up," that is, *should clear* up, not *clears*, which has reference only to a *present* and now *existing* state. "Do you think that the roads will be dirty this morning?" "Yes, if there *has* been much rain in the night." "Will you ride your horse to town next week?" "Yes, if he *have* (not *has*) recovered of his lameness before that time." "Though he *studied* (past) the work for twelve months, yet he did not make himself master of it. Though he *studies* (present) twelve hours a day, yet he makes little progress. Though he *study* twelve hours, he will not (future) be sufficiently prepared."

" *Were* I Alexander, I would do it. And *were* I Parmenio, I would do it." That is, were the state of things so altered, that I, as Alexander, should become Parmenio, then I would do it. But if in these cases, we substitute *was* in the place of *were*, the meaning of both sentences would be changed, and that subjunctivity, which is their very gist and essence, would cease to exist.

The substance of these observations on the subjunctive mood was written many years ago. Since that time, I have had the good fortune to fall in with Noah Webster's* fourth Dissertation on "The English Language," with introductory remarks by H. J. H.—the subject being the subjunctive mood. Of the numerous examples there given, whether supposed or real, I do not find one to which the above-mentioned principle does not apply, where the distinction of past, present, and future is clear and decided. Everything that is *past* or *present* is a matter of *certainty*, as far as the thing itself is concerned, though it may not be a matter of certainty as far as our *knowledge* is concerned. We speak it therefore declaratively or indicatively. Everything that is future we speak of as a matter subject to some condition, by which it may or may not be affected. In many cases, *shall* and *should* may be prefixed to that

* Mr. Webster is an American.

which has a subjunctive form, when it relates to that which is *future*, but never when it relates to that which is *past* or *present*.

Let us now try how far this consideration will apply to the following examples, given in H. J. H.'s introductory remarks:—

"If I *be* well *next week*, I shall call upon him."
"If he *be* there by *two o'clock*, he will be in time."
"If he *be* ready *when you call*, you shall have it."
"If they *be* unprepared, they will fail in the attempt."

Every one of these suppositions relates to a *future* contingency, and might be expressed by *should be* or *shall be*.

"If it *is* he, I am much mistaken."
"If it *is* raining, you had better not go."
"If I *am* the man you seek, why not confess it?"
"If they *are* guilty, they will be hanged."

Every one of these sentences relates to the *present* time, and is, therefore, expressed declaratively.

"If Cæsar *was* a tyrant, he deserved death."
"If I *was* in your company at A.'s, I have not the slightest recollection of it."
"If his mind *was* uncultivated then, it is far from being so now."
"If they *were* at York when I was, probably I should have seen them."

Every one of these sentences relates to the *past*, and is properly expressed by the indicative mood. If we give an answer to a supposition, which has reference to *present* or *past* time, that answer will be declarative; but not so in the case of a supposition, relating to *future* time. As,

"If Cæsar *was* a tyrant, he deserved death." "Cæsar *was* a tyrant, and therefore he deserved death."

"If it *is* he, I am much mistaken." "It *is* he, and therefore you are much mistaken."

"If I *be* well next week, I shall call upon him." "If you *should be* well, I hope you will call upon him."

H. J. H. then gives the following illustration of what he calls the present tense of the subjunctive hypothetic mood:—

"If I *were* in a situation to defend, I would disdain to flee."
"If he *were* in my situation, he would be unbearable."
"If it *were* not for its opacity, I could see more clearly."
"If they *were* present, you would not speak of them so contemptuously."

But sentences like these, and which, I believe, are confined to the verb *were*, seem to embrace both present and future time. As, "If I were in a situation at this moment to defend, or, should I be placed in a situation to defend."

The expression, being capable of a double combined meaning, with reference to time, *present* and *future*, is peculiar, and cannot be classed simply in the *present* tense. It is the participation of futurity that requires the subjunctive form. Were the meaning strictly confined to the present time, we should say, "If I *am* in a situation to defend, I will disdain to flee." The subjunctive form of the verb carries us on to a future point, at which point we *should* or *would* do this or that. In its present form, we are already at a point when we shall or will. "*Were* I Alexander, I would do it." This implies, in the first place, that I am not Alexander: and, in the second, that *were* my condition, *should* my condition be, so far changed that I *should* stand in the place of Alexander, I *would* do it. Such a sentence as the following, it is true, has reference to *past* time, and yet is put in the subjunctive mood; but then the subjunctive member of the sentence is future with reference to the primary and indicative member of it. "*It was my desire that he should come yesterday.*" The coming being posterior to the desire, and therefore future.

"After an attentive and accurate examination of this subject, I believe I may venture to assert (says Mr. Webster) that nine times out of ten, when the pretended subjunctive form of the verb is used after a conjunction, either in the vulgar translation of the Bible, or in our best profane authors, the sense is *actually future*, and, to render the sentences complete, it would be necessary to insert *shall* or *should.*"— *Webster's Dissertation,* p. 49.

If, in all cases of doubt as to the use of the indicative or the subjunctive mood, we should mentally try whether or not the auxiliary can, with propriety, be placed before the principal verb, we should at once see the principle upon which the form of expression *must* rest. We may go so far as to look upon the auxiliary as a *principal,* and the verb following as a verb in the *infinitive* mood; with the exception of the verb *were,* which is derived from the German *Ich war,* I was, and as a verb is irregular and defective, and does not harmonize with the usual form of an English verb. In the *Anglo-Saxon,* indeed, the verb following the auxiliary was evidently considered to be a verb in the infinitive mood; for this is distinctly marked by the termination *an,* which denoted the infinitive mood of the Anglo-Saxon verb. As, "Nu *wille* ic *faran.*" (*Luke* xiv. 19.) "Now will I go," an infinitive after *will.* "Hu *mæg* se man well *faran?*" "How *may*, or can, the man fare well?" *To fare*, an infinitive after *may.*

The propriety of using the indicative or the subjunctive mood will sometimes be determined by an adjunct of the verbs, which marks the time of an action. As, "*Were* I ever to recover from my lameness, I would make a pedestrian tour." "*Were* he to read hard for *the next six* months, he would probably accomplish his object." Futurity is the very essence of these sentences; and to write *was* in the place of *were* would be a monstrous solecism.

As a clear principle, there can be no contingency of a *fact* apart from *futurity.*

Lindley Murray gives the following phrase as a contingency apart from futurity:—

"If he thinks as he speaks, he may safely be trusted."

But surely the man either thinks as he speaks, or he does not think as he speaks. One way or the other is a matter of *fact*, only I do not know whether or not he speaks as he thinks; but my ignorance cannot alter the existence of a *fact*. Westminster Abbey either exists or it does not exist. If it exists, the ignorance of a Hottentot as to its existence could not affect that existence. The *subjective* contingency arises out of mere mental ignorance or uncertainty as to the existence of a *fact;* but in that which either *exists* or does not *exist, is* or *is not,* there can be no *objective* contingency at all.

The subjunctive mood, then, in English, is not used with

propriety, when we speak of that which is past, or of that which is present, but when the fact itself has not yet taken place, and is necessarily future.

This rule will bear the test of the numerous examples which have already been given, and will equally apply to the use or abuse of this mood in those which follow.

CHAPTER VII.

EXAMPLES OF THE PROPER USE OF THE SUBJUNCTIVE MOOD.

"Even so our eyes wait upon the Lord our God, until he *have* mercy upon us."—*Psalm* cxiii. 2.

The end or purpose of waiting is, that the Lord *may* have mercy upon us; that mercy not being extended to us as yet. If, in this case, we should say *has* mercy upon us, instead of *have* mercy upon us, the meaning would be altered. If *has* be used, the sentence would mean that our eyes are in the *habit* of waiting upon the Lord until he *has mercy upon* us, when they cease to wait upon him; but if *have* be used, then the sentence means, as it does here, that our eyes continue to wait upon the Lord our God *until*, at some future period, he *shall be pleased to have mercy* upon us. The subjunctive mood is here clearly and legitimately required.

"They deck it with silver and with gold, they fasten it with nails and with hammers, that it *move* not."—*Jer.* x. 4.

Here the end or purpose of fastening it is, that it *move*

not. In both these cases, a future end or purpose is in view.

"Men do not despise a thief if he *steal* to satisfy his soul when he is hungry."—*Prov.* vi. 30.

That is, as a general supposition, should a thief steal merely to satisfy hunger, then men do not in such a case despise him. *Steals*, in this case, would imply a habit, and not merely one individual fact.

"If thou *return* at all in peace, the Lord hath not spoken at all by me."—1 *Kings* xxii. 28.

Thy returning in peace will be a proof that the Lord hath not spoken by me. *Shouldst thou* return in peace, a thing not to be expected, then will it be a proof that the Lord hath not spoken by me; *if thou return*, having reference to a future contingency.

"If thou *have* a servant, let him be unto thee as thyself, because thou hast bought him with a price; if thou *have* a servant, entreat him as thy brother, for thou hast need of him as of thine own soul; if thou entreat him evil, and he run from thee, which way wilt thou go to seek him?"—*Eccl.* xxxiii. 30.

If, in this sentence, we read *hast* instead of *have*, the sentence would mean, If thou *hast* a servant at this present moment; but if we read *have*, it means, at whatever time thou mayest have a servant, entreat him "as thy brother." If *thou hast*, &c., would convey a specific precept with reference to a present state of things; *if thou have*, a general precept with reference to a contingent state of things.

"If thou *hast* a hundred pounds at thy present command, pray lend it to me." "If thou *have* a hundred pounds at thy command next January, wilt thou lend it to me?" That is, if thou *shall* have or should have, if *thou* have.

"With whom, if he *come* shortly, I will see you."—*Heb.* v. 8.

If, in a short time, he *should* come, or *shall* come.

"For these mid hours, till evening *rise*,
"I have at will." *Paradise Lost*, book v.

Rise, not rises; for Raphael is speaking of a future event.

"Unanswered, lest thou *boast*." *Paradise Lost*.

That is, lest, not having received an answer, thou shouldst hereafter be led to boast.

"No fear lest dinner *cool*." *Paradise Lost*.

That is, lest it *shall* or should cool.

"Thou shalt stone him with stones, *that* he *die*."—*Deut.* xiii. 10.

The end or purpose of stoning him is, that he *may* die, that he *shall be* stoned to death. They stoned him with stones, till he *was* dead: they had stoned him with stones till he *was* dead: they have stoned him with stones, till he *is* dead. In all these cases, the *end* or *purpose* is accomplished. But in the phrase "thou shalt stone him with stones, till, or that, he die, the end or purpose is yet *to be* accomplished.

"Though he *slay* me, yet will I trust in him."—*Job* xiii. 15.

Though he should proceed beyond all his present inflictions, and even *slay* me, yet will I trust in him. (Future.)

"Though he *were* dead, yet shall he live."

i. e. on the supposition that he should die, yet would he live; very different from *though he was dead*.

"The soul which hath touched any such shall be unclean until even, and shall not eat of the holy things, unless he *wash* his flesh with water."—*Lev.* xxii. 6.

That is, until he shall have washed his flesh, having reference to an act, not past or present, but as yet to be performed.

"That I may testify unto them, lest they also *come* into this place of torment."—*Luke.* xvi. 28.

The end of testifying is, that they may not come into this place of torment, lest they should *come* into this place of torment—*ne veniant*.

"If thy brother *trespass* against thee, rebuke him; and if he repent, forgive him."—*Luke* xvii. 3.

That is, if thy brother shall or should trespass against thee, rebuke him; and if, after this, he *shall* or *should repent*, forgive him.

"If ever he *have* child, abortive be it."
SHAKSPEARE, *Richard III.*

Not *has* child.

"And take heed to yourselves, lest at any time your hearts *be* overcharged with surfeiting."—*Luke* xxi. 34.

The purpose or object of taking heed is, "lest your hearts should, at any future time, be overcharged with surfeiting." In such a case, with a future purpose in view, to say *take heed* lest your hearts *are overcharged*, would be nonsense.

"If thou *seek* him, he will be found of thee; but if thou *forsake* him, he will cast thee off for ever."—1 *Chron.* xxviii. 9.

That is, he will be found of thee, if at any time thou shalt think fit to seek him; if thou *seek*, not seekest; and though the subjunctive mood is here used with propriety by the translators of the Bible, yet, in other cases of precisely similar import, we find the indicative; the translators, in such cases, deviated from the original, and using the indicative or subjunctive mood indiscriminately, and apparently without the slightest consideration.

"Then *shall thou prosper*, if *thou takest* heed to fulfil the statutes and the judgment which the Lord charged Moses with concerning Israel."

If thou *take heed*, then thou shalt prosper; if thou *seek him*, he will be found of thee; upon what principle shall we write *takest* in the one sentence, and *seek* in the other?

> "Beware,
> And govern well thy appetite, lest sin
> *Surprise* thee."   *Paradise Lost*, book vii.

Lest it *should*.

"And they shall pursue thee until thou *perish*."—*Deut.* xxviii. 22.

Not *perishest*. Until the end be accomplished, namely, that thou perish.

"What man of you, having a thousand sheep, if he *lose* one of them." &c.—*Luke* xv. 4.

That is, if he shall have lost one—*si unam perdiderit.*

"Which of you, intending to build a tower, sitteth not down first and counteth the cost, whether he *have* sufficient to finish it?"—*Luke* xiv. 28.

An had eat.

"I give thee charge in the sight of God, *that thou keep* this commandment without spot."—*Tim.* vi. 13.

Expressive of an end or purpose, whereas *that*, signifying a cause, and referring to present or past time, would require the indicative mood. As, I am sorry to hear that he *is* ill. I was sorry to hear that he *was* ill.

"So shall the lord bring upon you all evil things, until he *have* destroyed you," (*i. e.* until he shall have destroyed you.)—*Joshua* xxiii. 15.

Expressive of an object to *accomplish*. And Joshua smote him and his people, until *he had left* him none remaining. Expressive of an object *accomplished*.

CHAPTER VIII.

EXAMPLES OF THE PROPER USE OF THE INDICATIVE MOOD.

"If any of my readers *has* looked with so little attention upon the world around him."—*Adventurer*, No. 69.

Has certainly. The question propounded is, whether or not any of the author's readers has looked with so little attention upon the world around him. The fact is certain, one *way or the other*. There is no end or purpose in view.

"Though every funeral that passes before their eyes *evinces* the deceitfulness of such expectations."

Evinces certainly; that is, *evinces* the deceitfulness of such expectations the moment that it is passing.

"If Mr. Frolic *is* celebrated by other tongues than his own, I shall willingly propagate his praise: but if he *has* swelled among us with empty boasts and honors conferred only by himself, I shall treat him with rustic sincerity, and drive him, as an impostor, from this part of the kingdom to some region of more credulity."—*Rambler*, No. 6.

If he *is* celebrated at this time, and if he *has* (already) swelled, &c. The indicative mood is right in both cases.

"He that gazes upon elegance or pleasure, which want of money hinders him from imitating or partaking, comforts himself that the time of distress will soon be at an end, and that every day brings him nearer to a state of happiness, though he *knows* it has passed, not only without acquisition of advantage, but perhaps without endeavors after it."—*Adventurer*, No. 69.

He gazes at such and such things, comforts himself with such and such notions, at the same time knowing, though he *knows* that, &c. The indicative mood is required.

"If thou *canst* do anything, have compassion on us, and help us."—*Mark* ix. 22.

That is, if thou *canst*, at this moment. *Hast* thou the power to do this thing? if thou *hast* the power, have mercy on us, and save us.

"Thyself, though great and glorious, *dost* thou boast?"
Paradise Lost, book vi.

"Quem si fata virum servant, si rescitur aura
Ætherea." *Æneid*, i. 550.

Virgil here uses the present indicative, because the condition has reference to the present time; for, if the man is not alive now, he cannot be alive hereafter. With the speaker, therefore, it was a *present* condition, there being no contingency of fact. In the enunciation of general principles which, if existing at all, must always exist, though the expression may be conditional, the indicative mood is used with propriety; as, Is there a God? Yes. If, then, there *is* a God, that God, &c. Honesty *is* the best policy. If honesty *is* the best policy, then, &c. Man *is* mortal. If man *is* mortal, then, &c. These principles, if true at all, are true at all times; and the question is not, whether or not they may ultimately be found to be true, but whether or not they are so at this moment, have been so, and ever will be so.

"Will keep your own heart, if silence *is* best;
Though a woman, for once I'll in ignorance rest."
NOAH WEBSTER (*Quotation*).

Of this principle Mr. Webster observes, and justly, that the indicative mood is employed to express conditional ideas more frequently than the subjunctive, even by the best English writers (p. 43). And again, "When affirmation respects *present* time, the indicative form is the most correct, and the only form which corresponds with the actual present state of the language" (p. 45).

CHAPTER IX.

IMPROPER AND CONFUSED USE OF THE INDICATIVE AND SUBJUNCTIVE MOODS.

"IF a man *was* to compare the effect of a single stroke of a pickaxe, or of one impression of a spade, with the general design and last result, he would be overwhelmed with a sense of their disproportion."—*Rambler*, No. 43.

Were, not *was*. If any man should compare, &c. If a man *were* to compare; otherwise, we shall have a verb of the indicative mood past imperfect tense, with conditional and future signification. Let any one try to translate the phrase as it stands into another language, and the error will stand out glaring and palpable.

"But if it *be* true, which was said by a French prince, that no man *was* a hero to the servants of his chamber, it is equally true that every man is less a hero to himself."—*Johnson*.

If it *is* true; that is, if, as a *general* maxim, it *is* true, that no man *is* a hero to the servants of his chamber; not *was* a hero. The French prince lays down a principle, namely, that no man *is* a hero to the servants of his own chamber. *Was* refers to a past time, and cannot convey a general principle. *Be* and *was* are both wrong.

"Two young men have made a discovery, that there *was* a God."—*Swift, Argument against Abolition of Christianity*.

We naturally ask, at what time was there a God? does

a God continue to exist now, and will he exist hereafter? The phrase unquestionably ought to be *is* a God, the simple enunciation of an eternal principle. They have made a discovery, that there *is* a God. That there *was* a God! When? Last year?

"If the leg *does* not come off take the turkey to yourself."

"Madam," replied the man in black, "I don't care a farthing whether the leg or the wing *comes* off."—*Goldsmith*.

Do and *come;* for the parties are disputing upon the *result* of the lady's carving, and not upon the actual state of the turkey.

"If nobody within either *moves* or *speaks*, it is not unlikely that they may carry the place by storm; but if a panic should seize them, it will be proper to defer the enterprise to a more hungry hour."—*Idler*, No. 8.

If no person within either *move* or *speak;* not *moves* or *speaks;* for the author is speaking, not of anything present, but of what may happen, namely, that some one within may either move or speak, and cause a panic. *Should* no one either *move* or *speak*, then perhaps they may carry the place by storm; but, should any one *move* or *speak*, and on this account a panic *should seize* them, then it will be proper to defer the attack to a more hungry hour. The author himself says, in the second member of the sentence, but if a panic *should* seize them, not *seizes* them.

"If the hair *has* lost its powder, a lady has a puff; if a coat *be* spotted, a lady has a brush." *Idler*, No. 6.

Here we have *has* in one member of the sentence, and *be* in the other; the one indicative, the other subjunctive; the author being again inconsistent with himself. It is easy to give a future form to the sentence: "If the hair shall at any time *have* lost its powder, a lady has a puff; if a coat *shall* at any time be spotted, a lady has a brush."

"If similitude of manners *be* a motive to kindness, the Idler may flatter himself with universal patronage."—*Idler*, No. 1.

Is a motive to kindness. The author is speaking of a principle, which, if true now, was equally so a thousand years ago, and will be so a thousand years hence, and which simply either *is* or *is not;* and these general propositions, as it has already been shown in a former chapter, are properly expressed in the indicative present.

"If there *be* but one body of legislators, it is no better than a tyranny; if there *are* only two, there will want a casting vote."—*Spectator*, No. 287.

Inconsistent.

"And when the tempter came to him, he said, If thou *be* the Son of God, command that these stones be made bread."—*Matt.* iv. 3.

In the Latin and Greek of these passages, we find *ei* and *es*, both indicative, and properly so.

"If thou *be* the Son of God, come down from the cross."—*Matt.* xxvii. 40.

Again, *be*, in the Latin and Greek, is in the indicative mood, and ought to be so here.

"Now if Christ *be* preached, that he rose from the dead, how say some among you that there is no resurrection of the dead? But if there *be* no resurrection of the dead, then is Christ not risen. And if Christ be not risen, then is our preaching vain, and your faith is also vain."—1 Cor. xv. 12.

In all these cases, the translators have unnecessarily deviated from the original, and substituted the subjunctive for the indicative mood. The question was, not whether Christ should or should not be preached that he rose from the dead, but whether or not, at the time St. Paul speaks, he *is* or *is not* preached that he rose from the dead.

"For he must reign, till he *hath* put all enemies under his feet."—1 Cor. xv. 25.

Till he *shall* have put all enemies under his feet—*subjecit*. Till he *have*. *Till* carries us forward to a *future* time; *hath* fixes us down to the present.

"If thou *bring* thy gift to the altar, and there *rememberest*," &c. Matt. v. 23.

Here is a subjunctive and an indicative mood in one and the same sentence, and under precisely the same conditions. *If thou bring* required to be followed by *if thou remember*.

"And he said unto them, If they hear not Moses and the prophets, neither will they be persuaded, though one *rose* from the dead." Luke xvi. 31.

Though one *rise* from the dead. Though one *rose* means, though one did rise at some *former* period. Though one *rise*, that is, though one *should* rise is the meaning required, and also conveyed by the original.

"Nay, father Abraham, but if one *went* unto them from the dead, they will repent."—Luke xvi. 29.

That is, if one *went at a future time*, which is intense nonsense.

In these cases, with a clear and obvious principle before them, and with the guidance of the Latin and the Greek, as also in many other similar cases, we ask what could induce the translators of the Bible to be so frequently inconsistent with themselves? The answer is, that the English language had not then, nor has it yet, received that attention which is required.

"No one can thoroughly understand the Scriptures of the New Testament, unless *he be* well acquainted with those of the Old. No one can entirely comprehend the more perfect system of Christ, unless *he sees* it prefigured in the more imperfect system of Moses."—*Rennel, Sermon* 24.

Here we have unless *he be, subjunctive,* followed by unless *he sees, indicative.* No one can thoroughly understand the Scriptures of the New Testament, unless at the time he is endeavoring to understand them, *he is* well acquainted with those of the Old. No one can comprehend the more perfect system of Christ, unless *he sees* it at the time prefigured in the more imperfect system of Moses. In other respects, the sentence is bad; we have *more perfect* contrasted with *more imperfect;* and though perhaps degrees of perfection may be allowed, yet there is an incongruity between an ascending and a descending comparative. We expect more perfect and less perfect, not *more perfect* and *more imperfect.*

"So that, while to law we would commit the defence of society from all the aggressions of violence, and confide the strict and the stern guardianship of the interests of justice, we should tremble for humanity, lest it *withered* and *expired* under the grasp of so rough a protector; and lest, before a countenance grave as that of a judge, and grim as that of a messenger-at-arms, this frail but loveliest of the virtues, *should be* turned, as if by the head of Medusa, into stone."—*Chalmers, Bridgewater Treatise.*

Lest it *should* wither, and expire; and the author, in the next member of the sentence, says, lest this frail but loveliest of the virtues *should be* turned, being obviously inconsistent with himself.

"So he took the opportunity of declaring certain truths, which she might ponder in her heart till she *was* able to comprehend them more fully."—*Sermon,* " *Christ the Resurrection and the Life.*"

Should be able. I might with propriety say, she pondered in her heart certain truths till *she was* able, &c., because here would be an object accomplished; but in the case before us the object is future: "So he took the opportunity of declaring certain truths, which she might ponder in her heart," till she *should* be able to comprehend them more fully.

"Whether our conduct *be* inspected, and we *are* under a righteous government, or under no government at all."—*Priestley, Letter to a Philosophical Unbeliever:* quoted by Webster.

Inconsistent.

"Though *thou be* long in the first part of the verse."—*Sheridan, Art of Reading.*

"And though it *is* impossible to prolong the sound of this word."—*Ibid.*

Sheridan is here evidently inconsistent with himself.

"If any member *absents* himself, he shall forfeit a penny for the use of the club, unless in case of sickness and imprisonment." *Spectator.*

If any member *absent* himself, that is, shall absent himself, for the sentence has reference to a future and supposed violation of certain rules.

"Saxony was left defenceless, and if it *was* conquered, might be plundered," &c.—*Johnson, Life of the King of Prussia.*

Were conquered. The power of plundering Saxony depended upon the condition of its being conquered, which at the time it was not. The subjoined condition of plundering Saxony was its previous conquest. The sentence ought to be, "Saxony was left defenceless, and if it *were* conquered (should it be conquered), might be plundered."

CHAPTER X.

PROMISCUOUS ERRORS IN THE USE OF THE VERB.

"O God of my fathers, and Lord of mercy, who *hast* made all things with thy word, and *ordained* man through thy wisdom, that he should have dominion over the creatures which thou hast made."—*Wisdom of Solomon* ix. 1.

If *ordained* is here used simply without the repetition of the auxiliary *hast*, it ought to be *ordainedst*, that is, *didst* ordain, &c.

"Perhaps, lone wretch, unfriended and alone,
In hovel vile thou *gav'st* thy final moan,
Clos'd the blear'd eye ordain'd no more to weep,
And *sunk*—unheeded *sunk*—in death's long sleep."
Quotation in the History of Suffolk.

Gav'st is right in the second person, and *clos'd* wrong

in the third. *Sunk* in each place ought to be sank'st. *Sunk* is doubly wrong; the participle is used in the place of the verb; and the third person engrafted on it, in the place of the second.

These four lines comprehend *three* errors; *four*, including the repetition of *sunk*.

The following errors of a similar kind have also been noticed in Pope:

"Thou great First Cause, least understood,
Who all my sense *confin'd*;
To know but this, that thou art good,
And that myself am blind:

Yet *gave* me in this dark estate
To see the good from ill;
And binding nature fast to fate,
Left free the human will."

The relative *who*, being of the same person as the antecedent *thou*, of course requires this sequence of verbs *confined*, *gave*, and *left*, to be of the second person.

Again:—

"O *Thou*, my voice inspire,
Who *touch'd* Isaiah's hallow'd lips with fire." *Messiah*.

"If there arise a prophet among you, or a dreamer of dreams, and *giveth* thee a sign or a wonder."—*Deut.* xviii. 1.

Giveth is here altogether inconsistent with the preceding member of the sentence, and the pronoun *he* ought to be placed before the latter verb. As, if there arise among you a prophet or a dreamer of dreams, and (if) *he* give (that is, should he give) you a sign or a wonder, &c. Nothing can justify the sentence as it stands.

"Have we, during the last year, done the proportion of *work towards working* out our own salvation, *which,* suppose *we were* certain of the term of our life, *would be* the proper quantity in that time."—*Sermon, Eminent Divine.*

No one can read this sentence without being shocked by its hideous cacophony, independent of any other consideration. Such sounds and such a construction would have carried death into an Athenian mob. *Work, wards, working,* in an unmixed and unredeemed sequence, soon to be followed by *which, we, were, would,* might be very suitably set to that peculiar kind of village music which occasionally serenades some "lord of the creation" who may have been detected in asserting his prerogative by force of arms over his weaker half. The terms are

"Like hedgehogs, which
Lie tumbling in my barefoot way, and mount
Their pricks up at my footfall." SHAKSPEARE.

A sentence may be constructed with harsh and rugged terms by design, when the object of the writer is to make the sound accord with the sense. Thus, when Pope describes Sisyphus struggling to roll the huge stone to the top of the hill, the terms are so appropriately chosen, that we seem to hear his giant sobbings, and pantings, and groanings, in the performance of his laborious task.

"Up the *high hill he heaves a huge* round stone."

Five aspirates or breathers, four of them in immediate sequence, followed by a heavy spondee at the end of the line, give all that can be desired for fidelity of description. Deformity becomes a beauty, because intensely characteristic:—

Virgil makes thunder speak in tones which cannot be misunderstood:—

"*Iterum atque iterum fragor* intonat ingens."

The change, indeed, of a single word, the abstraction or addition of a single syllable, will sometimes mar the harmony of a well-balanced sentence.

"From every ship an island was seen, about two leagues to the north, whose flat and *verdant* fields, well stored with wood and watered with many rivulets, presented the aspect of a delightful country."—*Robertson.*

As Lord Brougham has well observed, change *verdant* into *green*, and the harmony of the passage is destroyed.

In the passage, however, from an "Eminent Divine," the nature of the subject affords no palliation for its rugged and uncouth construction. But what is meant by *in that time? The term of life* immediately preceding dwells upon the mind, and connects itself with the phrase *in that time.* But probably *in that time* refers to the last year, a reference which is by no means clear. Then again that which was a *proportion* becomes a *quantity;* and again *were* ought to have been *had been;* and *would be, would have been.*

"The right of man to the means of existence, on the sole ground that he exists, has been vehemently and loudly asserted; yet is a factitious sentiment, notwithstanding."—*Chalmers, Bridgewater Treatise.*

Yet *is it;* not, *yet i*.

"The worship and service of the glorified spirits in heaven *is* not represented to us as a cold intellectual investigation, but as the worship and service of gratitude and love."—*Wilberforce's Practical View.*

"Worship and service" *are,* not *is,* not.*

"From the same position he may turn his eye to the left of Goat Island, on the American side, and witness a still more lofty cataract, but more modest; not yet presuming to assert *such* profound pretensions, descending in a silvery sheet, as if from an artificial shelf, connecting the island with the shore, and dashing on the rocks below, *displays* a vast bed of fleecy whiteness, like a storm of the thickest and purest snow, reflected by the sun."—*Colton.*

The noun *cataract* is in the objective case, and all the participles and adjectives connected with it. We cannot, therefore, have the verb *displays* standing here without any nominative case. The author evidently gets confused, and sinks under the magnitude of his subject. "And dashing on the rocks below, *it* (the cataract) displays a vast bed of fleecy whiteness."

"Diodorus, whose design was to refer all occurrences to years, is of more credit, on a point of chronology, than Plutarch, or any other that *write* lives by the lump."—*Bentley, Dissertation on Themistocles' Epistles. Lowth.*

Any *other that writes,* or any *others that write.*

"Let us consider how many things we formerly knew, but now have either wholly forgotten, or but very imperfectly *remembered* for want of use."—*Rennel, Sermon 25.*

It may be said with propriety, that we have now

---

* Had the author a principle in view here? or is this an accidental error overlooked? See the question discussed under *Noun.*

at this present time, either wholly forgotten a thing, or but imperfectly *remember* it, but not *remembered,* for we are here speaking of the degree of present recollection, not of past.

> "In endless error hurl'd." POPE.
>
> "'Tis these that early taint the female soul." *Ibid.*

Hurl'd in error does not seem a very appropriate expression, whilst *'Tis these* (though perhaps the expression may be supported by other authorities) is, after all, a grammatical discord.

> "A single glance at his own engraving of this beautiful head, at the symmetrical and elegant formation of the whole fabric, the nice correspondence and adjustment of all (its) parts, the perfect harmony between the cranium and (the) face and in all the details of each, *demonstrate* most unequivocally, that it is a natural formation, and a very fine work of nature too."—*Lawrence's Lectures.*

The author is here confounded by a multiplicity of images, and seems to forget that a single glance at all these *demonstrates*—not *demonstrate;* besides, the beauty or the symmetry of an object is not demonstrated by a glance; the demonstration is inherent in the object itself. The truth of a mathematical proposition appeals to the reason of man, but it is not demonstrated by that reason. It is true, or false, in itself. The sight is the instrument by which we perceive beauty in an object, but it does not demonstrate it. Again, we expect all *its* parts, and not *all parts,* which is general instead of being particular; and in the phrase "the perfect harmony between the cranium and face," we expect *the* face, and not face only, because they are distinct and separate objects.

"Wherefore *kick* ye at my sacrifice, and at mine offerings, which I have commanded in my habitation, and *honorest* thy sons above me, to make *yourselves* fat with the chiefest of all the offerings of Israel, my people."—1 *Samuel* ii. 29.

There is, in this sentence, a strange confusion of persons, and an extraordinary abruptness of transition.

> "Its tufted flowers and leafy bands
> In one continuous curve *expands*,
> When herb or flowret rarely *smile*."
> *Glastonbury Abbey, A Poem.*

Here are two errors in three lines.

> "Tufted flowers and leafy bands
> In one continuous curve *expand*"—not *expands*.

Then herb *or* flowret being disjoined, the verb *smile* must be *smiles*.

> "The unwieldy elephant,
> To make them mirth, used all his might, and *wreathed*
> His lithe proboscis."   *Paradise Lost,* book iv.

Writhed would surely be more appropriate than *wreathed*.

"And the King said, If he be alone, there *is* tidings in his mouth."—2 *Sam.* xvii. 25.

Perhaps *is* may in this case be admissible, the word tidings being used in the plural form only, and may be considered as collective information. We say, what *is* the *news? Is* there any news?

"There is nothing on the part of God *to refuse* this victory to you, nothing in yourselves to make you incapable of enjoying the blessing."—*Sermon.*

The dependence which the infinitive mood *to refuse*

has upon the preceding part of the sentence is much too slight; the same may be said of *to make*. The meaning seems to be, there is nothing on the part of God which would induce him to refuse this victory to you. There is no reason, on the part of God, why he should refuse, &c.

"And Leah also with her children came near, and bowed *themselves;* and after came Joseph near and Rachel, and they bowed themselves."—*Gen.* xxxiii. 7.

The word *children* being in the objective case, cannot form a second nominative case, in conjunction with Leah, and therefore grammatically the verb *bowed* has but one nominative case, and that in the singular number. The pronoun *they* ought, therefore, to have been introduced before *bowed.* "And Leah also with her children came near, and they bowed themselves; and after came Joseph and Rachel near, and they bowed themselves."

"And Peter, fastening his eyes upon him with John, *said,* Look on us."—*Acts* iii. 4.

The verb *said*, in English, may be either singular or plural, and therefore leaves an important principle untouched, namely, whether a nominative case of the singular number, followed by another noun in the objective case, connected with it by the preposition *with*, and not by the copulative conjunction *and,* may be followed by a verb of the plural number; that is, whether the *virtual* meaning of a sentence shall supersede its *syntactical* principle. A variety of examples may be produced, on both sides of the question; so that, as far as authority goes, the matter cannot be decided.

In the case before us, the Greek has εἶπε, and the Latin, *dixit*, both in favor of syntactical rule.

"But a certain man named Ananias, with Sapphira his wife, *sold* a possession."—*Acts* v. 1.

Again: in English, *sold* may be either singular or plural: but both in the Latin and Greek the *equivalent* of *sold* is of the singular number, again in favor of the rules of syntax.

"Then went the captain, with the officers, and *brought* them without violence."—*Acts* v. 26.

Brought is again doubtful as to number; but in the Latin and Greek the verb again is singular.

Xenophon says, 'Ἐμβαλὼν σὺν τοῖς ἑξακοσίοις νικᾷ.

All these examples are in favor of syntax.

We now come to examples favoring the other side of the question.

"Cleander, with six hundred soldiers whom he had employed, *were* publicly executed."—*Goldsmith's History of Greece*, c. 14.

Here we get at the grammatical intention of the author in the verb *were*. If the sentence had run, Cleander *and* six hundred soldiers whom he employed were publicly executed, the expression would have been clear and grammatical, and the verb *were* would have been right. Grammatically, *were* is wrong. The question is, can it be admitted on the ground of the *virtual* meaning of the sentence? The authority of Goldsmith in grammar amounts to nothing, and ought not to enter into the question.

On the other hand, however, there are classical authorities in favor of this mode of expression; as,—

"Dum equites præliantur, Brutus cum peditibus, quos filius ejus adduxerat, neque in priore pugnâ adfuerant, postremam Romanorum aciem *incadunt.*"—*Sallust.*

"Syrus cum illo vestro *susurrant.*"—
TERENT. *Haut.* 3. 1. 64.

"Ilia cum Niso de Numitore *sati.*" OVID.

"Remo cum fratre Quirinus
Jura *dabunt.*" VIRGIL. *Æn.* i. 296.

"On the morrow when Agrippa *was* come, and Bernice, with great pomp."—*Acts* xxv. 23.

That is, when Agrippa was come, and Bernice was come. So far right; but, when it is added, "and was entered into the place of hearing," &c., the sentence is faulty. In the former member of the sentence, the terms are spoken of separately, and have separate verbs, in the one case expressed, in the other understood. In the second member of the sentence, they are spoken of in common, and have one verb in common, and therefore we expect *and they were,* not *was.* The English translation in this point deviates both from the Latin and the Greek:—

"Postero igitur die cùm venisset Agrippa, et Bernice, cum multâ ostentatione, et *introissent.*"

The Greek maintains the same principle, though under a different form:—

Τῇ οὖν ἐπαύριον ἐλθόντος τοῦ Ἀγρίππα, καὶ τῆς Βερνίκης, μετὰ πολλῆς φαντασίας, καὶ εἰσελθόντων.

Christ beheld by Faith. The title of a published sermon. This is an unfortunate title; for the grammatical and legitimate meaning of *beheld* is *saw,* not *seen.*

Christ *beheld*, or *saw*, something by faith. But the meaning intended is, Christ *seen* or *beholden*, by faith. *Beheld* is the imperfect past tense of the verb, grammatically and legitimately. *Beheld* is sometimes used as a participle; but when so used is wrong nevertheless, and most certainly ought not to be used when by such use *ambiguity* is occasioned, and the balance of propriety decidedly against it. "Christ *seen* by Faith" would have answered every purpose, and "Christ *beholden* by Faith," would have been in accordance with Scriptural phraseology, at the same time that an ambiguous use of the term *beheld* would have been avoided.

Contraction of the Verb and Participle.

In the Scriptures, words ending in *ed*, whether verbs or participles, seem to have been, as a general rule, pronounced distinctly, so that the termination *ed*, formed a separate syllable. We still find this pronunciation among our peasantry; and the parish clerks of country churches, perhaps without an exception, continue to give full force to the final syllable of verbs and participles ending in *ed*. It is amongst these that we must trace the tenacity of custom, and judge of that which has been from that which is. In the Psalms, in particular, and in the rhythmical parts of Scripture, the retention of *ed*, as a distinct syllable, is often imperatively demanded. We find, however, that, in the present age, even in the reading of Scripture and the liturgy, no regular principle is observed, and every minister seems to follow the bent of his own inclination; so that one man reads the following testing passage with the abbreviation of ed into d, whilst another reads it with the distinct enunciation of the final syllable:—

"Brethren, I declare unto you the Gospel which I preach-ed unto you, which also ye have receiv-ed, and wherein ye stand; by which also ye are sav-ed, if ye keep in memory what I preach-ed unto you, unless ye have believ-ed in vain. For I deliver-ed unto you first of all that which I also receiv-ed."—1 Cor. xv. 1.

It seems, however, but right that Scripture should be read in the same way in which it was read at the time when the translation was made. Every sentence is, or ought to be, constructed with due regard to harmonious proportion; and the curtailment of a verb, or a participle, of its final syllable will often as effectually mar this object, as it would do were we to contract the dissyllables of Chaucer and Spenser into monosyllables. If we preserve the style of Scripture and its antique phraseology, why should we adapt to it the tripping enunciation of modern times?

When we leave the field of Scripture, modern usage has sanctioned the fusion of the final syllable of certain verbs and participles with the preceding consonant, more particularly when ed is preceded by a liquid, or with z or v, for the sound of these two letters is continuous, and glides with facility into the following ed. The contraction of ed is, of course, formed by the elision of e, leaving d and not t remaining. Custom has sanctioned the contraction of a few words from ed into t, as feel felt, smell smelt; and in some of these words there is no violation of euphony; but it must be borne in mind, that this usage is by no means applicable to our verbs and participles generally; for to admit *t* in the place of *d* is not a *contraction* simply, but a *substitution*. It violates the grammatical analysis of the term, and, where it has not euphony to recommend it, becomes a barbarous deformity. The sound of *t*, compared with that of *d*, is harsh, wiry, and curt, and when preceded by a mute, grates like a crushed pebble in the machinery of articulation. In verbs or participles in which *d* coalesces with ease, *t* is often altogether abhorrent; we can say *spurn'd*, and *kill'd*, and *climb'd*, and *prov'd*, and *remov'd*, and *graz'd;* but we indistinctly shrink from *spurnt*, and *kilt*, and *climbt*, and *provt*, and *removt*, and *grazt*. He must be a bold man, or else a vain man, who on his own authority, presumes to introduce such mutilated cripples as these upon his pages. Yet, in six pages forming the preface to "Guesses at Truth," third edition, we find the following terms: *distinguisht, furnisht, reacht, increast, lookt, affixt, nourisht, developt, fixt,* followed by specimens of a similar kind in the body of the work. Words like these are sufficient to justify the description of Byron already quoted, where he stigmatizes the English language as

"Our harsh, northern, whistling, grunting, guttural,
Which we're obliged to hiss, and spit, and sputter all."

In justice to the English language, it must, however, be observed, that these words are not English, and that it would be equally just to exhibit, as a fair specimen of the English population, some unsightly creature

"Curtailed of his fair proportion,
Cheated of feature by dissembling nature,
Deform'd unfinish'd,"   SHAKSPEARE.

as to parade these gurglings, and hissings, and snappings, as average examples of the structure of our verbs and participles. "Guesses at Truth" is an interesting work, and a successful one, and it needed not these adventitious mutilations to attract attention. Few animals, indeed, can be improved by lopping off their natural elongations, and substituting a short, impertinent-looking tail.

Are we doomed to admit into the English language such terms as *quackt, stackt, awakt, nakt, digt, fagt,* &c.? Should some reckless innovator attempt it, may we have the satisfaction of writing over him,

> "He with his horrid crew
> Lay vanquished!"   Milton.

SECTION VII.

THE PARTICIPLE.

CHAPTER I.

ITS CHARACTER.

EVERY complete verb is expressive of an *attribute*, of *time*, and of an *assertion*. Now, if we deprive the verb of its vitality, that is, of assertion, there will still remain the attribute, and the time or tense. The part of speech which expresses an attribute and time is called a *participle* or participator, inasmuch as it partakes of a verb in marking time, and of an adjective in expressing an attribute. The English participle is subject to inflexion with reference to time, and also varies in its active from its passive condition: as, *loving, about to love, loved, about to be loved;* but it undergoes no inflexion, or change in *number, case* or *gender*. *Loving*, as a participle, never varies. The same may be said of *about to love, loved, about to be loved*. We are not, however, on this account to suppose that our participles have neither number, case, nor gender. The same form of the word serves under intellectual distinctions, just as *amans*, loving, is either masculine, feminine, or neuter. At the same time, ambiguity can seldom happen from this cause, since the juxtaposition of the participle to the noun, of which it expresses an attribute, is sufficient to form an inseparable connection between the two. There is, therefore, not much room for error in the use of the participle.

The language is not answerable for any ambiguity that may arise from the misplacing of a participle: as in the following examples:—

"And all the people followed him *trembling.*"—1 *Sam.* xiii. 7.

The term *trembling* referring to the people, and not to *him* (Saul), is misplaced: "And all the people *trembling* followed him."

"Thy *father* and I have sought thee *sorrowing.*"—*Luke* ii. 48.

The participle *sorrowing* may agree either with the terms *father and I*, or with the term *thee.* "Thy *father* and I, *sorrowing*, have sought thee." The sentence so constructed would not, however, read so well as under its present form.

CHAPTER II.

VERB IN THE PLACE OF THE PARTICIPLE.

In speaking of the participle, I feel it necessary again to revert to the confusion that exists in many of our authors, with respect to the use of the past tense of the verb in the place of the participle. To use the words of Harris:—

"It would be well if all writers, who endeavor to be accurate, would endeavor to avoid a corruption, at present so prevalent, of saying it *was wrote*, for it *was written*; he was *drove*, for he was *driven*; I have *went*, for I have *gone*; in all which instances, a verb is absurdly used to supply the proper participle, without any necessity from the want of such word." *Hermes*, c. ix

OF THE PARTICIPLE. 331

A great deal of mischief has arisen in this respect from versifiers, who find the past tense of the verb more convenient as a rhyme, than the participial termination, and sometimes, having neither scruples of conscience nor knowledge of grammar, do not hesitate to adopt a sound which suits their present purpose. What a godsend is *hid* in the place of *hidden*, in the following lines from "The Golden Grove:—

> "That vertue which in happie state
> Is darke unknowen, and *hid*,
> Appeares, and shews itself more bright
> Adversitie *amid*."

Milton, in this respect, is frequently inconsistent with himself, using the past tense of the verb in the place of the participle or not, just as it happened to suit the metrical arrangement of his verse. He says rightly—

> "The roof
> Of thickest covert was *inwoven* shade,
> Laurel and myrtle." *Paradise Lost,* book iv.

Not so in the following:—

> "And to the ground
> With solemn adoration, down they cast
> Their crowns, *inwove* with amaranth and gold."
> *Ibid.* book iii.

> "At last
> Words *interwove* with sighs found out their way."
> *Ibid.* book i.

> "To be avenged
> On him who had *stole* Jove's authentic fire,
> Too divine to be *mistook*." *Ibid.*

"And the widows of Ashur were loud in their wail,
And the idols are *broke* in the temple of Baal,
And the might of the Gentile, *unsmote* by the sword,
Hath melted like snow in the glance of the Lord."

      Byron, *Destruction of Sennacherib.*

To put this corruption in its full aspect of deformity, let us take a series of irregular verbs, and use the past tense of the verb instead of the participle.

Present.		Imperfect.		Participle.
Bear,	*To bring forth.*			
	The child was	bare,	instead of	born.
	The wind had	blew,	"	blown.
	They had	chose,	"	chosen.
Cleave,	*To adhere,*			
	They had	clave,	"	cleaved.
Cleave,	*To split,*			
	They had	clove,	"	cloven.
	The wood was	clove,	"	cloven.
	The cock had	crew,	"	crowed.
	The bird was	flew,	"	flown.
	The money was	gave,	"	given.
	The people were	went,	"	gone.
	The tree was	grew,	"	grown.
	The tree was	hewed,	"	hewn.
	The lesson was	knew,	"	known.
	The man was	saw,	"	seen.
	The men were	slew,	"	slain.
	The stone was	threw,	"	thrown.

Glaring and hideous as these examples are, they are grammatically in the very same condition as a thousand others, which might be produced from every grade of English literature. They are on a par exactly with the "*unsmote* Gentile" and the "idols are *broke*" of Byron, and the "too divine to be *mistook*" and "words *interwove* with sighs," of Milton, &c. &c. &c. Many examples of this kind are given under the head of the verb, and form an anomaly not to be found, one would hope, in the language of any other civilized people on earth.

CHAPTER III.

PROPER USE OF THE PARTICIPLE.

It is gratifying to turn from these ungrammatical medleys to any passage in which the participle is not displaced, but gracefully woven into the texture of the verse, as in the following passage:—

"But let us leave Queen Mab awhile,
Through many a gate, o'er many a stile,
That now had *gotten* by his wile
    Her dear Pigwiggen kissing;
And tell how Oberon did fare,
Who grew as mad as any hare,
When he had sought each place with care,
    And found his Queen was missing."
Drayton's Nymphidia.

"Grease that's *swealen*
From the murderer's gibbet."   Shakspeare.

"At mortal battailes had he been fifteen,
And *foughten* for our faith at Tramissene."
Chaucer's Canterbury Tales.

"On the *foughten* field."   Milton.

> "The barren ground was full of wicked weeds,
> Which she herself had *sowen* all about,
> Now *growen* great of little seeds." — SPENSER.

"For he hath *broken* the gates of brass and *smitten* the bars in sunder."

Who could tolerate *broke* and *smote*, in the place of *broken* and *smitten?*

> "His countenance meanwhile
> Was *hidden* from my view, and he remained
> Unrecognized; but, *stricken* by the sight,
> With slacken'd footsteps I advanced." — WORDSWORTH'S *Wanderer.*

> "The bold youth,
> Of soul impetuous, and the bashful maid,
> *Smitten* while all the promises of Life
> Are opening round her." — *Ibid.*

Grammatically speaking, Wordsworth is perhaps the purest of English poets.

CHAPTER IV.

CONFUSION OF NOUNS AND PARTICIPLES.

WHENEVER a participle takes an article, it becomes virtually and grammatically a *noun*, and is subject to precisely the same regimen.

"Almighty God, by whose providence thy servant John Baptist was wonderfully borne, and sent to prepare the way of thy Son our Saviour by preaching *of* repentance." — *Collect.*

In the first place, why not *the* Baptist, in accordance

with the terms of Scripture ὁ βαπτιστης? Then the omission of the article *the* before *preaching* throws the sentence out of grammatical order, and changes its meaning. *The preaching* of repentance, *preaching* being under such construction a noun, would have rendered the passage clear and correct. As it stands, it is wrong in grammar, and wrong in sense. A man may preach *of* repentance without preaching repentance; but the object of John was to preach repentance, and enforce it, and not to preach *of* or *concerning* repentance, which preaching might be against repentance, and not in favor of it. In this passage, the error of confounding the noun and the participle is striking and obvious.

As in this sentence an error arises from the introduction of the particle *of*, so the following passage is ungrammatical from the want of it:—

"Since I have intimated that the greatest decorum is to be preserved, in the *bestowing* our good offices."—*Spectator*, No. 292.

Here we must either have "in the bestowing *of* our good offices," or "in *bestowing our* good offices; in the first case *bestowing* being a noun, in the second a participle, with an active transitive signification.

"But he had another errand in Persia than buying *of* slaves."—Bentley.

This sentence is liable to the same objection. Ought to be "than *the* buying *of* slaves."

"And when they saw the chief captain and the soldiers, they left beating *of* Paul."—*Acts* xxi. 35.

The phrase "left *beating of Paul*" savors strongly of

the nursery, and is totally unjustifiable, at any period of the English language.

CHAPTER V.

PREFIX BEFORE THE PARTICIPLE.

Such phrases as "I am a-coming," "he goes a-begging," frequently occur both in conversation and print; and, though an educated person would not say "I am a-coming," but "I am coming," yet the same person would not scruple to say, "he goes a-begging;" such is the authority of custom. In matters of euphony, we might often take a lesson from our own domestics; and, supposing *a* in such case to be a prefix, and not a preposition abbreviated in the grammatical sense of a preposition, *a* coming is in many instances, as a matter of articulation, far preferable to *coming*. In *am coming*, the collision between *m* and *c* is anything but agreeable, the first being close, the latter open. There is none of that imperceptible gliding from one letter to another so grateful to the musical ear of the Greek and the Roman. The sensation is that of being *stumped*, as the American would appropriately describe it. The introduction of *a* between *m* and *c* renders the pronunciation easy and flowing. Considered as a prefix, the question of grammar would not be affected by it. Some expressions of this kind, as *a*-begging, *a*-fishing, &c., have established themselves in the English language, and are therefore deserving of our attention.

The phrases just alluded to are by some interpreted as *at* coming, *at* begging. At other times, however, *on*, rather than *at*, is required, and even expressed; and this prefix *a* has on the whole a very general and a very loose application. Again, it is not unusual to find *a* used in a similar manner, where *on* seems to be required.

"It would be pretty hard to believe that he would send *a*-begging to Sicily."—*Bentley.*

That is, for the purpose of begging—*on* begging.

Again:—

"Yet the same man here, in his great wisdom, would have a learned university make barbarism *a*-purpose" (i. e. *on* purpose). —*Bentley, Dissertation on Phalaris.*

"They take coach, which costs them ninepence, or they go *a*-foot, which costs them nothing" (*on* foot).—*Goldsmith, Citizen of the World.*

"The depths *a*-trembling fell."   HOPKINS.

"And when he thinks, good easy man, full surely
His greatness is *a*-ripening."   SHAKSPEARE.

"Our grandfathers left more glory by their exploytting great acts, than we shall do by forging *a*-new words and uncouth phrases."

Unless *a* is in this case a misprint, and ought to be joined to *new* (anew), it must stand here for *of*. The sense, however, does not require *anew*, but *of* new.

Here, then, we have the particle *a* apparently used for *at*, for *on*, and for *of*, and the abbreviation or corruption has probably arisen from our natural tendency to cut words as short as possible in familiar conversation. In the Anglo-Saxon Gospel, as Lowth has pointed out, what in our English is translated "I go *a fishing*" (John xxi. 3), is there, "Ic wylle gan *on* fixoth," I will go *on* fishing, *a*-fishing. We say twelve o'clock for *of* the clock, or *on* the clock, on the same clipping principle. He is *aloft, on the* loft.

It is quite possible, however, that some of our present English words, which take *a* before them in the participle, as *a*-coming, may have only retained the common Saxon prefix *ge* and *be* under a different form. Thus *geclypode*, or *beclupod*, *becleopod*, *beclyped*, has become *yclepid*, *yclep'd*, *iclep'd*, from the verb *clypian*, to call, invite. "Manega synt *geclypode*," Many are called (Matt. xx. 16). So *gecuman* might be changed into *a-coming*, without much violence in pronunciation. In defence of this supposition, we have an example in the following old verses:—

> "Sumer is *i* cumen in,
> Lhude sing cuccu,
> Groweth sed, and bloweth med,
> And springeth wde nu.
>   Sing cuccu, cuccu."

Here we have *i cumen*, not *a coming*, just as *yclypode* became *yclypede*, and *iclypode*, and *iclept*. Again, *on* was a common Anglo-Saxon prefix before nouns and verbs: as *on-drœding*, fear, *on-drœdan*, to fear, *on-cuman*, to come, to enter; and this prefix, like *ge*, *be*, *y*, in most cases, did not alter the signification of the word to which it was attached. We might, therefore, say: "Sumer is *on-cumen* in," considering *on-cumen* grammatically as no more than a simple participle; or,

"Sumer is a-coming, be-coming, ge-comen, y-comen, i-comen." "In fact," says Bosworth, "if a word cannot be found under *a*, it may be sought for under *be, for, ge,* or *to;* or, rather, under the first letter that remains, after rejecting these prefixes." We now say, to "*stow* away articles;" but the Bible says, "And when he came to the tower, he took them from their hand, and *bestowed* them in the house."—2 *Kings* v. 24.

Besides, in many cases, we have dropped the initial Saxon *a* of words: as *a*slidan, to slide; *a*slidende, sliding; *a*standan, to stand; *a*standende, standing;— *a*slidende and *a*standende, neither expressing nor implying a preposition, sound very much like *a*-sliding, and *a* standing. We have both live and alive, from the Saxon *alybban*, to live, participle *aleofod*, living, in the first case having dropped, in the second having retained, the initial *a*. We may look at these abbreviations, therefore, partly as abbreviations of the prepositions *on*, or *at*, or *of*, partly perhaps as the Anglo Saxon prefix, under a different form.

CHAPTER VI.

PARTICIPLES ENDING IN EN, ING, ED, T.

Mistaken and *Mistaking.*

Dr. Carey, in his "English Prosody" (note), ranks *mistaken* with such passive participles as *sworn, drunken, fallen, grown (growen), rotten, swollen.* "Thus, a *sworn* broker may not be a *swearing* broker, a *fallen* tree is not a *falling* tree, a *rotten* branch is not a *rotting* branch." *Mistaken* refers to an act accomplished, *mistaking* to a past or present continuous state.

Mistaken is the passive form of To mistake, yet custom has authorized its use with an active signification. I am mistaken, is used to signify I *mistake, misunderstand.* My meaning is mistaken, *misunderstood.* Thus the same form is used both actively and passively.

It is inconsistent with the English idiom to use the auxiliary verb and the participle in the place of the principal verb, whenever the principal verb has a continuous signification—that is, a signification having reference both to past and present time. We say, "I am *listening* to you," for this expresses only a present continuity; but we do not say "I am *hating* you," for this supposes past and present time—a state of feeling—a condition of the mind resting upon some antecedent cause; and we therefore say "I *hate*," a term which does not limit the signification to a present operation. I *hate*, I *love*, I *mistake*, are English; but not I am *hating*, I am *loving*, I am *mistaking*, in the same sense. When, therefore, we say "I am mistaken," instead of "I mistake," we avoid the un-English expression "I am mistaking." Custom has authorized "I am mistaken" in the place of "I *mistake* or *misunderstand*," and custom has authorized "his meaning is mistaken or *misunderstood*," and there the matter rests.

It is in vain, in cases of this kind, "to kick against the pricks." We say "he has the wish, but the means are *wanting*," when the means are *wanted*.

Instead of *owing*, we ought, in many cases, to use the passive participle *owen*, instead of the active form *owing*. It was *owen* to my exertions, not *owing*. The debt was *owen* to him, not *owing*. It is my *own;* that is, my *owen;* i. e. it is *owen* to me. Liberalism itself will not, however, allow, "I am beholdi*ng* to him," instead of "I am beholde*n.*"

There is a phrase, at present, fluctuating between an active and a passive form. As, the house *is building*, that is, in the act of being built, and the house is *being built*, the import aimed at being the same in both. In German, the passive form is used in speaking of things done by *the assistance of* man; as *Das Schiff wird gebaut*, the ship is building, becomes built, is becoming built—the active form, in expressing the *operation of inanimate objects;* as, *Das Feuer brennt*, the *fire is burning*. Is the object of this distinction gained by the English phrase, "The ship is *being built?*" The phrase "is *being built*," and others of a similar kind, have been, for a few years back, gradually insinuating themselves into our language; still they are not English. If we use the phrase, "*The house is building*," we speak of it as a thing from its very nature *not acting* itself, and we use the term *building* as expressive of a passive progressive condition of the house. If we say "The *men are building*," we then have active instruments, and the term *building* is an active participle, requiring to be followed by a noun: as *building a wall, a castle*. No mistake can, therefore, arise from the use of such phrases as *The house is building, Preparations are making*. We use the participle in *ed* both actively and passively;

29*

as, I *have loved*, I *am loved*. The French do the same, as J'ai aimé, I *have loved;* Je su's aimé, I *am loved*. If the passive form *ed* can thus be used both actively and passively, the active form, on the same grounds, may be used passively and actively. Certain it is, that phrases similar to *The house is building, Preparations are making*, are scattered profusely over our literature; whilst The house is *being* built, Preparations are *being* made, are phrases not only foreign to our language, but, under certain modifications, difficult to deal with. Let us take such a phrase as the following: "*He will find, on his arrival, that the house will be being built.*" Or, "When he *arrived, he found,* on inquiry, that, when the accident *happened, the house had been being built.*" Are we to say, "*I knew the house to be being built,*" instead of "*I knew the house to be building?*" Are we prepared to carry the principle thus far, for the sake of an innovation, to say the least, unnecessary? Besides, *built*, or *builded*, implies a thing effected, an act accomplished; whereas *being* implies something continuously present, —a continuous condition. Where a verb denotes *continuous* action, *being* may properly be applied to it, as consentaneous with the action of the verb: as, *being feared,* expressive of a continuous condition; but a house is either *built* or *not built*. *Being built* includes incompatible terms, *progression* and *accomplishment*. It combines *perfect* and *imperfect* action. *Becoming* built —the house is *becoming* built, *i. e.* approximating to accomplishment, would come nearer to the intended meaning. Dr. Beattie says, "One of the greatest defects in the English tongue, with regard to the verb, seems to be the want of an *imperfect passive* participle;" yet he does not scruple to say, "*Actions that* are now *performing.*" "Creusa, who was *missing*," &c.

Mr. Pickburn (page 78), speaking of the participle ending in *ing*, observes, "The tenses of the passive voice compounded with the participle in *ing*, are never used but in the third person, and with relation to *inanimate objects;* or, at least, *such as* are incapable *of the actions* mentioned. They can, therefore, in no case occasion obscurity: for, whenever the imperfect participle is joined, by an auxiliary verb, to a nominative *capable of* the action, it is taken actively; but, when joined to one incapable of action, it *becomes passive.*"

In no way can we express the difference between an act accomplished and an act in the course of accomplishment, so readily or effectively as by considering the participle ending in *ing*, under the conditions already mentioned, as an *imperfect passive participle.*

To the same purport is the opinion of Mr. Grant, in his "Grammar of the English Language," namely, that "the imperfect participle is to be substituted when *progression* is to be denoted; as, the *letter is writing, was writing, has been writing, will be writing;* the house *is building, was building, has been building, will be building. Written*, or *built*, would, on the contrary, denote perfection or completion."

If we object to participles in *ing*, as having an imperfect passive signification, on what principle do we justify such expressions as, "the *verses read* well," when an external agency is applied to the verses, and they in fact *are* read?

Clearly in such a case, *read* is an imperfect passive verb: that is, a verb denoting *progression* or *imperfect accomplishment*. The same may be said of such phrases as, the *ingredients mix well*, the *fields plough well*, the *corn threshes well*, this is good *to eat*, this is good *to drink*, a house *to let*, an estate *to sell*. The agency in these cases is external, and the object does *not act*, but is *acted upon*.

It is, however, to be borne in mind, that, when a participle ending in *ing* is connected by an auxiliary verb to its subject, and that subject a nominative case, *sentient* and *capable* of action, the participle *must* be taken actively, and from its very nature cannot be taken passively in the same form; as, he was *reading, writing, painting*. These phrases cannot be understood as *passive*, either perfect or imperfect. In the case of verbs implying sensation, we do not use the auxiliary and the participle to express our meaning, but the simple verb; not, *I am fearing*, but, *I fear*. The reason is that these verbs express a continuous affection of the mind *without* an auxiliary. That verbs expressing a continuous affection of the mind have a different bearing from ordinary verbs expressive of action, may be exemplified in phrases like the following: "*If you feared me, you would avoid me;*" which means, you would at this time avoid me, if you were *under the influence* of fear. If *you feared*, does not then relate merely to time *past*, but to time *present* also. It indicates the *continuity* of a certain state of the mind. But a verb of *decisive* action does not convey such a meaning without the addition of the auxiliary verb. "If he *struck* him," refers to an action which did or did not take place at a certain time; but there is no *continuation* of the action, as in the case of a verb expressive of sensation.

Passing.

"Where *passing* fair
 Allured them."
      Milton. *Paradise Lost.*

That is, where something *passing* or *surpassing* that which is fair allured them.

"And *passing* rich with forty pounds a year."
      Goldsmith.

More than rich.

Rapt, carried away.

Care must be taken not to confound *rapt, carried away,* with *wrapt, enveloped,* the former being derived from *rapio, raptus,* borne away, hurried along, the other signifying folded up.

"Not *rapt* above the pole."   *Paradise Lost.*
"*Rapt* in a chariot drawn by fiery steeds."   *Ibid.*
"*Rapt* into future times the bard begun."   Pope.
"High *rapt* ambition."   Savage.

Wrapt, enveloped.

"Go less than woman in the form of man,
To scale our walls, to *wrap* our tow'rs in flames,
To lead in exile the fair Phrygian dames."   Pope.

"Not with more rage a conflagration rolls.
Wraps the vast mountains, and involves the poles."   *Ibid.*

It may be observed that *rapt* is used in the *participial* form only, there being no English root in the sense of to *rap*, derived from *rapio*.

We may say "*Rapt* by the God;" but we cannot say that the God *rapt* him, in the same sense. In the case of *wrap*, we have the root to *wrap*.

Time not expressed by the Participle abstractly.

English participles, whether ending in *ing*, or *ed*, or *en*, or *t*, do not express time *abstractly*. I can say, "I was *reading*, I am *reading*, I will be *reading*; the book is *printed*, it was *printed*, it will be *printed*." The participles *reading* and *printed*, whether *past*, *present*, or *future*, have undergone no variation. The tense of participles is thus expressed by concomitant auxiliaries.

SECTION VIII.

ADVERB.

CHAPTER I.

ITS NATURE.

The term *adverb* is derived from the two Latin words *ad*, to, and *verbum*, word. The Greek term επιρρημα has also precisely the same signification as *adverbium* in Latin, and *adverb* in English. As its name denotes, it is used as an attributive to some other word, either in order to qualify its *simple* intension, or, when used comparatively or superlatively, its *relative* intension. The word, to which it is joined, is not necessarily a *verb*, in the limited acceptation of the term *verb*; for it may be joined to a participle, as *bitterly* hating; to an adjective, as *exceedingly* fair; as well as to the verb: as, he spoke *fluently*. It is obvious that an adverb, being an attributive, and springing out of the nature or condition of some object or action, cannot stand alone. Hence the word *adverb*. Besides expressing a *simple* and an absolute condition, when joined to another word, the adverb expresses also a relative condition; as, A. speaks *fluently*; B. *more fluently*; C. *most fluently*. Variation of intensity is as necessary in an adverb as in an adjective. We speak of anything done, either *abstractly* and without reference to the manner in which it may be done elsewhere, or we speak *comparatively*, and with reference to the mode in which it may be done elsewhere. The same principle applies to the adverb, when it is an attributive of the adjective or of the participle. In these, also, there must be gradations of condition and of action.

The position of an adverb, and its proper use in a sentence, are often objects of the greatest moment, and this position and use I shall proceed to illustrate by a variety of examples, proper and improper.

CHAPTER II.

EXAMPLES OF ADVERBS.

Position of the Adverb.

Not.

THE negative adverb *not* follows, and in modern usage never precedes, the principal verb to which it refers. We cannot now say "I *not* offend," as in Dryden, or "She *not* denies it," as in Shakspeare.

Only, Merely.

"Reason informed us—*only* of the necessity of the thing, revelation has prescribed the terms. Philosophy conjectured—*merely* its existence, the gospel has announced the mode of its consummation."—*Rennel.*

The adverbs *only* and *merely* are in their proper places in this passage. In the former sentence, the antithesis is not between the terms *informed* and *prescribed*, but between the *necessity of the thing* and *the terms of the thing*. In the latter, the antithesis is not between the terms *conjectured* and *announced*, but between the *existence of the thing* and the mode *of its consummation;* and this is properly expressed. At least, if we place *only* in any other position than that in which we find it, the passage would be more liable to ambiguity than it is at present. If properly read, a slight pause ought to take place after *informed*, by which the meaning would be defined; and an emphasis laid on *only*. In print, the pause may be indicated visibly as above. *Merely* is subject to the same remarks. Both sentences are tricky, and ought to be remodelled.

"But on inquiry, we find that the words were not *only* uttered by a mortal man like ourselves, but by one who was more than most others constantly exposed to death, and expecting it."— *Published Sermon.*

From the position of *only* before *uttered*, we expect the sentence to run, that the words were not *only* uttered by a mortal man, but something more that uttered; whereas, the antithesis is between a mortal man, simply as such, and a man constantly exposed to death, and expecting it. Place *not only* after uttered, and all is clear. These words were uttered *not only* by a mortal man, like ourselves, but, &c. The sentence would, however, be still more distinct by the arrangement, "These words were uttered by a man, not only mortal like ourselves, but by one who was more than most others constantly exposed to death, and expecting it."

If we take the following sentence, we shall find that it is susceptible of three different meanings, according to the situation of the adverb *only:* "I *only* am left to tell thee," *i. e.* I, and *no one* besides; "I am left *only* to tell thee," *i. e.* I am left for *no other purpose* than to tell thee; "I am left to tell thee *only*," *i. e.* and to tell *no other person* than thyself. The position of the adverb *only*, which so materially affects the meaning of a sentence, is worthy of much more consideration than it usually receives. In conversation, mere emphasis will often come in aid of the meaning intended; but in written language the arrangement of a sentence ought to be such as not to be susceptible of any other meaning than that which it is intended to convey.

Again, in the following sentence, the adverb *only*, from its position, gives a turn to the meaning quite different from that which the author intended:—

"He had suffered the woodward *only* to use his discretion in the distant woods. In the groves about his house, he allowed no marking-hammer but his own."—*Gilpin's Forest Scenery.*

The sentence means that he had suffered the woodward, and no other person than the woodward, to use his discretion in the distant woods; whereas, from the sentence that follows, it is evident that Mr. Gilpin meant to say, "he had suffered the woodward to use his discretion in the distant woods *only*." The sentence arranged as follows, would be clear: "It was in the distant woods *only* that he suffered the woodward to use his discretion. In the groves about his house, he allowed no marking-iron but his own."

"Her bosom to the view was *only* bare." DRYDEN.

"Her bosom *only* to the view was bare."

"The province of Gaul seems, and indeed *only* seems, an exception to this universal toleration." *Gibbon, Decl. c. ii.*

Mr. Gibbon is here speaking of the religious toleration which all the nations under the dominion of Rome enjoyed. He then adds, "The province of Gaul seems, and indeed *only* seems, an exception to this universal toleration." As the passage stands, it means that Gaul was in reality no exception at all; but that it *only* seemed so—*only* seems an exception; whereas Mr. Gibbon means that the sanguinary religious rites of the Gauls, under the Druids, were not tolerated by the Romans, and that the restraint imposed upon the exercise of those rites was the only exception to the toleration which the whole Roman world freely enjoyed.

"The first (pestilence) could be *only* imputed to the just indignation of the gods."—*Gibbon.*

According to this form of expression, the pestilence of which the author is here speaking could be imputed, and *nothing more than imputed*, to the just indignation of the gods; whereas he means to say that the pestilence could not be attributed to the wicked administration of Commodus, but *solely*, and *entirely*, to the just indignation of the gods—*only* to the just indignation of the gods.

"But, by learning, the Apostle does not mean empty and barren speculation, but learning unto salvation; not *merely* to render us better scholars, but better men: not *only* to satisfy us in useless curiosity, but to confirm us in the belief of Christianity."—*Rennel,* Sermon 24.

The words *merely* and *only* are both mischievous. It was no part of the object of Scripture to make us better scholars, and most certainly no part of it to satisfy us in useless curiosity.

Examples.

Double Negative.

Amongst writers of a certain date, it is not unusual to find a double negative, which in the present age would not be admissible; as,

> "I never was *nor never* will be false."   SHAKSP. *Rich. II.*
>
> "*Nor did not* with unbashful forehead woo
>   The means of weakness and debility."   SHAKSPEARE.
>
> "He *never* yet *no* vilanie *ne* sayde."   CHAUCER.
>
> "She mounts her chariot in a thrice,
>   *Nor* would she stay for *no* advice,
>   Until her maids, who were so nice,
>   To wait on her were fitted."   DRAYTON'S *Nymphidia.*

Such expressions as these ought, perhaps, to be estimated by the age in which they were used; but they cannot be used with propriety now.

> "It is all along bounded by lofty mountain-ranges on both sides, never narrows into a defile, *nor never* expands into a plain."—*Inglis, Tyrol.*

The same excuse cannot be made for the *nor never* of Mr. Inglis, which is applicable to authors of a much older date.

Excessively, Exceedingly.

> "Excessively drunk."—*Goldsmith.* Not "*excessive* drunk."
>
> "Exceedingly fair." Not "*exceeding* fair."
>
> "Eusibhart, who was secretary to Charles the First, became exceeding popular."—*Spectator,* No. 14.

An attempt is made to justify the expression *exceeding fair*, and others of a similar kind, by supposing *exceeding*, in such a case, to be a participle—as exceeding that which is fair. It savors, however, very strongly of error, and may be ranked with such expressions as the following:—

"The sellers of the newest patterns at present give *extreme* good bargains."—*Goldsmith, Citizen.*

" In a word, his speech was all *excellent* good in itself."—*Fuller's Andronicus.*

Exceedingly is usually applied in a good sense—*excessively* in a bad sense; as, *exceedingly* beautiful, *excessively* ugly.

Peculiarly, Particularly.

Peculiar and *peculiarly*, *particular* and *particularly*, have distinct significations, and cannot, without impropriety, be confounded; as was briefly noticed under the head ADJECTIVE. *Peculiar* may be said to mark a property *absolutely*, *particular* the *degree* of a property common to more objects than that to which it is applied. For, as Harris justly observes,

"Every thing in a manner, whether natural or artificial, is in its constitution compounded of something common, and something *peculiar*; of something common, and belonging to many other things, and of something *peculiar*, by which it is distinguished, and made to be its true and proper self. Hence, language, if compared according to this notion to the murmurs of a fountain, or the dashings of a cataract, has in common this, that like them it is sound. But then, on the contrary, it has in *peculiar* this, that whereas those sounds have no meaning, or signification, to language a meaning or signification is essential."—*Hermes,* c. i. b. 3.

"This happy region seemed *peculiarly* sequestered by nature for his abode."—*Goldsmith.*

Peculiarly, not *particularly.* Cashmere possessed advantages in this respect, of a kind *peculiar* (*propria*) to itself—advantages such as no other country possessed.

"But the far greater part retained those arms to which the nature of their country, or their early habits of life, more *peculiarly* adapted them."—*Gibbon, Decl.* c. i.

Here Mr. Gibbon presumes that the difference of country and of the habits of early life had produced, in some of the auxiliaries of the Romans, an aptitude for the use of certain arms, which aptitude did not exist in any other part of these auxiliaries. This aptitude, or degree of aptitude, belonged to them *distinctly,* and not in *common* with the rest, and was therefore *peculiar* to them.

Farther, Further, Forther.

Farther, further, and *forther.* All these forms have been used in the same sense, though *further* is the word now generally in use. From *far* would regularly be derived *farrer* and *farrest,* not *further* and *furthest,* unless we suppose the *th* to be used for the sake of euphony. *Further* and *furthest* are justified by *custom* only, and not by analogy. It is a corruption of *forth, forther, forthest,* to go *forth, forther, forthest.* In this sense it is used by Chaucer in his "Canterbury Tales:"—

"But natheless, while I have time and space,
Or that I *forther* in this tale pace."

But Chaucer does not write *far,* but *fer:*—

"With was his parish and his houses *fer* asonder."

And from this he deduces *ferrest:*—

> "In sikenesse and in mischiefe to visite
> The *ferrest* in his parish."

Heywood, also, in his "Epigrams," as quoted by Lower, writes *fer:*—

> "A foole's bolt is soon shot, and fleeth oftimes *fer*;
> But a foole's bolt and the mark cum few times ner."

But the Scotch poet, William Dunbar, who was born about 1465, in his poem of "The Thistle and the Rose," writes,

> "In field go *furth*, and fend the laif."

And Johnson, in his "History of Early English Poetry," observes that "the Scotch of both Douglas and Dunbar was not materially different from the language of the best cotemporary English writers."

Sir David Lindsay, a Scotch poet of a period somewhat later, being born in 1490, in his tale of "Squire Meldrun," writes *furth:*—

> "She slippit in or evir he wist,
> And feynitlie past till ane kist,
> And with her keys oppenit the lokkis,
> And made her to take *furth* ane boxe."

It would appear, therefore, from these authorities, that the word written *fer* by Chaucer and Heywood was used in the sense of the modern term *far*, and that from *fer* was derived the superlative *ferrest*, and that the comparative would, if regularly formed, be *ferrer*; *fer ferrer, ferrest:* but the word *further*, used by Chaucer, is a different word, and derived from *forth*, a term still holding its place in the English language, though, so far back as Dunbar and Lindsay, written *furth*. It is clear, therefore, that the word which now fluctuates between *further* and *farther* ought to be written *forther*. Custom will have it *further*. *Far* is a corruption of *fer*, leading to other corruptions, *further*, and *furthest*, in the place of *fer, ferrer, ferrest*, now obsolete. To go *forth* implies no particular distance; to go *far* is so far definite that it excludes nearness.

Never, Ever.

"It produces that slow Alexandrian air, which is finely suited to a close, and for this reason such lines *almost never* occur together, but are used in finishing the complet."—*Blair's Rhetoric*.

Better, "*very seldom* occur."

"The Lord is king, be the people *never* so impatient."—*Psalm* xcix. 1.

"For, though a man be *never* so perfect among the children of men."—*Wisdom* ix. 6.

"If I wash myself with snow-water, and make myself *never* so clean."—*Job* ix. 30.

"Charm he *never* so wisely."—*Psalm* lviii. 5.

"His face was easily taken, both in painting and sculpture, and scarce any one, though *never* so indifferently skilled in their (his) art, failed to hit it."—*Wellwood's Memoirs*.

"Besides, a slave would not have been admitted into that society had he had *never* such opportunities." *Bentley, Dissertation on Phalaris*.

"Let the offence be of *never* so high a nature."—*Spectator*, 181.

But Harris, whose authority is worth a thousand authorities such as those above mentioned, writes, -

"Be the language upon the whole *ever* so perfect."—*Hermes*, p. 122.

Dr. Carey, in his "Treatise on English Prosody," page 64, note, has the following observations on the subjoined couplet:—

> "Though *ne'er* so rich, we scorn the elf
> Whose only praise is sordid pelf."

"*Never so rich.*"—"Some modern grammarians," says he, "condemn phrases of this kind as improper, and recommend *ever so*. I would very cheerfully subscribe to their opinion, if I only could understand the latter phrase, so as to extract from it a satisfactory meaning; but *that* I own is a task which exceeds my abilities. For example, 'It is a fine day—will you take a walk?' 'No; if it were *ever* so fine a day I would not go out.' To discover the meaning of this reply, I first consider that *ever* signifies *always*."

After begging the question, and assuming that *ever* signifies *always*, he proceeds to argue the case, and paraphrases the expression thus: "If this day were fine to such degree that *never so fine* a day has smiled from the heavens, I would not go out." But *ever*, in such a situation, has nothing to do with *time*. It is an adverb of *degree*, and not of time, and is constantly used as such under analogous circumstances; as, "If I take *ever* so little of this drug, it will kill me." That is, *however* little. "If I take *ever* so much of this, it will not hurt me." "How much *soever* I may take of it, it will not hurt me." Let any one translate one of these phrases into another language, and he will find that *ever* presents itself as a term expressive of degree, and not of *time* at all. "Charm he *ever* so wisely:"— Quamvis incantandi sit *peritus*, aut peritissimus. In the second quotation (from Wisdom ix. 6), the Greek has τέλειος, the Latin *perfectus*, and the French *consommé*. In the fourth quotation (Psalm lviii. 5), the Latin has "vocatis incantationibus *peritissimi.*" The doctor's fallacy lies in the assumption that *ever* must signify *always*, and nothing else. In such cases, then, *ever* and not *never*, is required. The doctor's explanation is circuitous and unnecessary.

"Seldom *if* ever," not "seldom *or* never," "seldom *or* ever."

Adverbs in ly, *formed from Adjectives in* ly.

Though an adjective may end in *ly*, the usual termination of the English adverb, yet this ought not to deter us from adding *ly* to the end of an adverb formed from such adjective, and changing the first *ly* into *li;* and this in order to distinguish it from the adjective, out of which it is formed. In the Old Testament, we find *wilily* from *wily*, and in the New *holily* from *holy*. The combination of the syllables *li*, *ly*, it is true, on some occasions may have a disagreeable effect; but, where the exact similitude of the adjective is preserved in the adverb there is also something offensive, as a matter of sense. It is a question, therefore, between sense and sound, as in the second collect for Good Friday, "May truly and *godly* serve thee." Whenever a decidedly inharmonious effect is produced by such a word as *godlily*, *masterlily*, the phrase ought to be recast. It was *masterly* done, is bad; It was *masterlily* done, no better: but we *can* say, It was done in a masterly way or manner.

No, Not.

"If that be all, there's no need of paying for that, since I am resolved to have that pleasure, whether I am there or *no*."—*Goldsmith, Citizen*, 105.

"Whether love be natural or *no*, replied my friend gravely, it contributes to the happiness of every society into which it is introduced."—*Ibid.*

If we supply what is wanting, we shall see that expressions of this description require *not* in the place of *no*. Whether I am there, or *not* there. Whether love be natural, or *not* natural.

SECTION IX.

PREPOSITION.

CHAPTER I.

ITS NATURE.

THE English preposition is simple, and easy of application. In the Greek language, some prepositions are followed by one case only, some by two, some by three, according to circumstances. The use of the Greek prepositions often, therefore, rests upon shades of distinction not very strongly marked. In English, the preposition is *always* followed by the objective case: and, as the objective case of the noun never varies from the nominative, the chance of error is reduced within a very small compass. The old Anglo-Saxon genitive case, resolved into *of* before the noun, ceases to be a case; as, *Thomas's* book, or the book of Thomas. The term *Thomas* undergoes no change, whether we say this is *Thomas*, this is the book *of Thomas*, or give it to *Thomas*.

But though the absence of variation in the English noun reduces the chances of error in connecting it with the preposition, still there may be misapplications of the prepositions themselves, either when standing alone, or in composition. The variation of the pronoun, according to its use in the nominative, possessive, or objective case, is frequently the source of error, though that kind of error which a very slender stock of grammatical knowledge, with ordinary attention at least, ought to avoid. Such expressions as, "Take it from *she*, and give it to *I*," are by no means uncommon southern* provincialisms, and these not always confined to the farmyard or the stable. Under the head of PRONOUN, some examples of this kind may be found, in a former part of this work.

CHAPTER II.

ADOPTION OF LATIN, GREEK, AND FRENCH PREPOSITIONS.

PREPOSITIONS taken from the Latin and Greek enter largely into the present constitution of the English language. In the present state of our literature and

* Referring to England.

science, they cannot be dispensed with. They have become necessaries of life. About *twenty* Latin prepositions, capable of standing alone, coalesce readily with words that now form an undisputed part of the English language. *Five* more, which may be regarded as inseparable prepositions, that is, not found alone but in composition only, have also become children of adoption. To these may be added fourteen prepositions from the Greek, easily combining with different parts of speech. These, with our own indigenous prepositions, are amply sufficient to supply all our wants; and if, in this respect, and as far as the use of prepositions is concerned, we do not express our meaning with sufficient perspicuity, it is not from the want of terms, but from our own ignorance or negligence in their application. In some cases, we have recourse both to Latin and Greek prepositions in composition, and adopt two words, both signifying the same thing, as, *periphery* and *circumference*. Sometimes we combine an English preposition with a Latin term, as, *overplus;* sometimes a French preposition with an English term, as, *surcharge*, that is, *overcharge; surpass*, to pass over or beyond. We even adopt a Latin preposition, and form a noun from it, as, "He is an *Ultra;* yet custom will not allow us to say "He is a *Beyond;*" so entirely is language in the power of this earthly deity. Prepositions of foreign origin cannot, of course, be duly appreciated, without reference to the languages from which they are derived. They perpetually minister to the use, the precision, or the elegance of the language, and, as such, are worthy of minute attention.

CHAPTER III.

PLACE OF THE PREPOSITION.

The very term *preposition* indicates that it is connected with something that follows; otherwise, it could not be a prefix, or preposition. Yet the preposition sometimes ostensibly becomes an adverb, and in such cases it has no object *expressed*, as, *above*, *beneath*—the heavens *above*, the earth *beneath*. It would appear, however, that a noun is here *tacitly* implied. The heaven *above* is the heaven above *something*. The earth beneath is the earth beneath *something;* though that something may not be expressed.

Again, prepositions sometimes serve the place of adjectives, as, an *after*-thought, an *under*-current, "thine *often*-infirmities."

But, though the term *preposition* indicates something placed before, it is not so on all occasions. *Formally* the preposition may be far separated from its dependent noun, or pronoun, though in grammatical construction it necessarily precedes it. By an idiom, peculiar, perhaps, to the English language, the prepositions *of, to, in, for*, &c., are sometimes placed at the end of a sentence, and quite apart from the noun that depends upon them. As, "These are matters which he is entirely ignorant *of;*" or, "What he is an entire stranger *to;*" "Which he is engaged *in;*" "The sum which he sold it for;" i. e. *of which, to which, in which, for which.*

The particle *of*, whether looked upon as a preposition,

or the sign of the genitive case, admits the same construction.

> "These more sterling qualities of strict moral conduct, regular religious habits, temperate and prudent behavior, sober industrious life—qualities which are generally required of public men, even if more superficial accomplishments should be dispensed with—he had absolutely nothing *of*."—*Lord Brougham's Statesmen, Life of Wilkes.*

Here the particle *of* is placed at the end of the sentence; in the following sentence, at the beginning:—

> "*Of* the lighter but very important accomplishments, which fill so prominent a place in the patriotic character, great eloquence and a strong and masculine style in writing, he had but little."—*Ibid.*

The first and last words of each of these sentences are grammatically connected; as, "he had absolutely nothing of those more sterling qualities;" and "he had but little of the lighter," &c.

The particle *of*, in such a position as we find it, at the end of the former sentence, and also the wide interval between *of* in the beginning of the latter sentence, and the term *little*, with which it is grammatically connected, are quite consistent with the idiom of the English language.

The following sentence from Bentley, exhibiting the same position of the preposition, is grammatically faulty:—

> "And so begin his examination in such articles as he could raise the greatest bustle *in*."

The relative being here supplied by the particle *as*, the preposition *in* has nothing to which it can adhere. The sentence might have run: "And so begin his examination in those articles in which he could raise the greatest bustle;" or, "which he could make the greatest bustle in." To say, "And so begin his examination in those articles in *as* he could make the greatest bustle" is nonsense. Yet this is the grammatical resolution of the passage. So again:—

"This surely was too slender a thread to trust a business of that weight to."

This sentence requires to be reconstructed: "This surely was too slender a thread to be trusted in a business of that weight."

The following phrase is colloquial, but nothing more:—

"The only animal we saw for some time was an opossum, which the native discovered in a tree, and climbed up for."—*Landor's Bushman.*

The relative *which* here depends upon two different parts of speech, *discovered* and *for*, a verb and a preposition. Though the sentence is not grammatically faulty, yet in its construction it certainly presents nothing worthy of imitation.

There may, however, be cases in which the disjunction of the preposition and its dependent noun is not only the cause of an inharmonious cadence, but where, as a grammatical principle, it is inadmissible; as,

"He betrothes himself oftener to the devil in one day, than Mecænas did in a week to his wife, that he was married a thousand times to."—*Butler's Remains*.

Here we see the preposition *to* placed at the end of the sentence; yet we cannot convert the phrase, "his wife, that he was married a thousand times *to*," into "his wife *to that* he was married a thousand times." Yet this is the real test of its propriety. In a case like this, *that* must give way to *which* or *whom.*

When *that* is demonstrative, it will admit a preposition before it; as, "Give it *to that* man;" "Take it *from that* man." But when *that* is a relative, we cannot say, "This is the man *to that* the book belongs;" or, "This is the man *from that* he took the book."

CHAPTER IV.

DOUBLE PREPOSITIONS.

The following passage affords the unusual application of two prepositions, one *before* and the other *after* the noun to which they have reference:—

"With noise like the sound of the distant thunder,
Roaring they rushed *from* the black gulf *under.*"
Translation from Schiller.

That is, *from under* the black gulf. There is nothing here that offends against the idiom of the English language; but ambiguity lurks in the phrase, "from the black gulf under." "*From under* the black gulf" conveys a meaning different from that which is conveyed by "*from* the black gulf *that is* under," supposing the phrase to be elliptical.

When *two* prepositions come before the noun to which they refer, the meaning may be quite clear and quite consistent with the structure of our language; as, "*From about* the age of twenty years." In this case, the terms "about the age of twenty years," though verbally distinct, form a concrete noun grammatically and logically in the objective case, and depending upon the former preposition *from*. We cannot, however, place the latter preposition *about* at the end of the sentence.

In such a phrase as "*over against* the church," the prepositions have reference to two distinct nouns; as, "*over* the way, *against* or *opposite* to the church."

CHAPTER V.

COMPOUND AND SIMPLE PREPOSITIONS.

In, To, Into.

In implies a *state of being; into* an *act.* We pour water *into* the pail; when there, it is *in* the pail. This distinction in Greek and Latin requires a different case.

Horace has been censured by some critics for writing "igne," when he meant *at* the fire; but as no motion *towards* or *to* the fire was meant, the expression is correct; and, if he had said "in ignem," it would have been equivalent in English to "they roasted thrushes *to* the fire."

As the preposition *in* implies *rest*, and *into, motion* to, it is obvious that, when two verbs have a diversity of meaning, one implying *motion* and the other the place *where*, they cannot properly be followed by one and the same preposition. Thus:—

"After killing his wife and children, he laid them upon a pile which he had erected for that purpose, and thus setting fire to the whole, *rushed* and *expired in* the midst of the flames."—*Goldsmith's History of Greece.*

That is, "rushed *into*, and expired *in*, the midst of the flames." The preposition *in* is not applicable, in common, to both these verbs, and the terms are inconsistent.

The preposition *in*, when used in composition, denotes negation; as, *indirect, indecent, inhuman,* &c.; that is, *not* direct, *not* decent, *not* human. Words of this kind are derived from the Latin; yet in words clearly of Latin origin we have not in all cases been satisfied with a correct example. Ovid says,

———"Non est habitabilis æstu."

We also say, "the habitable globe;" and if "habitable globe" signifies a globe capable of being inhabited, why should not *inhabitable*, on the same principle, signify incapable of habitation? To effect this signification, we have prefixed to it *un*, and thus get *uninhabitable.* Yet Sandys, in his annotations on Ovid's "Metamorphoses," writes, "The frigid zone, held *inhabitable* for extremitie of cold:" *inhabitable* then having the same signification as *uninhabitable* has now.

In the case of *immortal*, we have *mortal* and *immortal* opposed to each other; an *un* prefixed to *immortal* would reduce the meaning of the term to *mortal; unimmortal,* that is *mortal.* Milton has it so:—

"*Unimmortal* made
All kinds."   *Paradise Lost*, b. x.

The addition of *un* to an epithet already compounded, in the following passage from Milton, is a magnificent conception:—

"All too little seems
To stuff his maw—this vast *unhidebound corpse.*"

The epithet *unhidebound*, applied to the sin-born monster Death, is singularly happy,—a monster not confined within superficies, and therefore by nature insatiable.

Up, On, Upon.

On and *upon* ought at least to have different significations, on the same principle as the signification of *in* differs from that of *into*. The promiscuous use of *on* and *upon* is, however, sufficiently prevalent, if not to constitute a rule, at least to establish a legalized confusion. Yet do not such phrases as the following involve a difference in the meaning of these prepositions? "The bird flew *upon* (*up on*) the house, and when there sat *on* the roof." In the first case, *motion to* is implied; in the second, simply a *state of rest*. Again, *up on* (*upon*) would properly signify *elevation* and a *state of rest*. The Greek preposition ανα seems to have the same import as our preposition *up*; and ειδα ανα σκαπτω (Pindar), that is, ανα (η) σκαπτω corresponds with our phrase, "sleeps *up on* (*upon*) the sceptre." *Upon*, however, in its present use does not always imply *motion up* or even *elevation*; for we say, "He threw himself *upon* the ground;" "Send down *upon* our bishops and curates;" "Pour *upon* them the continual dew of thy blessing."

Custom has, in fact, irretrievably confounded the use of *on* and *upon*; though *uppan*, the old form, seems always to have had reference to elevation, as, " *Uppan* ðisne stan," "upon this stone" (Matt. xxi. 44): "*Uppan hys heafod*," "upon his head" (Matt. xxvi. 7): *Uppe-land, up*-land; *up*-ric, *up*-kingdom, heavenly kingdom.

The preposition *on* is sometimes confounded with *of*, as, "Take hold *on* it." We lay hold *on* a thing, but we take hold *of* it.

"Blessed is the man that doeth this, and the son of man that layeth hold *on* it."—*Isaiah* v. 6.

"Every one that keepeth the sabbath from polluting it, and taketh hold *of* my covenant."—*Ibid.* lvi. 6.

With and *By*.

With properly denotes concomitancy or assistance; *by*, the proximate cause; as, "The soldiers entered the breach *with* loaded muskets: their leader fell mortally wounded *by* a musket-ball." In the former case, *with* is adjunctive; in the latter, *by* is instrumental.

When Ovid says,

"Terrificam capitis concussit terque quaterque
  Cæsariem, cum quâ terram, mare, sidera, movit."
                                  (*Metamorph.* i. 179),

he does not mean, that the shaking of Jupiter's hair was the cause which moved the earth, sea, and stars; but that the shaking of his hair accompanied this act of power. We may say, "*With* prayers and tears he supplicated pardon;" but in such a case prayers and tears would not be instruments, but adjuncts or concomitants, *cum* precibus et lacrymis. "He drew water from the well with a rope." The man (*he*) is the instrument, the rope an adjunct.

CHAPTER VI.

TERMS COMPOUNDED WITH PREPOSITIONS.

As a general rule, a term compounded with a preposition will require after it a preposition of similar import, should a preposition be required at all. Thus we say, in compliance *with;* not in compliance *to,* as in Swift, "It was perfectly in compliance *to* some persons;" nor, as in Bacon, "Diminution *to* (of) their greatness."

The same principle will apply to verbs compounded with prepositions; and we dissent *from* a proposition, not "dissent *with* it," as in Addison, "Whig Examiner."

Practically, however, this principle is not always strictly carried out. The secret operations of the mind will sometimes exert their influence and modify certain phrases at pleasure. Thus custom will have the preposition *to* and not *from* after *averse;* a practice altogether at variance with the etymology of the term *averto,* "to turn *from."* Thus Bentley follows custom when he says, "Out of a natural aversion *to* all quarrels."

In the phrase "aversion *to,*" Mr. Grant has noticed that a similar phrase is found both in French and Spanish; as, "J'ai une grande aversion pour (ou à) cette manière de vivre;" and "Tengo una aversione grande á (to) este modo de vivir." We must look, then, to the secret operations of the mind for this form of expression. Now *aversion,* or *a turning away,* is only the *result* of a feeling, and not the feeling itself. Dislike is the feeling, and aversion, or turning away *from,* is the consequence of dislike. We have a dislike *to*—cherish a dislike *towards*—an object, and we turn from it. In the expression, "aversion *to*," we therefore fall back upon the primary operation of the mind, and we embody the result of the feeling with that primary operation *dislike*. "Aversion *from*" might in fact, in particular circumstances, convey a meaning different from that of "aversion to;" as, "From these considerations I have an aversion to the journey."

In more ancient authorities, however, we find the preposition following *aversion* consistent with the etymology of the noun; as,

"There grew in the Brittaines a great aversion *from* their king."—*Verstegan*.

"Aversion *to*" seems now to have fully established itself.

CHAPTER VII.

ERRORS IN THE USE OF PREPOSITIONS.

I know nothing *on* (of) it.
More than I thought *for* (of).
I was thinking *on* (of) that.
I changed *to* (for) the better.
Depending *of* (on) his relations.
In compliance *to* (with) your request.
Agreeable *with* (to) your request.
The master *with* (and) his servant were lost.

Without (unless) you see miracles.

They quarrel amongst *one another* (themselves).
Amongst refers to numbers collectively, and does not apply to *one* individually; hence not *one* another, but themselves.

Among (in) a nation so civilized.
Nation is here a *unity*, and *amongst* a unity would be nonsense.

Made much *on* (of).

No need *for* (of) that.

Free *of* (from) blame.

Different *to* (from) what is said.

It was divided *between* (among) fifty.
Between has reference to two parties only; *among*, to any number more than two. *Between* is compounded of the Anglo-Saxon *be*, *by*, and *twam*, or *tweon*, the dative case of *twa*, *two*. It was divided *between two;* it was divided *among twenty.*

However phrases like the following may have been sanctioned or tolerated in the use of the preposition at the time, custom and etymological propriety, in most cases, reject them now:—

"Value ourselves *by* (upon) drawing."—*Swift.*

"Bestowed your favors *to* (upon).—*Ibid.*

"Such occasions as fell *into* (under) their cognizance."—*Ibid.*

"That variety of factions *into* (in) which we are still engaged."—*Ibid.*

"To restore myself *into* (to) the good graces of my fair critics."

"Accused the minister *for* (of) betraying the Dutch."—*Swift.*

"Congratulate *to* themselves."—*Dryden.* To superfluous.

"He is resolved *of* (on) going to the Persian court."—*Berkeley.*

"Swerve ... *from* ... Ben Jonson.

"Prevail *upon*" (over).—*Addison.*
"Observance *after*" (of).—*Swift.*

Let it not be supposed that attention to these connecting particles is a matter of indifference. It is precisely from the improper use of them that ambiguity and obscurity generally arise; and, unfortunately, authors of high character, who have been so repeatedly referred to in the course of this work, instead of serving for unerring guides, often sink us more deeply into error by their unhallowed example. Particles are the cement of sentences, and bind them into order, consistency, and stability.

CHAPTER VIII.

REPETITION OF THE PREPOSITION.

"Exhausted *by* the abuse of her strength, *by* America, and *by* superstition, her pride might possibly be confounded, if we required such a list of three hundred cities, as Pliny has exhibited under the reign of Vespasian."—*Gibbon's Decline,* c. ii.

The particle *of* is used with similar effect in the following sentence:—

"In their dress, their table, their houses, and their furniture, the favorites of fortune united every refinement *of* conveniency, *of* elegance, and *of* splendor, whatever could soothe their pride, or gratify their sensuality."—*Ibid.* c. ii.

"*In* journeyings often, *in* perils of waters, *in* perils of robbers, *in* perils by mine own countrymen, *in* perils by the heathen, *in* perils in the city, *in* perils in the wilderness, *in* perils on the sea, *in* perils amongst false brethren, *in* weariness and painfulness, *in* watching often, *in* hunger and thirst, *in* cold and nakedness."—2 *Cor.* xi. 26.

By the repetition of the preposition in these passages, the mind is made to dwell emphatically on each object of interest.

In the Litany of the Church of England (one of the most tender, beautiful, and forcible of human compositions), the preposition *from* occurs sixteen times in four short clauses; and what an earnestness is thrown into the other two clauses following, by the repetition of the preposition *by* before each separate member of prayer!

"*By* the mystery of thy holy incarnation; *by* thy holy nativity and circumcision; *by* thy baptism, fasting, and temptation, Good Lord, deliver us."

"*By* thine agony and bloody sweat; *by* thy cross and passion; *by* thy precious death and burial; *by* thy glorious resurrection and ascension; and *by* the coming of the Holy Ghost."

Examples of this kind might be greatly multiplied. The principle is founded on the natural impulse of our affections—it is the language of nature.

When Livy describes the melancholy reflections of the Romans, on being obliged to deliver up their arms to the Samnites, and pass under the yoke, he amplifies and diversifies their grief by the repetition of the preposition or the adverb, as the sense might require:—

"Se color sine vulnere, sine ferro, sine acie victos; sibi non licuisse gladios, non manum cum hoste conserere; sibi nequicquam arma, nequicquam vires, nequicquam animos datos."—L. b. ix.

So in Cæsar, "De Bello Gallico:"—

"Et eo pene uno tempore, et ad silvas, et in flumine, et jam in munitionibus nostris, hostes viderentur."

SECTION X.

THE CONJUNCTION.

CHAPTER I.

ITS NATURE.

The object of a conjunction, as its name indicates, is to join together, *con-jungo*. In plain English, it might be denominated a *bind-word*. Conjunctions then connect either two or more words in a sentence, or they form one compound out of two simple sentences. Conjunctions are either copulative, that is, they unite, or they are disjunctive, that is, they separate. Disjunctive conjunctions seem to be a contradiction of terms. In form, at least, they are so; but in bringing two or more objects under consideration, the operation of the mind will either unite or disunite them, in the process of comparison, and *disjunction* may be as natural a result as *conjunction*. Two objects brought conjointly before the mind may be disunited by their inherent differences; hence the objection to *disjunctive* conjunctions is *formal* rather than *real*. Horne Tooke maintains that many of our conjunctions are the imperatives of Anglo-Saxon verbs, as, for example, *if* from *gif*, and that from *gifan* to give. *If*, however, was spelt in at least a dozen different ways, some of them deviating from *gifan* much more than *if* in its present form. In this case, at least, the conjecture wears an air of probability. Thus, we may say, "*If* he take sufficient pains, in all probability he will succeed." That is, *give*, *grant* that he will take sufficient pains, in all probability he will succeed. Many of our conjunctions, however, are not so probable in their etymology as this.

The moods required by conjunctions under particular circumstances, have already been explained under the head, *Verb*. As, however, the position of a conjunction in a sentence will often modify, and sometimes entirely alter the meaning of such sentence, and as there are certain conjunctions, whose correlatives ought to be carefully attended to, the conjunction, as regards correctness and effect, is well worthy of grammatical consideration. And first, of correlatives.

CHAPTER II.

CORRELATIVE CONJUNCTIONS.

I am the same to day	*as* yesterday.
It was exactly *such*	*as* this.
The same man	*that* (Rel. Pron.), not *as* I spoke of
This man is *as* tall	*as* that, *i. e.* as that is.
He is not *so* worthy	*as* she,—*as* she is.
Both this	*and* that.
Whether this	*or* that.
Either this	*or* that.
Neither this	*nor* that.

No other . . . . *than* (not *but*) this.
Though degraded . . . *yet, nevertheless.*

All comparatives require to be followed by *than*, or *as*, or *because*, according to circumstances; as,

This man is stronger *than* that.
The more acceptable, *as* being unexpected.
The more available, *because* unasked.

CHAPTER III.

CONJUNCTIONS COPULATIVE AND DISJUNCTIVE.

As conjunctions couple like cases of nouns, we cannot say, "The measure was acceptable to my friend and *I*," but to my friend and me, that is, *to* me. "He blamed her more than him," that is, "He blamed her more than he blamed him." "He runs faster than I," that is, "than I do." Simple and obvious as this principle is, yet it is perpetually violated.

Nor can we, with propriety, couple together different parts of speech. As, "men sincerely loving their fellow-creatures, and *who hate* oppression, will," &c. The terms *who hate*, in such a situation, ought to be *hating;* otherwise we couple together discordant materials. Nor can we, with propriety, couple together an adverb and an adjective, though poets sometimes take liberties in this respect, as Shakspeare (Richard III.),

"Scarce made up,
And that so *lamely* and *unfashionable.*"

We must suppose such phrases to be elliptical—made up so *lamely*, and, when made up, *unfashionable*.

The disjunctive conjunctions are of course subject to a similar construction. Though formally they may *disjoin*, yet *intellectually* they conjoin.

And and *An*.

And and *an* at a certain period were used in the place of *if*.

"No marry (quoth he) that wot I well enough, but what *and* he call it a horne, where am I then?"—*Thomas More.*

"I trust to God, *and* her teeth were well graft, to have her grace in another fashion than she is yet."—*Lady Byron's Letter to Lord Cromwell.*

"Ha! said the King, I have so long desired to fight with the Frenchmen, and now I will fight with some of them, by the grace of God and St. George; for truly they have done me so many displeasures, that I shall be revenged, *an* I may."—*Southey's Naval History, Quotation.*

"I must give over this life, and I will give it over by the Lord, *an* I do not I am a villain."—*Shakspeare.*

This form of expression is now obsolete, though I believe it is to be heard occasionally among our peasantry.

Also.

"And Saul sent messengers to take David, and when they saw the companies of the Prophets prophesying, and Samuel standing as appointed over them, the spirit of God was upon the messengers of Saul, and they *also* prophesied."—1 *Samuel* xix.

The word *also* is here in its proper place, conveying the meaning that not only Samuel, and the companies of the prophets prophesied, but the messengers *also*. Yet in the next verse we find,

"And Saul sent messengers again the third time, and they prophesied also."

They *also* prophesied—that is, they, the third set of messengers, as well as the preceding sets of messengers, also prophesied.

The introduction of *also* in the following passage renders it absurd:—

"And when they found not his body, they came, saying, that they had *also* seen a vision of angels, which said that he was alive."—*Luke* xxiv. 23.

We cannot connect an entity with a non-entity. The sentence amounts to this: They did not do a certain thing, and they did something besides. If we strike out *also*, the passage is clear and consistent. "And when they found not his body, they came, saying, that they had seen a vision of angels, which said that he was alive." Both the Greek and Latin of this passage, however, require *also* to be in the position in which we find it: Λεγουσαι και οπτασιαν αγγελων εωρακεναι, "dicentes se etiam apparitionem angelorum vidisse."

It may here be incidentally mentioned, that the term *was*, in this passage, is capable of a meaning not intended, and indeed, strictly speaking, distinctly conveys that meaning. If I say, he *was* alive, I confine the act of living to a certain time passed, and not continuing up to the *present* time. He *was* alive at that particular time. The meaning ought to have been expressed in the form which the angels would make use of in speaking of a present state, saying, "he *is* alive," cum vivere, αυτον ζην.

Likewise.

"And when it was told Saul, he sent other messengers, and they prophesied *likewise*."

And *they likewise* prophesied. The meaning of the passage is, that not only Samuel and the companies of the prophets, and the messengers sent on a *former* occasion; but these messengers *likewise, they also* prophesied. If we say they prophesied *likewise*, we imply that the messengers did something or other, and prophesied *likewise*.

Both.

"Give unto thy servants that peace which the world cannot give, that *both** our hearts may be set to obey thy commandments, and *also*," &c.—*Collect. Evening Prayer.*

The term *both* is ambiguous, for it may signify the hearts *of both* of us. Better, "Give unto thy servants that peace which the world cannot give, that our hearts may *both* be set to obey thy commandments, and also," &c.

Even.

"But if it be of God, ye cannot overthrow it, lest haply ye be found *even* to fight against God."—*Acts* v. 39.

Lest your attempts to put down and silence the disciples of Jesus be of such a nature, with reference to his assumed position, as to exhibit you in the character even of fighters against God, and not against man only,

---

* [The word *both* is omitted in the Book of Common Prayer of the P. E. Church of the U. S. of America.— Am. Pub.]

μηποτε και θεομαχοι ευρηθητε, lest you should prove even *God-fighters.*

• It is evident that, according to the sense of this passage, the term *even* should have followed, and not preceded, the words *to fight*—" lest haply ye be found to fight *even* against God."

Such in the place of So.

The use of *such* in the place of *so* is a very common error. *Such* denotes quality, *so* degree. If I say "I never saw *so* high a spire," the term *so* denotes degree of height, but I cannot say "I never saw a spire *such* high;" for, as *so* denotes the degree of a quality, and *such* a quality itself, they cannot be applicable in the same sense. In this case, the *quality* or *condition* is expressed by the term *high*, the *degree* of that quality by the term *so*. I might say, "I never saw *such* a tree *so* high," because *such* then denotes the quality, and *so* the degree; that is, I never saw a tree of this kind *so* high—a phrase which conveys a meaning very different from "I never saw *so* high a tree." The former phrase relates to trees of a particular class, the latter comprehends trees of every kind.

"*Such* a great character being given of it."—*Bentley.*

That is, "*so* great a character being given of it."

But in the place of Than.

"For the sun is no sooner risen with a burning heat, *but* it withereth the grass."—*James* i. 11.

"This is none other *but* the house of God."—*Gen.* xxxviii. 17.

"Yet no sooner does the morning dawn, and daylight enter his room,] d this strange enchantment vanishes."—*Harvey's Medita-tions.*

"They have no sooner fetched themselves to the fashion of the polite world, *but* the town has dropped them."—*Spectator.*

In all these cases, *than* is required in the place of *but*.

But.

In the following passage, *but* is used antithetically according to its usual acceptation, where no antithesis is required:—

"The Arabian Nights' Entertainments are the production of a romantic invention, *but* of a rich and amusing imagination."—*Blair's Rhetoric.*

Romantic invention and *rich and amusing* imagination are not opposed to each other, but on the contrary are perfectly compatible.

In the first commandment, *but* is used as a preposition, followed, as usual, by the objective case:—

"Thou shalt have none other Gods *but* me."

The passage, however, ought to have been translated *besides* me, *præter* me.

And, Or.

The conjunctive nature of *and*, and the disjunctive nature of *or*, must be kept in view throughout a sentence.

"A man may see a metaphor, *or* an allegory in a picture, as well as read *them* in a description."—*Addison's Dialogues on Medals.*

"It must indeed be confessed that a lampoon *or* a satire do not carry in *them* robbery or murder."—*Spectator*, No. 23.

Or, in both these sentences being disjunctive, requires

it in the place of *them*, and in the latter sentence *does* in the place of *do*.

CHAPTER IV.

OMISSION OF CONJUNCTION.

MANY passages in the classics, as well as in English authors, depend very much for their vividness, energy, and propriety of description, on the omission or repetition of the conjunction, as circumstances may require.

If Cæsar, in his celebrated despatch, had said *et* veni, *et* vidi, *et* vici, the connecting particles would have given an air of tardy deliberation to the execution of the victory.

Again, Virgil—

"Ferte citi flammas, date tela, scandite muros."
VIRGIL, *Æneid.* ix. 37.

Again,

"For there is wrath gone out from the Lord—the plague is begun."—*Numbers* xvi. 46.

Here, there is no lingering. The wrath of God and the plague—its effects are simultaneous and coincident.

"Thou didst blow with thy wind—the sea covered them, they sank like lead in the mighty waters."—*Exodus* xiv. 10.

"Thou stretchedst out thy right hand—the earth swallowed them."—*Ibid.* xiv. 12.

A sublime description of God's power, and of the prompt connection of cause and effect.

When St. Paul says of Charity, that "she beareth all things, believeth all things, hopeth all things, endureth all things," he gives a beautiful summary and condensation of the properties of this maternal virtue. The introduction of the copulative between each member of the sentence would have spoiled the effect.

How fearfully does the absence of the conjunction represent the horror and confusion of that dismal world, in which the damned spirits, when fallen from heaven, were doomed to wander!

> "Through many a dark and dreary vale
> They pass'd, and many a region dolorous;
> O'er many a frozen, many a fiery Alp,
> Rocks, caves, lakes, fens, bogs, dens, and shades of death,
> A universe of death." *Paradise Lost*, b. ii.

> "And every eye
> Glared light'ning, and shot pernicious fire,
> Among th' accursed, that wither'd all their strength,
> And of their wonted vigor left them *drain'd,
> Exhausted, spiritless, afflicted, fallen.*" *Ibid.* b. vi.

What a concentration of calamity is here pictured!

> "*drain'd,
> Exhausted, spiritless, afflicted, fallen.*"

> "Under thee, as head supreme,
> Thrones, princedoms, powers, dominions, I reduce." *Ibid.* b. iii.

Here the absence of the copula is to mark a close concentration of power.

As the regular connection between the members of a sentence, by means of the copula, would mark order and regularity, so its absence in the following passage is descriptive of wild confusion: —

> "Then might ye see
> Cowls, hoods, and habits with their wearers toss'd,
> And flutter'd into rags—then *reliques, beads;*
> *Indulgences, dispenses, pardons, bulls.*
> The sport of winds."   *Paradise Lost,* b. iii.

> "Yet when I approach
> Her loveliness, so absolute she seems,
> And in herself compleat, so well to know
> Her own, that what she wills to do or say
> Seems *wisest, virtuousest, discreetest, best.*"   *Ibid.*

In this passage, the affection of Adam for Eve, with the acknowledgment of the ascendency which she had gained over him, very naturally vents itself in an uninterrupted series of superlatives, which disdain a mixture of anything that might diminish their intensity. We recognize the same principle in the following lines:—

> "O fairest of creation, last and best
> Of all God's works, creatures in whom excell'd
> Whatever can to sight or thought be form'd,
> *Holy, divine, good, amiable, sweet.*"   *Ibid.*

The desperate energy of a murderous contention is forcibly expressed in the following lines from Byron, "Corsair," canto 2d:—

> "One effort, one to break the circling host,
> They *form, unite, charge, waver*—all is lost!
> Within a narrow ring *compress'd, beset,*
> *Hopeless, not heartless,* strive and struggle yet,
> And now they fight in foremost file no more,
> *Hemm'd in, cut off, cleft down,* and trampled o'er."

When Timon gives vent to his bitter and furious hate, the violence of his feelings hurries him on, and causes him to disregard those connecting particles which a calmer state of mind and orderly arrangement would naturally dictate:—

> "Piety and fear,
> Religion to the gods, *peace, justice, truth,*
> *Domestic awe, night-rest,* and neighborhood—
> *Instruction, manners, mysteries,* and trades,
> *Degrees, observances, customs,* and *laws,*
> Decline to your confounding contraries." SHAKSPEARE.

In fact, wherever strong emotions of love or hate or vengeance are struggling for immediate utterance, we cannot expect that the words expressive of such emotions will be clogged with expletives. On the other hand, an affectionate remembrance would rather dwell upon the subject, there being nothing acting immediately upon the senses, so as to produce a sudden excitement; accordingly, when Adam speaks of Eve, and contrasts her loveliness with the sin to which she had seduced him, he is made to say:—

> "This woman, whom thou mad'st to be my help,
> And gav'st me, as thy perfect gift, so good,
> So fit, so acceptable, so divine,
> That from her hand I could suspect no ill—
> * * * * *
> She gave me of the tree, and I did eat."

Beautiful picture of a generous confidence, and of the affection which, in spite of adverse circumstances, still lingers in the breast of Adam!

CHAPTER V.

REPETITION OF THE CONJUNCTION.

When Milton wishes to exhibit the effect which sin had wrought upon our first parents, he places, in order, the different passions that had been engendered in their breasts, and exhibits them in a series, link by link:—

"Love was not in their looks, either to God,
Or to each other, but apparent guilt,
And shame, *and* perturbation, *and* despair,
Anger *and* obstinacy, *and* hate, *and* guile."

Again, when the poet, in that sublime hymn to light, speaks of the different objects from which he had been cut off by blindness, those objects seem multiplied by the interposition of the particle *or*, and a lingering sorrow is attached to the consciousness of each individual privation:—

"Thus with the year
Seasons return, but not to me returns
Day, *or* the sweet approach of ev'n, *or* morn,
Or sight of vernal bloom, *or* summer's rose,
Or flocks, *or* herds, *or* human face divine."
Paradise Lost, b. ii.

"If there be a royal solitude, it is a sick bed. How the patient lords it there! What caprices he acts without control! How king-like he sways his pillow, tumbling, *and* tossing, *and* shifting, *and* lowering, *and* thumping, *and* flatting, *and* moulding it to the ever-varying requisitions of his throbbing temples."—*Elia, Essays*.

This is a graphic description. The repetition of the

conjunction diffuses the action, and presents it under a variety of forms. The royal patient is exhibited under a wearisome and distressing multiplicity of efforts in search of repose.

The conjunction is repeated before each member of the following sentence for the sake of amplification:—

"Italy teems with recollections of every kind; for courage, *and* wisdom, *and* power, *and* arts, *and* sciences, *and* beauty, *and* music, *and* desolation, have all in their turn made it their dwelling-place."—*New Monthly*, No. 103.

"They brought beds, *and* basins, *and* earthen vessels, *and* wheat, *and* barley, *and* flour, *and* parched corn, *and* beans, *and* lentiles, *and* parched pulse, *and* honey, *and* butter, *and* sheep, *and* cheese of kine, for David, and for the people that were with him." 2 *Samuel* xvii.

What a profuse variety of necessaries do these thirteen conjunctions scatter over the camp of David! Take, again, the following passage, and see how beautifully the article and the conjunction are interwoven with the narrative, and how forcibly they depict, under various aspects, the loveliness of the promised land:—

"For the Lord thy God bringeth thee into a good land, a land of brooks of water, of fountains and depths that spring out of valleys and hills; a land of wheat, *and* barley, *and* vines, *and* fig-trees, *and* pomegranates; a land of olive oil, *and* honey."—*Deut.* viii. 7.

The attention and kindness shown by the good Samaritan towards the wounded traveller, are set forth to the greatest advantage by the repetition of the conjunction before each member of the sentence. His good offices seem multiplied in every direction. Humanity, like a guardian angel, seems to flutter over the wounded man with an officious kindness.

"But a certain Samaritan, as he journeyed, came where he was, and when he saw him he had compassion on him, *and* went to him, *and* bound up his wounds, pouring in oil and wine, *and* set him on his own beast, *and* brought him to an inn, *and* took care of him."—*Luke* x. 30

"The Lord shall smite thee with a consumption, *and* with a fever, *and* with an inflammation, *and* with an extreme burning, *and* with the sword, *and* with blasting, *and* with mildew, *and* they will pursue thee until thou perish."—*Deut.* xxviii. 22.

What an awful extent of calamity is here presented, afflictions multiplied, amplified, worked up, exaggerated, and operating with individualized energy in the work of destruction! For this the passage in all its sublimity is, in a great measure, indebted to the repetition of the conjunction, the preposition, and the article.

The Adjective, the Article, and the Pronoun, in the Place of the Conjunction.

These different parts of speech are sometimes used with great effect in the place of the conjunction.

"Tell him all terms, *all* commerce I decline,
Nor share his council, nor his battle join." *Pope's Iliad.*

Again,

"Go then to Greece, report our fix'd design,
Bid all your councils, *all* your armies join;
Let *all* your forces, *all* your arts conspire,
To save *the* ships, *the* troops, *the* chiefs from fire."
                                                    Ibid.

"For thankless Greece such hardships have I brav'd,
Her wives, *her* infants by my labor sav'd."

In this last case, *her* in the place of *and* is more forcible than the copulative, because it expresses personality, and depicts Greece under a tender and feminine character.

SECTION XI.

THE INTERJECTION.

An interjection is a mere exclamation, arising out of a peculiar condition of the mind, as affected by joy or grief, or some less definite emotion. As such, it is capable of indefinite variety. It will stand alone, at the beginning, in the middle, or at the end of a sentence; but the sentence will not be affected by it, whatever may be the position of the interjection.

An interjection is not significant by compact, or *institute*, and in no way enters into the artificial texture of language. It is an effort of Nature to unburden herself of some pressing emotion. As its name indicates, it is thrown in among the members of a sentence, and is altogether adventitious. The English interjections are such as Oh! Alas! Ah! The Latin such as Oh! Heu! Hei! Vae! In Greek, they are more numerous than they are either in Latin or English. These inarticulate or unjointed sounds are common even to the brute creation. The expression of pain would probably not differ very materially in individuals of the same species, to whatever country they might belong; while laughter, peculiar to the human species, may be considered a continuous or protracted interjection. In the "Persai" of Æschylus, we meet with various modifications of the interjections. The poet has resorted to almost every form of ejaculation, in which abject misery could be expressed, in order to furnish gratification to the Athenians, in beholding their once proud enemy humbled to the dust, and pouring out the bitterness of affliction, to the very last dregs.

Such words as Farewell! Adieu! Welcome! are not inarticulate sounds, and are to be looked upon as elliptical forms of speech rather than interjections: as, *farewell!* may you fare well; adieu ! *à Dieu*, to God, I commend you to God. Can Good-by or bye be a corruption and contraction of God be with you? Welcome, *well* or *opportunely* come?

The following words enter into the composition of a sentence, and properly speaking, therefore, cannot be looked upon as mere interjections: Woe is *me!* That is, woe is *to me!*

" O well is *thee*."—*Psalm* cxxviii. 2.

To thee.

" Well is *him* that hath found prudence."—*Ecclus.* xxv. 9.

To him. Yet in Ecclesiasticus xxviii. 19, we find, " Well is he that is defended from it;" which phrase, having abandoned its basis as an objective case, has no grammatical standing at all, unless we suppose the phrase to be an inversion of " He is well."

CONCLUDING REMARKS.

A spoken language is subject to perpetual changes. Words gradually and imperceptibly lose their meaning, and become antiquated and inapplicable; not perhaps from any etymological impropriety, but from the caprice of custom, and sometimes from the passive obstinacy and tenacity of downright ignorance. A sluggish, stolid, and doltish indifference to propriety is a far more dangerous enemy to encounter than a lively, erratic imagination. Human efforts and human patience sink under the daily and hourly pressure of a dead weight, and conviction resigns itself helplessly and hopelessly to the rude tyranny of popular caprice. This does not, however, always furnish an apology for the numerous errors which are so profusely scattered over our literature. We must look for them in the want of attention to the peculiarities of the English language, and to the foolish supposition that the grammatical construction of languages, wide as the poles asunder from that of our own, will prove a safe and unerring guide in the analysis of the English tongue. Foolish, indeed; else why should the literary giants of preceding ages, imbued, as they doubtlessly were, with classic information in a high degree, be exhibited under a load of negligence and error, aggravated by the very eminence of their position. The purification of the English language is worthy of our holiest and never-ceasing devotion. It will bear to future ages the sentiments of a free, generous, and singularly energetic race of men. It already overspreads a large portion of the world, and is diffusing itself, east, west, north, and south. It carries with it the cherished and sanctified institutions of its native soil, and, under the influence and adventurous spirit of the parent and her vigorous offspring in America, is materially changing, or modifying the destinies of mankind.

In all the great essentials of language, we have arrived at a degree of copiousness such as few languages possess. But English literature furnishes us with no positive and recognized standard of grammatical accuracy. What was the result of the well-founded pride of Greece in the excellency of her own language? What the result of the unwearied pains which her orators, poets, historians, and philosophers bestowed upon their compositions? The delicate perceptions of the Grecian ear would not allow a word, a syllable, a letter, to be out of its place, to form a disagreeable collision of sounds, or a cadence which did not leave a pleasing effect upon the senses. The result was a language which, perhaps, will never be equalled in the future generations of mankind; a language which has become as necessary to the intellectual wants of European civilization as bread is for bodily support.

The French and Italians have paid great and praiseworthy attention to the formation and accuracy of their respective languages, and Germany is following their example. We have societies of various descriptions, founded on the intellectual, social, or physical wants of the community; but we have no society of a purely literary character, to which the language can appeal in the case of doubt or difficulty. The consequence is that the vagaries of affectation, and sometimes even of ignorance, will be seized on as authorities worthy of confidence and imitation, words will be moulded in their spelling to accord with the transitory and ever-varying pronunciation of the day, etymology will be lost sight of, and error present a front of brass against the hand of correction. But if the very "salt shall have lost its savor," if men of high literary character shall think the grammatical structure of the English language a secondary consideration only, we must not be surprised if the sickness of the head should communicate itself to each individual member. It is no unusual thing for men of great classical attainments to say: "I can understand the grammatical construction of a Greek or a Latin sentence, I can comprehend its syntactical arrangement, and the mutual dependence of its several parts; but in English I see nothing but the force of custom, and the unbridled licentiousness of idiom." But, it may be asked, have these gentlemen ever paid a fiftieth part of the attention to the construction of the English language which they have paid to that of classical literature? The Greek and Latin languages to them have been the study of a life: the English frequently little more than an incidental acquisition, a matter of ear and imitation rather than of grammatical principle.

But surely there is much in our native English which deserves a separate attention on the part of those to whom the education of youth is intrusted; and no men would be more likely to apply themselves with success to the grammatical analysis of their native tongue, than those who already have made language their study, and pondered over the exquisite concatenations of Greek and Roman sentences.

The errors which have been brought forward in the course of this work are but as grains of sand picked from countless and immeasurable heaps. The difficulty has been in rejecting rather than finding examples of error. The author has frequently been apprehensive of overloading a position with testimony; at the same time, he is well aware that many things worthy of attention must have altogether escaped his observation. He is indeed sensible of the imperfection of his labors; not only as far as his own individual ability is concerned; but from the fact that a work made up from a variety of separate parts must, from its very nature, remain imperfect, and capable of indefinite addition and improvement. Literary error is indefinite in its forms. It meets us under a variety of aspects; sometimes presenting a bold and unblushing front, sometimes shy and retiring, sometimes of doubtful character. It slips from the mind unperceived, it eludes investigation, it goes forth before the public, and when too late, we perhaps feel obliged to acknowledge the force of the trite maxim "fugit irrevocabile verbum."

THE END.

www.ingramcontent.com/pod-product-compliance
Lightning Source LLC
Chambersburg PA
CBHW032016220426
43664CB00006B/260